When You Wish Upon a Wideout

A **SECOND CHANCE** AT **FIRST LOVE**

CATHRYN CARTER

from the author

Please note that *When You Wish Upon a Wideout* comes with gentle content warnings that some readers might find sensitive or triggering including: mentions of suicide and depression, the death of a loved one/family member, and medically fragile children.

for those who believe each day is a second chance

every wish i ever made

DEAR DIARY,

Diary. That's what Dad called you. I've never had a diary before. I guess I never had much to talk about. Or maybe I did. But I used to have people to talk to in Nashville. And here I am back in Brookwood, Texas—where I haven't lived for almost ten years—with no one to chat with.

I'm exaggerating. Obviously, there are people here. Not many, though. Brookwood is basically one long street with a grocery store, a bar, a pharmacy, and a few random shops sprinkled in between. I don't really remember anything about living here, but apparently, everyone remembers us.

The doorbell rings nonstop. I'm not sure if that would be the case under different circumstances. Would people stop by with casseroles and pies to welcome the prodigal football coach back to town? Or are they only doing it now because they feel sorry that the prodigal football coach came back as a widower with two teenagers to raise on his own?

I use "raise" loosely here. Dad is a robot, and there isn't much raising left for me and Henry. We're almost seventeen, and we resume our junior year of high school tomorrow. Apparently, the hiatus after losing your mother to suicide is pretty short. It's been twenty-four days. Yes, I count. I'm struggling to remember what life was like beyond day twenty-five. That's the last day I was myself—happy, outgoing, someone with a mother. And a lot has happened in that short time. We buried Mom, packed up our house, and moved. This move was supposed to happen a few months from now, in August. But Dad couldn't stay in the house where she did it much longer.

But even though it's been busy, it's been quiet. Only small talk. And small talk is basically a whisper, considering how loud my thoughts are. There will be more noise and whispers tomorrow with us starting school.

It would be nice if I could talk to Henry—I should be able to. He's my brother. But he's also the one who found Mom. So, Henry doesn't talk much. But I guess I should tell you about him anyway. Even though we're twins, we're not the same. He's smart. Like so smart—NASA kind of smart. Insanely good at chess and Scrabble and is allergic to peanuts. Henry also walks with crutches these days because he broke his leg and had surgery two months back.

Mom used what was left of his pain pills.

That's who I want to talk to.

I want to tell my mom how much I hate Brookwood and how much I miss Nashville. I want to tell her that if she really loved us, she would've stuck around. I want to tell her we loved her exactly how she was—flighty, enthusiastic, and fun. We loved her even though she thought she had a beautiful voice but was tone-deaf (seriously, who can mess up Amazing Grace?) We also loved her when she was down and depressed. We loved her through everything, and we would've loved her through anything. I guess she didn't believe that. And do you know what, Diary? I kind of hate her for it. Because she lit up everything—every room, a stranger's heart, my own life—and now it's not just dark. It's pitch-black.

There's a lot of irony there considering how obsessed she was with the night sky. Ever since Henry and I were little, the night before every birthday, the three of us would lay in the grass and she'd tell us to make our wishes there and not wait for the cake tomorrow.

"Stars are more powerful than candles," she'd say.

We did this for her birthday, too.

I'm looking at the stars right now. I guess what's nice about the new house is that it's a ranch, so it's easy to climb out my window, up the trellis and onto the roof. It's April, and my birthday is in October, but I'm making wishes anyway in case one of them might stick and become a dream come true.

I wish I would make a friend, just one, so I have someone to talk to.

I wish I could talk to you, Mom. I wish I could tell you I still need you. A lot. Especially right now. I wish I could've told you that before. And I wish I could tell you I'm angry because you should've just known that.

Maybe that's what I'll use this diary for. Maybe this is how I'll talk to you. Maybe you'll talk back to me sometime. I don't want to picture you as a bird or anything like that. I think you're actually a star, Mom. I never told you this, but every wish I ever made, you made come true.

Love,

Sienna

chapter one

THE STEAM FLOATING from the mug burnt Sienna's nostrils, but her focus on the pamphlet in front of her didn't waver. *I should've tossed it,* she mutely fumed. Somehow, that glossy piece of paper with the smiling kid in a wheelchair had followed them home from the hospital. Sienna couldn't remember which trip to the hospital it was, or even from what year.

Setting her mug down, she grabbed the paper and scoffed at it—*The Golden Penny Foundation, Where Dreams Come True.* A line at the bottom didn't quite sit well with her. "The Golden Penny Foundation aims to support families and children with serious disease," Sienna read before she folded the pamphlet and tossed it in the trash.

"What about my wig?" Grace's voice yanked Sienna from her thoughts.

Sienna's eyes floated down her daughter's bare legs. "That's mine," she said about her daughter's outfit. "And for the record, it's a shirt, *not* a dress."

Grace rolled her eyes. "On *you,* maybe. Not all of us need extra length in our pants."

You might one day.

Grace had been off the charts in length from the moment she

was born fourteen years ago, which led Sienna to wonder if her daughter might take after her in the height department. With a gun to her head, Sienna couldn't remember how tall Grace's father was. *Six two, maybe?* She had only seen him twice. The first, she had downed too much tequila and remained mostly horizontal, and the second, a month later, Sienna was too focused on the positive pregnancy test in her shaking hand to even look at him.

"Go put on leggings. It's January, not July."

"And my wig?"

Her daughter pointed to her short, light brown pixie cut, which Sienna found adorable but Grace had deemed "absolutely atrocious," quick to point out it was "easy for the one with luscious locks to say."

Sienna didn't care about her long, blonde hair. In fact, she found it quite annoying, but couldn't find time to visit the salon for a hefty trim. She had shaved her hair after Grace's had fallen out during her first round of chemotherapy—following her initial diagnosis five years ago—and hadn't cut it since.

"You know, I could use a haircut," she told Grace.

Sienna loved her daughter's confidence—a loud, commanding voice, a beaming smile no matter where she went. But it hurt her mother heart that she was still so self-conscious about her hair—or lack thereof.

Grace narrowed her eyes. "*Don't* get any ideas, especially right before we go. We're going to be on *TV*," she reminded her mother. "Don't ruin that for me by shaving your head with Henry's clippers like you did last time."

Sienna reached for her mug, a splash of coffee dripping on the counter. "Your wig is in my bathroom. I washed, dried, and curled it when I got home last night."

It had been less of last night and more of this morning because Sienna wasn't able to close the bar until after two. But her only bartender, Emily, just had a baby, and as the owner, she filled in where needed.

"Thanks!" Grace beamed before spinning on her heel.

Wiping the mess with a paper towel, Sienna opened the trash again. The pamphlet had unfolded and, though creased, continued to taunt her. *Serious disease*, she scoffed in her head. Cancer was a mountain of serious disease, one that when Grace was initially diagnosed, Sienna had vowed to hack into pebbles with a chisel even if she had to hold it with her teeth. She would fight it one piece at a time. But every piece that broke off—blood draws, bone marrow aspirations, chemo inductions, infections, stem cell transplants—showed her that cancer was more than an illness.

It was a thief, a quiet one, taking small things, like the Fourth of July parade, a ballet recital, and bigger things, like a growth spurt, puberty, birthdays, and Christmases. Cancer and its accomplices carried off the will to believe, to hope, to dream. Silently and sneakily, they never stopped. Even when the words "disease free" flowed from the doctor's mouth, cancer still stole your breath. And it held it while you waited and waited until you heard the word "recurrence." Your breathing never returned to normal after that, each inhalation too short, too worried, too overwhelmed by what it took to parent a sick child.

Sienna knew this because it wasn't her first rodeo.

Grace had been disease free from leukemia once before. Sienna learned from her daughter's recurrence that the one thing she could never let this vicious disease take was her fierce determination to fight it. But cancer constantly found a way to one-up its opponent. Because even though Sienna would give Grace anything she could—from blood and platelets to all her energy—this was something her daughter had to fight entirely on her own, and that had to be the least fair thing in the entire world.

Grace's voice squealed from the front of the house.

"The limo is here!" she announced. "Mom, come on. Are you ready?"

"A limo? Why did you ask for a limo?"

"Because it's *my* day," Grace proclaimed. "Henry! Let's go."

Sienna could hear her brother shuffling down the hallway. "Nice wheels, kid."

"Kickoff isn't until five. We have some time." Sienna took a heavy swig of her coffee.

"I'm doing the coin toss!"

Hot liquid scalded her mouth, and she spit it back into the mug. "The *what*?"

"The coin toss!" Grace repeated, returning to the kitchen. She reached for a pack of gum on the counter, pulling out a piece. "I'll be on TV. I already texted everyone. Will you hurry? I *cannot* be late!"

When Sienna had read the email from the Golden Penny Foundation, alerting her that Grace's wish had been granted, she had been surprised for two reasons. The first being Sienna didn't know Grace had even applied. And the second was Sienna knew that if Grace *had* applied, her wish certainly would have included some sort of meet and greet with whatever popstar she was currently obsessed with.

After Sienna read The Golden Penny Foundation's email stating they would honor Grace's wish to attend "in VIP style, as requested" the upcoming home game for the Dallas Sparks, instead of telling her daughter, she wrote the foundation back, explaining that there must be a mistake. Her daughter hated football—just like Sienna.

When she told Grace the news, Sienna expected her daughter to confirm that it *was* a mistake, to be disappointed, and demand Sienna call them back. But instead of freaking out, Grace jumped on the bed.

"This will be the best day of my life!"

"Did you put her up to this?" Sienna asked Henry, leaving Grace's room when she began to call all her friends.

Her brother shook his head, looking surprised. "Why would I do that? Basketball is my thing. But we get to sit in those boxes with the buffet and open bar. Could be kind of cool."

"Kind of cool? We can watch a football game and eat at home."

Henry stared curiously, his green eyes matching hers. "Walker still plays for the Sparks, you know."

Sienna folded her arms across her chest defensively. "They've won one game all season, so he doesn't play very well obviously. Maybe they shouldn't renew his contract."

Henry smirked. "I thought you hated *football."*

"I do. But we live in Texas. You can't buy milk at the grocery store without someone talking about the Sparks." And you can't live in small, sleepy Brookwood without anyone mentioning Beau Walker, *she added in her head.*

Her brother continued to stare.

"What?"

"Nothing," Henry said, shaking his head. "The one who got away, huh?"

Sienna swallowed. No. The one who left me behind, *she wanted to correct him, but instead said, "We were kids, Henry."*

Sienna placed her mug in the sink. *We were kids,* she reminded herself. *That was over fifteen years ago.* It didn't matter if occasionally Sienna Googled Beau Walker or if she pulled up game footage on YouTube, awaiting the moment the camera might catch his face. But all those clips and internet searches did was remind her that Beau was no longer a kid, but a man, with thirty pounds more muscle, who almost always seemed to have a five-o'clock shadow. But even though his hair was no longer shaggy, his arms no longer lanky, some things about Beau stayed the same, like his bold brow, his broad shoulders, and his signature half smile that had made Sienna a swoony teenager.

No longer eighteen and living around the corner, Beau was an NFL veteran who, at some point, was ranked the best wide receiver in The League, having played in New York, Los Angeles, and finally, an hour away in Dallas.

Grace continued to prance and Sienna sighed.

This is her day, she thought, trying to ignore the nerves that brewed in her stomach, twisting her gut anxiously. *Let Grace have her day. Don't even think about him. He's just one player on the field in a stadium filled with thousands of people.*

"Is it straight?" Grace asked, tugging on the ends of the dark brown wig.

Sienna turned back to Grace. "Looks great."

"Are you ready?"

"Are you sure you want to do this?"

Grace nodded enthusiastically.

"Since when do you like football?"

Grace rolled her eyes. "Mom, I'm going to be on TV. *Everyone* watches the Sparks so *everyone* will be watching. Besides, I already have tickets to see Simon Gorges in March. The only thing better would be meeting him, which"—she paused, pointing to her wig—"I *refuse* to do without my own hair."

Even though she nodded, Sienna frowned inwardly. "Go on out with Henry. I'll be out in a minute."

Sienna watched Grace trot through the house and out the front door, still skeptical of her daughter's excitement considering Grace loved the Hallmark Channel more than Sportscenter. But Grace's wants had been shoved to the side for too long.

If she's this excited, Sienna thought, picking up a wrapper from Grace's gum that hadn't made its way to the bin, *who am I to say no?*

She wanted to ignore the pamphlet she saw again in the trash when she went to throw away the wrapper. This time Sienna laughed at the tagline.

"The Golden Penny Foundation aims to support families and children with serious illness by making wishes come true," Sienna read aloud, shaking her head. "They don't know what they're talking about. If wishes actually came true, cancer would've been long gone by now."

Sienna grabbed her purse from the table and keys off the hook. *And if wishes came true, I wouldn't care that I'm about to see Beau Walker because I never would've met him in the first place.*

Janet from the Golden Penny Foundation met Sienna, Henry, and Grace in the garage, leading them through a maze of hallways to an elevator.

"You'll just wait right here," Janet said when they came up into a tunnel.

Sienna's eyes were drawn to the right, toward the opening that led to the field, roaring with fans. But the pounding pulse in her ears muffled the crowd's noise. She hadn't felt that kind of thumping in so long—the kind that makes your body nearly jump with each bulging beat in anticipation. *He's here*, her brain was trying to tell her, but Sienna's racing heart already knew.

"They'll give us the signal when it's time for the coin toss," Janet told them, flashing an overenthusiastic smile.

Slumping against the cold stone wall, Sienna looked at Grace bouncing beside her, well past the point of annoying, but she let it slide. *Her day.*

"Wow," Grace said nervously. "There's a lot of people out there, yeah?"

"Don't shake so hard when you flip the coin," Henry told her from across them, pushing his glasses up. "You don't want to mess up."

Grace immediately locked her knees. "Can you mess up a coin toss though? It only needs to hit the ground, right? Was I supposed to practice?"

"Just make sure it doesn't hit anyone else *before* the field." Henry pushed up his tortoise-framed glasses, smirking at his sister.

Turning to her mother, Grace pursed her lips. "What are the chances I *actually* mess it up?"

Sienna rolled her eyes, not wanting her brother to see how hard she chewed on the inside of her cheek. "Don't be nervous."

She wasn't sure if those words were only meant for Grace. *He'll be on the sidelines with the rest of the team and wouldn't put two and two together anyway. Grace is doing the coin toss, not me.*

"Are you ready?" Janet asked Grace eagerly. "We'll walk out to the middle of the field with the referees and captains."

Sienna watched Grace's throat bob before she turned to her. "Mom?"

"You'll be great," Sienna told her with an affirming nod. "You can't mess up a coin toss."

But Sienna knew from experience, you kind of could.

Janet stood at the front of the tunnel with a stadium attendant, both looking at Grace anxiously.

"Mom?" she asked again.

Sienna looked at her brother. "Henry will go with you."

"No, I'm good," Henry said.

"Just go with her," Sienna muttered quietly.

"You go."

Janet looked uncomfortably between the three of them. "Grace, why don't we—"

"Mom?"

Sienna pushed off the wall, taking Grace's hand. "This was *your* wish," she reminded her as they followed Janet out of the tunnel. Her feet angrily stomped on the turf but feeling Grace's fragile, trembling fingers wound in her own, she slowed her pace and softened her heart. "You're the bravest person I know."

Blood draws, bone marrow aspirations, chemo, stem cell transplants, and you're worried about all these people? But Grace was her mother's daughter and hated crowds as much as Sienna.

"There's just *so* many people."

Sienna held her breath as she looked up, overwhelmed by the thousands of faces. "If you want to be an actress, you need to get over your stage fright. Picture them all naked."

Her daughter laughed.

"See? It works."

"Not really," Grace said, turning her head to the sidelines. "Number twenty-two on the other team is kind of hot."

"Stop it."

Grace sighed. "Maybe I should've taken some Zofran."

"You're not *that* nauseous. Just smile and toss the coin and let's go up to the suite and eat candy."

And drink wine, Sienna added mutely. *Lots of wine.* Sienna was about to tell Grace she bet there was ice cream too, when her voice got stuck in her throat. *Yeah, a lot of wine. Because we have a driver and because* he's *standing right there.*

Beau was yards away, as tall as ever, even broader in his pads and white uniform, with the royal-blue star right smack on his chest as he stood in the center of it all—the small huddle, the middle of the field. It seemed fitting, considering he had been the center of Sienna's universe once upon a time—her shooting wideout.

Wishes don't come true, Sienna reminded herself.

She tried to maintain a calm smile aimed solely at the lead referee as they approached. Her cheeks stung from the tightness as she counted the stripes of his black-and-white uniform with her teeth clamped shut, her eyes unblinking. She refused to give Beau this moment—Grace's moment.

Don't look, don't look, don't look. Her internal lecture was nearly a scream, one so loud that Sienna barely heard whatever was said over the loudspeaker announcing Grace as the GPF's guest of honor. What she could feel, thankfully, was the loosening of Grace's shoulders beside her and the movement of her hand as she reached out to take the coin from the referee.

The visiting team called heads, and Sienna's knees gave out slightly before she corrected herself, standing firm and trying to ignore that even though Beau was feet in front of her at the moment, they might as well have been standing with a mere breath between them.

"Heads or tails, I love you no matter what."

"Give it a good flick," Beau's voice sounded, and Sienna

gritted her teeth, angry that she could hear *his* voice over the loudspeaker, over the players joking back and forth as Grace tossed the coin, over the roar of *thousands* of people.

But hasn't it always been that way?

Sienna had once found Beau, her childhood best friend, after a decade and a thousand miles apart, picking right up as teenagers where they had left off, the closest of friends—and then some, as first loves.

Following the trail of the coin to the ground, Sienna held her breath as it landed—tails up—between her feet. And she held it even longer, watching a large hand retrieve it. A large hand leading to a thick wrist, a powerful forearm dusted with dark hair except for a small scar where Sienna knew—by heart—nothing would grow from the wounded tissue.

"Keep it for good luck," Beau said, handing the coin back to Grace before he turned to her, his big brown eyes of the past meeting her green ones, desperate to forget it ever happened. "Just in case you need it."

Sienna trembled when Beau turned with his teammates, returning to the sidelines. The shake that overtook her wasn't because he was walking away. It was because he still wore sixteen—her lucky number—even after all these years.

chapter two

THE DALLAS SPARKS had lost fifteen games this season. Beau Walker knew that their only win until today—the second of the year—was because of a bad call from a ref who wrongly ruled an incomplete pass a fumble, giving the Sparks the ball right on their own eight-yard line. He had made the catch that kicked up the score with a minute left, outjumping a defensive back more easily than he would have cared to admit considering his age. But that touchdown—his only of the game—helped his teammates collectively turn the game around and bring a win back to Dallas.

Today, the Sparks, for the first time all season, didn't just win by the skin of their teeth—they dominated. Because even though he was no longer a teenager, some things always remained the same whether he was five or approaching thirty-five—like his enthusiasm for impressing the blonde with the emerald-green eyes. Eyes that Beau spent countless hours staring into during his youth, eyes that went on to haunt Beau for nearly sixteen years.

"You landed on that shoulder funny," a trainer yelled as he bypassed the ice tubs. Beau had already managed to skip an interview with ESPN. "And your leg—"

"Still works," Beau joked as he jogged down the hall, tugging his jersey and chest protector off.

"Where are you going? I've got Rebecca and a camera—"

Beau rolled his eyes at the sound of his agent's voice and pushed open the locker room door. *No boundaries. This guy's got no boundaries,* he thought before saying, "Need to shower."

Chase was quick on his heels. "It's an on-field interview. They don't care."

"Not doing it."

"You need to," Chase hissed, following him into the near-empty locker room, looking out of place in his sharp, well-tailored suit. "That was your best game all season. Maybe last season, too. Watch, I bet there's a bidding war for you by morning. Dallas won't let you go so easily after this."

Beau chewed his lip. *Good. I don't know If* I *want Dallas to let me go after this.*

Today concluded Beau's contract with the Sparks, whom he had signed with coming off a broken tibia, two surgeries and an enormous amount of rehab. Few teams had offered him at that point—concerned about his injury and his age given the rise of young competition.

Chase had advised against it. *"You're a champion. Dallas hasn't been* the *team in a decade. Let's wait."*

But Beau had spent a decade playing for the best teams. He had been a field goal away from a Super Bowl Championship. But coming off a serious injury, he knew he had to go where the opportunity presented itself—even if it was playing for a mediocre team that put him further from his goals. And signing with the Sparks wasn't just another opportunity to play. It was an opportunity to go home to Texas.

To Sienna.

But Beau realized he talked a lot of game, even in his head. He never could bring himself to make the drive back to his hometown of Brookwood and face her. Instead, Beau put all his focus back on football, performing well enough that his former team began to inquire about bringing him back to Los Angeles.

Even though he had initially planned to retire in a year, the move back to the sunshine state had been exactly what he wanted.

Until today.

After this game—after seeing Sienna again—Beau was no longer so sure.

"They see Beau Walker is back—"

"I never *went* anywhere, Chase."

Chase gripped his clean-shaven jaw. "Well, since you're ending the season on a personal best, let's remind people you're still looking to play."

Tossing his gear into a bin, Beau made his way to the shower. "I said everything I need to say on the field. We're done for this year."

Apart from exit interviews, Beau was officially in the off-season stretch, which meant he wouldn't report for camp or official team practices until the summer. Unofficially, it meant Beau would train just as hard—if not harder—than he did during the season, taking part in captains' practices with whomever was in town. But it would be on his terms and quiet—exactly how he liked it.

"You're not done for *next* season, Beau. You've been saying you have one more year in you before retirement—"

"If any team cares more about one interview than how I play, they can light their contracts on fire and put on a show for everyone to watch."

"Call me crazy, but *I* care about those contracts."

"You should. You're my agent *and* manager. So, manage it." Beau flipped on the water. "And Chase, go ask someone about that Golden Penny girl." *And her mom.* "If they're upstairs, make them wait."

Narrowing his eyes, Chase cocked his head. "Why? You *hate* sick kids."

"Who doesn't?"

It was a valid question, but Chase had a point. The Golden Penny Foundation was local to Dallas, and the Sparks were heavy sponsors, yet Beau avoided events. Some things that meant well came with a heavy, emotional cost Beau wasn't ready to pay.

Sick kids meant hospitals. Hospitals meant distressing memories, like waking up in one when he was eleven with eighteen stitches in his head and no idea what day it was or that his brother had died pushing him out of the way of a speeding car.

But if there was anyone Beau could be brave for, it would be Sienna.

He stuck his head into the hot stream of water, his dark hair matting as other memories—what seemed to be a lifetime's worth—flashed before his closed eyes. One stuck out in particular, the last time he saw Sienna. It was over seven years ago, when that young girl, now with the obvious dark wig, was small enough to sit on Sienna's hip, when her hair was as blonde as her mother's, so similar Beau didn't know where one's started and the other's began.

The last time Beau had seen Sienna was from a distance at her father's burial, when he didn't want his presence to detract from honoring Jack Clarke's memory. Beau had watched from the footpath along the cemetery, cringing, knowing he had broken his promise to Coach Clarke. He hadn't always treated Sienna right. He hadn't looked out for her for years. As they lowered the coffin to the ground, Beau prepared himself to right the wrong and do just that. He waited for the moment he could pull Sienna aside and into his arms, to whisper countless apologies that he had waited so long to come back. *I'm here now,* Beau imagined telling her. *You're not alone.*

But through the waning crowd, Beau saw she wasn't. Sienna had a daughter—a family—and Beau wasn't prepared to step back into her life and ruin that for her.

The young girl on the field today—the one who brought Sienna right to Beau's turf—was the reason he walked away again all those years ago. But on the field, he had seen something in Sienna's eyes as she tried to avoid his own. There was hope, a sense of longing, and even though it was clouded by hurt and disappointment, it was still present enough that Beau knew he wouldn't be able to walk away so easily this time, no matter the circumstance.

"Not again," Beau said, pressing his palms against the slick tile with the water beating his back, bowing his head as if in prayer. "Not today."

Returning to his locker ten minutes later, Beau glanced at his phone, reading Chase's text.

Your GPF crew is in Suite B. On a flight to LA tonight, back in Dallas next week. We'll talk.

Beau quickly toweled off and slipped back into his clothes, trying as quickly as possible to move through the teammates that had begun to pour into the locker room.

"You sprinted back here quick." Giles unlaced his cleats. "Lot of people were waiting on you."

Beau stuffed his foot into a sneaker. "Yeah, I gotta jet."

Lifting a curious eyebrow, Giles folded his arms across his chest. Giles might have been a professional teammate for only a season, but he and Beau had known each other since college, when they began their collegiate athletic careers at Florida State University.

"Jet where?" Giles asked because he knew better than anyone else Beau had no place to really be. He lived a quiet, single life, and apart from work and making appearances at team events, Beau mostly kept to himself.

He grabbed his wallet and keys, slapping Giles on the shoulder as he moved past. "I'll fill you in later." Beau left the locker room, seeking the right set of elevators—the ones that would carry him to Sienna.

"Come on, come on," Beau begged, gnawing on his bottom lip as the elevator ascended painfully slow. His legs bounced—from eagerness or nerves, Beau wasn't sure. The drumming of his pulse in the tight space forced Beau to take a deep, full breath when he stepped onto the highest floor of the stadium.

Shaking in my boots. Great, Beau silently sneered as he made his way down the hall to Suite B, where a dozen people lingered. Beau ignored how the wide eyes of the Golden Penny Foundation representative lit up when she saw him. He wasn't looking for crystal blue orbs. He was in search of vibrant green—a pair of emeralds that mirrored both freshly cut grass in the spring and the pine needles of Christmas trees. Sienna's eyes weren't seasonal. They were annual and always.

Just like her brother's, who was standing right in front of him.

"My dad would roll over in his grave knowing you're a Spark."

Beau could only nod at Henry Clarke, still lanky, still wearing glasses. Unable to read the look on Henry's face—something stern and serious—Beau cleared his throat to recuperate his voice.

"You're right. Your dad would've rather me play basketball than play for Dallas. But here I am."

Henry folded his lips into a firm line.

Okay, so he hits me, Beau thought. *He wouldn't be the first Clarke to.*

But Henry smiled, and after inwardly sighing in relief, Beau did too.

"No. He would've been proud."

The smile fell from Beau's face. *Would he?*

Henry started to continue but stopped when the young girl appeared by his side. She looked like Henry because Henry looked like Sienna. The mouth on her heart-shaped face hung open, highlighting her strong cheekbones and wide eyes. But their color was dark brown, similar to Beau's and his heart fluttered at a thought.

In another place, at another time, she could've been mine.

Even though that was what Sienna had wished all those years ago, Beau knew it wasn't possible.

And I couldn't handle a kid, let alone a sick one, he told himself but found some relief because, even though Sienna's daughter was smaller in stature, with protruding wrist bones and knobby hands, there was a pink tinge to her cheeks and her mouth pressed into a smile after she closed it. If she were sick at the moment, it didn't show.

"It's you, right?" her daughter asked. "You played for my Papa Jack."

"Once upon a time."

"He died."

Beau took a deep breath. "I know."

"He said *you* were the best goddamn wideout he's ever coached."

"Grace Clarke," Sienna hissed. "Language."

Beau braced himself before he lifted his head to look beyond Grace, where he was certain those green eyes would practically bleed disappointment and heartbreak right into him. Instead, Sienna was focusing on her daughter, and Beau could see the silent communication between them—one he could never understand. When she finally looked at Beau, there wasn't disappointment—there was nothing.

Beau's stomach plummeted.

Sienna tucked a blonde lock behind her ear. "Come on. It's getting late. We've overstayed our welcome, and Beau probably has somewhere to be. I bet the team wants to celebrate their win."

Beau wondered if anyone in the room could hear his heart thumping against his sternum. *With you. I should be with you. I should've always been with you.*

"I don't waste too much time celebrating the moment." Beau

looked at Sienna. "Seconds later, you might miss something great."

Sienna placed a hand on her daughter's shoulder. "Well, we wouldn't want you to miss the next great thing. Come on, Grace."

Grace ignored her mother in the way only a teenager could. "You played real good today."

"Really well," Sienna corrected, folding her arms and glancing down at her feet before adding, "Congratulations on your win."

Following Grace's lead, Beau ignored Sienna. "Did you have fun today?" he asked Grace.

Grace beamed.

She has her mother's smile too.

"There's an all-you-can-eat candy bar up here." Grace motioned at Sienna before lowering her voice. "And wine too."

Beau smirked. "I hear they keep all the good stuff for the really special people." He gently lifted his gaze to Sienna. "They got any Swedish Fish? Those are my favorite."

Grace spun on her heels. "I'll get you some."

"You hate Swedish Fish," Sienna said when Grace was out of range.

But you love them.

Beau bit his bottom lip. "I've come around. But nothing beats—"

"Nerds Rope."

A smile ran through Beau's body, up his legs, through his chest, and to his face before his fingers twitched at his side, eager to brush another piece of hair that had fallen in her face. Frustrated, he pocketed his hands before looking at Grace, digging through candy bins enthusiastically with a small plastic shovel.

"She seems like a good kid."

"She's a great kid."

Beau wanted to ignore the plethora of swag from the Golden Penny Foundation littering the room, reminding him of why they were all there. Before Beau could even ask, Sienna gave him the answer.

"Beginning stages of remission. Leukemia."

He tried not to wince. "How long has she been in remission?"

"Eighty-four days now. Last time we cleared nearly two years."

The news was a blow to Beau's gut. "Last time?"

He could see Sienna chew on the inside of her cheek, as if she were contemplating telling him anything more.

"She was diagnosed about two years after my dad died. But, you know, health is never a guarantee. Even if you fight really hard for it."

About two years after I should've stayed for you.

Sienna bounced awkwardly. "You played great. They said it was your best game all season. Most yards or something like that."

"Yeah," he said, rubbing the back of his head. "Someone mentioned that."

Beau usually left the stadium after every game knowing his stats. But that was less for bragging rights and more for fueling his fire—*You can do better.*

It was always about being better, ever since the day he woke up in the hospital, reinforced on the day he returned home to a house that now had one less child, to a mother and father who were so blinded by unspeakable heartache, they couldn't see that they still had one left. He wanted to be a better son—the one who could sprinkle light into his parents' deep, hollow eyes, returning their gazes to how they were when he used to be not an only living child.

And for his brother, Greg, who had lost his life and saved Beau's, he was determined to achieve the dreams Greg couldn't. He would play for his brother's favorite college team. He would make it to the NFL and dominate. And he would, one day, win a Super Bowl Championship.

It was a dream he had shared with Sienna when they were

getting to know each other again after she had moved back to Brookwood. He thought about the day he first saw her again in the guy's locker room at school. Taking in how she had changed from the young girl with constantly scraped knees he had followed around the neighborhood to the *beautiful* young woman with endlessly smooth legs and pouty lips, Beau knew it wouldn't be easy rekindling only their friendship without wanting something more.

Standing in the stadium suite, even though a decade and a half had passed, even though gray had begun to paint his dark brown hair and he donned an ever-present five-o'clock shadow, looking at Sienna, Beau felt no older than a day over eighteen.

"I was racing to the end. I wanted it to be over quickly," Beau admitted, as if his yardage or touchdowns made any difference in the length of the game.

"Why?"

"So I could get to you sooner."

Sienna's head jolted back, and she opened her mouth to speak but promptly pressed her lips tightly together, as if it took every ounce of strength to battle against her words, to keep them from falling out. Beau didn't want that.

"Can we talk?"

Shaking her head, Sienna picked at invisible lint on the sleeves of her dark, navy coat. "This is Grace's day."

Tackled with embarrassment, Beau nodded. *It's not about me. It's about her daughter.* Beau's heart squeezed. *But it never was just about* me. *It always was about* us.

The representative from the foundation approached Beau and Sienna. "Oh, wonderful. Beau, how about we get some photos with the Clarke family?"

It wasn't until he heard the word *family* that it dawned on Beau a very prominent member was absent. But he had been too blinded by Sienna to notice that apart from team officials, foundation reps, Henry, Sienna, and Grace, there was no one else with them.

No dad, Beau thought, chewing on the inside of his cheek.

Grace pranced over with bags of candy, including one filled with Swedish Fish that she shoved at Beau.

"Save it for later, okay?" Grace motioned at the baggy before pushing it, along with a folded-up paper, discreetly into his hand. "Don't open until you get home."

Knitting his brow, Beau looked down, but the seriousness on Grace's face forced him to nod, and he shoved both items into his pocket.

"Right here," the woman called. "In front of the window with the stadium as a backdrop."

Glancing at Sienna, who begrudgingly shuffled her feet, Beau waited for her to move before following.

"Stand there, Beau, if you don't mind."

Beau didn't mind because the woman pointed to the spot beside Sienna, who pressed her hands to the top of Grace's shoulders when Beau bumped into her side. He held his breath and could feel her doing the same. The tension palpable, the nearly invisible space between them holding an abundance of memories, of words said and unsaid, of broken promises and dreams, of everything Beau had done wrong and all he wished he had done right.

But good or bad, Beau wanted to hold on to all of it. He slid his arm carefully and cautiously behind Sienna, resting his hand against her back as she swayed.

The photographer stood a few feet in front of them, clicking away. "Lovely. Let's do one last final shot. One, two. . . "

By the time the photographer hit three, Sienna had leaned into Beau's gentle and cautious hold, as if to bind the gap in their story, sealing all the memories safely between them where they had always been.

But Beau knew their story wasn't done yet. And when he pulled back after the photo, his fingertips slid down her back, feeling the tremble that shook Sienna's body beneath her jacket.

At that moment, Beau silently vowed he would finish their

story the way it always should have ended—packed to the brim with happiness, so the chapter of heartache and hurt was an afterthought instead of the entire plot.

He watched Sienna try to look anywhere but at him, and Beau smiled when she failed.

Second chances don't happen every day. And third, like miracles, almost never. Better not waste it.

After Grace had collected bags filled to the brim with Sparks memorabilia—signed balls, jerseys, photos, mugs—Beau hovered to the side, unsure of his place.

"The driver is on level three to take you home," Janet told them. "I hope you had a special day, Grace. It was wonderful to have you and your family join us. I'm sure the Sparks would love to have you for another game next season when they get their act together." She looked over her shoulder at Beau.

They left the suite, gathering in the hallway and waiting for Henry to return from the bathroom. Beau reached out and placed a hand on Janet's shoulder and lowered his voice. "If I wanted to contact them, how would I do that?"

"I'm sorry?"

Beau grit his teeth. "How do I *call* her?"

Janet's eyes rounded, concerned. "Grace?"

"Her mother," Beau corrected immediately. "I mean, if I wanted to send something. Season passes for next year, or I don't know, something else."

My heart on a silver fucking platter, he offered in thought.

Janet pulled out a business card. "Just arrange it through my office. We can send whatever you'd like. That's kind of you, Beau."

"Thanks," he mumbled. *Get Chase on it*, Beau thought, but he could already hear the dozens of questions his agent would ask and decided it would be best if he figured it out on his own.

Sienna was quick to push the button for the elevator when Henry entered the hallway.

"I'll take them down. I'm on three, too." Beau pushed past Janet into the elevator, ignoring Henry's questioning gaze when he enthusiastically pressed the close button.

Sienna continued to avoid his stare, smoothing down the ends of Grace's wig.

"Did you make it to NASA yet?" Beau asked Henry.

"My chances of being an astronaut were about as high as you winning the Super Bowl this year," Henry quipped. "No. I teach math at our alma mater. We're still in Brookwood."

We. Beau realized. *He said we. Which means she's still there.*

"We still live in Papa's house," Grace offered. "The three of us. Me. Henry. Mom."

Beau could feel the wrath of Sienna's stare burn into Grace, as if she were furious her daughter let Beau know all he needed to—there was no one else in the picture.

The elevator opened, and Beau moved aside for Henry to exit first, followed by Grace. When Sienna stepped in front of him, Beau slipped the bag of Swedish Fish into her jacket pocket.

"Can we stop at the diner for a milkshake? I want everyone to see me in this limo," Grace said.

Sienna shook her head. "Your day is over. And I think you made enough passes at the candy buffet."

Huffing, Grace trudged to the limo, where the driver was waiting by the open door. She turned back to Beau and smiled. "Thanks for making my wish come true."

Beau cocked an eyebrow, confused.

"The Sparks won. I guess miracles do happen." Grace shrugged before sliding into the limo.

"Take care of yourself, big guy." Henry gave Beau a pat on his back before following Grace.

Nodding, Beau chewed on his lip as Sienna approached the door.

"Sienna," he said quietly, and he could see the reluctance in her body as she stopped beside him. "I'm happy I got to see you."

Sienna said nothing, and Beau sighed heavily. *It's not our night.*

Sienna glanced around the near-empty parking lot. "Is your car even down here?"

"My car? No." She was mid-eye roll when Beau pointed and continued, "My bike, yeah."

He watched Sienna follow his finger and could see in the smallest twitch of her shoulders the way she held her breath for a moment before shaking her head, her blonde waves cascading down her back.

Your bike. Our bike. Beau wanted to cup her cheek and hold her close. *I didn't forget. I could never forget.*

But Sienna's face remained hard and cold before she stepped closer to the car to join Grace and Henry.

"Sienna," Beau called out again, and she sighed so strongly her shoulders raised and dropped. "You did a good job with her." He motioned to the limo where Grace was continuing to go on about milkshakes.

"I know," was all she said before stepping in, not waiting for the driver to close the door and shutting it behind her.

Beau let out a heavy breath, still hearing Grace yammer on about that milkshake. "Hey," he called out to the driver, following him behind the limo. Beau pulled out his wallet, handing him a hundred-dollar bill. "Get them some milkshakes, would you? From wherever the girl wants."

With a skeptical look and nod, the driver cautiously pocketed the money, and Beau headed to his bike, not wanting to see Sienna drive off. Straddling the seat, he reached into his pocket for the key, his fingertips colliding with the creased, paper he had shoved in earlier. With the limo out of sight, Beau pulled it out and opened it, finding a piece of paper flooded with ink.

Dear Mr. Walker,

Alright, I'll be honest. I don't really care that much about football. Don't take that personally. I'm sure you're a great wide receiver, even if your record this season tells me otherwise. But the truth is, the day I decided to submit my application to the Golden Penny Foundation was the day I found out two important things: 1) my stem cell transplant worked, and even though I wasn't cancer free right then and there, the doctors were happy and 2) my uncle Henry bought me tickets to the Simon Gorges concert this spring, and that's what I was going to ask for in the first place. I would've asked for backstage passes but I refuse to meet him without my own hair.

Another thing happened that night. I got up to use the bathroom (sorry for the TMI), and when I walked down the hall, heard my mom crying. It wasn't a happy cry, you'll have to trust me on that. I like to think I know her best. The truth is, she cries a lot. Like a lot, even though she'll never admit it. I hate to make her sound so sad, but she just is so *sad.*

And then I realized that if she couldn't be happy on the day that should be the happiest moment of our lives, she's the one who deserves the wish, not me.

Beau's hands trembled as he continued to read the letter, each painful word slicing into him. His phone shrilled from his pocket, and he sent the call to voicemail.

And the second one too.

The third time Chase called, Beau answered it with a huff. "What?"

"Voicemail? I'm your *agent*."

Beau ran a hand over his face. "Is there an agent emergency? I thought you had a flight to catch."

"No. But I take back everything I said before about what a mistake it was blowing off the interview. That Golden Penny group has already posted photos of you and the kid—"

"Grace," Beau corrected him.

Chase cleared his throat. "Right. There are some pictures of you and *Grace* already on the social media circuit. So good going with that one."

"For fuck's sake, Chase," Beau exclaimed. "It wasn't a media op."

"I'm saying—"

"Turning on vacation mode now. Talk to you next week."

Beau hung up the phone and slid it into his pocket. He sighed, unfolding the letter and continuing to read, his chest coiling with hurt and guilt. By the time he reached Grace's signature, Beau had to pause and take a deep breath before continuing to the final blurb.

PS: It's pretty much a mortal sin to not grant the wish of a sick kid. I'm not technically sick right now, but I have been for long enough. Just make my mom happy the way you did all those years ago. I don't tell her enough, but she deserves it. If you're short on ideas on how to do that, there's a list on the back of this paper.

PPS: This stays between us.

Beau turned the letter in his hand, eyeing the list. The breaths of his laughter echoed in the near-empty garage, and his bike wobbled between his spasming thighs.

Number twelve on Grace's list of suggestions was a motorcycle ride.

just one more day

DEAR MOM,

It's day twenty-seven, and I wanted to let you know one of those wishes came true, but in a weird way.

School is fine. It's about as fine as you can imagine it would be if you transferred to a new school in May because your dad couldn't live in the house where his wife killed herself. So, it's shitty. I ignore the stares and hope that by tomorrow people don't care as much. But I guess it's kind of hard to do that because I'm 5'10", and Henry is even taller and on crutches.

It started with his crutches. Or his crutch.

I was taking a long bathroom break from PE when I saw him hanging outside the guys' locker room. He was sulking (the norm these days). But there was something not normal. And that was that there was only one crutch up against him when he needs two. He obviously didn't leave it somewhere.

"What's going on?"

Henry huffed. "Nothing, Sienna. Just go."

"Go? And how are you *supposed to go anywhere?" I could tell he was having a hard time standing.*

"Nothing. I told you. Leave."

His eyes met mine, and Mom, I knew. *Kids are so awful. I looked at the door of the locker room. "In there?" I asked, but before he could even answer, I pushed the door open and almost vomited from how gross it smelled, like sweat and boy.*

I avoided eye contact with the half-dressed guys as they gasped and whistled and hollered.

*"You're new here, but the sign says '*men,*'" one shouted.*

"Then what are you *doing in here?" I retorted, purposely eyeing him up and down as he clutched the towel around his waist. "I am* new. *And so is my brother—"*

Henry hissed my name from the doorway. If he didn't need the other crutch to stand, he might've hit me with it.

"Give me back his crutch," I demanded, feeling all eyes on me. "I know it's in here. Either you give it to me, or I'll search every small*"—I paused and gave the loser another up-down—"inch of this place until—"*

"Sienna—"

I was about to wave Henry off again before something approached me from the left. I say something because it was a scent, a pleasant whiff of the past—like freshly cut grass and lemonade and warm blueberry pie.

But it was a guy, in case you're wondering, Mom.

I snatched the crutch from him, holding it back to Henry. Narrowing my eyes, I turned back to the guy who had the audacity to speak.

"I'm not sure if you remember. I'm—"

"The only thing you should introduce yourself as is an asshole," I growled.

I went to leave before the unapologetic jerkoff spoke again.

"I didn't—"

He didn't have the chance to finish his sentence because I hit him. Right in the nose. He didn't look hurt, so much as he did shocked, even though it was a good punch. But do you know what he did right after, Mom? He smiled. *For a second, I thought I had hit him hard enough to rattle his brain.*

And even though I tried to hide it, I smiled back. Do you know what the grin on his face felt like? Kind of like the anticipation of an awesome thing, like when you've been waiting for the most important person in your life to come home after being away, and you finally hear keys opening the door.

"The last time you hit me was with a Wiffle ball bat."

That smile on my face? It dropped. Actually, I *dropped. Right back to a decade ago when we lived in this town, when I used to ride bikes and climb trees with the short boy with the long brown hair.*

"Beau?"

I felt stupid for not recognizing him, but to be fair, I was in a fit of rage. And honestly, Mom? He looks the same. There's just more of him.

"You got taller," I whispered.

"You're still pretty."

My cheeks burned when the left side of his mouth lifted into a smirk.

I know now, Mom, that you can smell a memory. A happy one. And for the first time since you died—for the first time in nearly a month—I felt *happy, and do you know what I was thinking about? This place.*

I remembered the crack on the sidewalk to the right of our old driveway and how Beau always *got his bike stuck in it. I remembered his mom ran a baking business from her kitchen and how he always smelled like candied sugar and vanilla. I remembered us being chased out of that kitchen after trying to grab a spoon full of cookie dough. It all whooshes through my mind on video—riding bikes, playing tag, selling lemonade, climbing trees—a tornado of sounds of childhood laughter, teasing, and fun.*

Everything I now recall about living here has to do with Beau. And it's all I could think about when I got home and faced Dad.

"You slugged *my wideout?"*

"Your what-out?"

"Beau Walker is going to be one of my starting receivers next fall. Probably a captain. And you hit *him?"*

I lifted the foil covering another casserole and closed the oven. "It was a misunderstanding."

Dad sighed. "That's what I told the principal. But you, *I'm telling you something different. You never raise your hand to anyone unless you're being attacked."*

"Henry was being attacked."

"Standing up for him and doing what you did are two different things."

"Mom would've been proud of me."

I know, Mom, you would. Because it's the same as when we were little. You'd always say, "You only have each other to take care of." *So I did. And I will, even when he's upset with me for doing just that. Because if you won't go to war for the ones you love, who will? You used to remind us of that too.*

I said nothing else, and neither did Dad. Because something I've learned is when you play the dead-mom card, you really win the hand. I apologized to Henry, but he found my "Sorry, I'm not sorry" apology pretty lackluster.

After a silent dinner, I slid out my window and climbed onto the roof.

That's when I saw Beau walking to the front door.

"What are you doing?"

Beau looked up and scratched the back of his head with his free hand. "Shouldn't I be asking you *that?"*

I motioned at whatever he was holding. "What's that?"

"My mom wanted me to bring it over."

"Does she know I hit you?

"Yes."

"And she baked something?"

"Yes."

"Why?"

He looked at the front door and back at me. "Are you going to let me come up?"

I scooted closer to the edge. "Why did your mom send you over here with a pie after I *hit* you?"

"She didn't. It's a cake."

I rolled my eyes even though he couldn't see me do it, and before I knew it, he moved to the side of the house. He clanged loudly on the AC unit.

"I use the trellis," I told him, laying back down. "It's quieter."

Beau grunted and pushed the pan closer to me as he hoisted himself up. "You were always better at climbing than I was. Why are you up here?"

"Space."

I didn't tell him I come up here to talk to you, Mom. Because I didn't know how he'd react if I told him I come up to the roof to talk to my dead mother through the stars. And even though I wanted space, I suddenly didn't mind Beau next to me.

"I heard about your mom," he murmured. "That's why mine sent this over. She thought maybe you were going through a hard time."

I said nothing.

"Greg died six years ago."

My face dropped. Beau's brother was older than us. I pushed my brain to try and remember if there was something wrong with him when we were younger.

Beau pulled his knees to his chest, resting his chin on them. "He was watching me. I ran into the middle of the street to get a ball, and there was a car."

Beau stopped talking, but he might as well have continued because I could feel everything he didn't say. When he tapped the side of his head, I noticed the scar I hadn't seen earlier, one that definitely wasn't there when we were kids, of that, I'm sure.

"When I woke up, he was gone."

I didn't tell him I was sorry. Because I knew that no matter how apologetic I felt about Beau's loss, it was nothing compared to how he felt.

"It took me a while to feel normal."

"What does normal feel like?" I asked.

I can't imagine how anything could ever feel normal without you, Mom.

"Less angry."

I took a deep breath. "What helps?"

Beau shuffled closer. "Time. And talking."

But I don't want to talk about *you, Mom. I want to talk* to *you.*

"I talk to him, about him. I talk about everything," Beau admitted. "Plans, things I want to do."

I tilted my head away and banished the tear from my face with my thumb. Mom, we planned so many things. Big and small things. So many that I'm afraid I'll forget.

"Like what?"

"College ball. NFL."

I could hear the pain in Beau's voice, and my heart hurt knowing he's felt this longer than I have.

"Wishes or dreams?"

"No. Those things are dreams."

Cocking my head, I asked, "What's the difference?"

"You dream with your head. And wish with your heart."

I swear, Mom, my heart stopped beating because that was something you might say, and for a second, I wanted to tell him goodnight and shimmy back down the trellis into my room so I could catch my breath.

But before I could do that, he continued, "A dream you can work toward. But a wish you put out there and hope it happens, even when you know it probably won't. It's only about hope."

I had to look away from Beau because I know that's true. Because Mom, I wish I could hug you, and I know that's not possible, but part of me—my heart, my bones—still hopes that one day it might be true.

Taking a deep breath, I mirrored Beau's position and laid my head on my knees, facing him. He was picking dried leaves off a shingle between us.

"What do you wish for?"

Beau looked right at me, and I felt, even in the waning light as night fully approached, like he was looking right into *me.*

"Just one more day."

I want one more day too, Mom. I want one more day to tell you how angry I am that you thought I could do this alone. I want to hug you and hit you at the same time and beg you to stay, beg you to know just how much we all need you around. But then I'd use the rest of the day to do everything we had planned—and wished—to do together.

Remember, Mom, when I told you I wished for a friend? I found one.

So, maybe Beau was wrong about wishes only being about hope. Because on the roof, as we sat eating the cake with our hands, wiping our sticky fingers on our shirts, talking about all the things we would do if we had more time, I knew Beau was that wish come true.

Love,

Sienna

do you want to know a secret?

DEAR MOM,

It's been forty-four days since you died and a few weeks since I punched Beau in the face and he showed up with cake. We see each other at school and talk, but not as much as we do on the roof after the sun goes down and Dad goes to sleep.

His mom baked nothing today, so he brought Swedish Fish, and I smiled because they've always been my favorite since I was little, but Beau really hates them. But my smile was less about the firm, gummy sweetness and more about Beau remembering that. I didn't say anything, though.

I ripped open the bag and poured sixteen fish into my hand.

"Why do you do that?"

I shrugged. "Sixteen is my lucky number." It's also the number of pieces of candy I can eat without getting a stomachache.

It's so different on the roof with Beau. Is it because we're closer to the stars? Even though we're only a story off the ground, I feel like we're in our own little world, and it only took Beau visiting a few times before I realized we had created a safe space.

A few days ago, with a cracking voice and aching heart, I told Beau everything, Mom. I told him I come up here because I feel you can hear me. I told him about our shared love for the stars, for making wishes.

And even though I would've bet all the Swedish Fish in the world that he'd laugh uncomfortably and think I was crazy, Beau only nodded and said, "That's cool."

Tonight we were flat on our backs when we saw it—a shooting star clear as day.

"Quick, make a wish," Beau told me.

I felt kind of on the spot, and I think he could tell.

"What? You don't have a running list or something?"

I laughed. "It's not like a Christmas list. We only do it on birthdays. Hers and ours."

I didn't tell Beau I went rogue and made a wish for a friend when we moved back.

Beau shrugged beside me. "It should be like a Christmas list. You should always be ready. You never know what can happen. Maybe you wasted that one."

It wasn't a wasted shooting star, Mom, because I felt in the moment that it was you. But maybe he was right. I didn't know that our last birthday eve together would be the *last.*

Beau turned on his side. "Start a list," he told me. "And don't wait. Just find a really great star and have at it."

"What, now?"

"Why not?"

"I don't have any paper," I told him.

"If they come from the heart, you'll remember them."

His words struck me, and I felt even more on the spot. "What if they're silly?"

"Silly?"

"Like," I began, "I don't know, nothing all that meaningful."

"What's number one on your wish list?"

I pursed my lips in thought. "I guess it's not really in any order. But the ocean. I want to see the ocean. And I want to go on a sailboat in *the ocean."*

"Okay, why?" Beau's tone was just inquisitive enough.

"We planned to do that, me and my mom." The admission stung, but I felt safe enough to continue.

And I told him all the things I would've wished for if you were still around. It's not just sailboats or how I want to go to France and dance in Provence's lavender fields like you did in college—something you promised we would do the summer after I graduate from high school—or how I only want to go back to Disney World so I can eat my weight in Dole Whips. Or visit Graceland (that was more your thing than mine).

There are two things I didn't realize until I finished listing everything in my head and heart. One, they're memories I already wished I had, and two, I was crying.

Beau reached out as if he were about to wipe my face, but his hand stalled midair before he fisted his fingers and dropped his arm. Instinctively, I turned my head to banish my tears away on my sweatshirt, but Beau stopped me.

"I don't like seeing you upset, but I wish someone had told me it was okay to cry." He scooted closer. "It's okay to cry, Sienna."

Beau's words opened the dam, and I couldn't have stopped it even if I wanted to.

Crying won't bring you back, I know that. I've always known that. But as tears flooded my face, I realized that what it does is make you feel real—something more than a memory. All this time, I've been so afraid of you becoming just *that. But talking about everything I wished we could do together with Beau makes it seem like you're still around and still a part of me.*

And my tears? They came from my heart. Like all the wishes I'll never have the chance to make with you by my side.

"We can do those things sometime," Beau said. "You and me."

I looked up at him through teary eyes. "Really?"

"Yeah. I'll go to the beach, but I won't eat Dole Whips. I hate pineapple."

That made me laugh. "You can have a turkey leg," I joked, but then I remembered. "You said wishes don't really happen."

Beau shrugged. "I know I said that. But then I gave it some thought. You coming back, maybe you changed my mind." When he stopped talking and grew silent my heart began to pound. "I've been meaning to ask you something."

Beau finally reached out to wipe my cheeks. His hand was cool against my flaming skin, and I tried not to lean too hard against him.

"What?" I asked with a crackly voice.

He studied me for a minute, chewing on his lip. "Did you forget about me after you left?"

I wanted to tell him I did, but not in the way he might think. Because how could you forget the person who was the first thing you thought of when you woke up? How could you forget the last person you thought about before you went to sleep? Back then, it was about adventures, tricks, having fun. I'd lie on my pillow at night, reminding myself to tell Beau not to forget his net so we could catch toads in the creek, or to ask him to show me again how to tie a sailor's knot.

When we moved, I cried the entire drive to Nashville. I didn't care that I was leaving the only home I had ever known or the treehouse Dad had built for us. I cried because I was leaving my best friend. And it was you, Mom, who told me I'd see him again one day when the time was right.

And then you did what Moms do—you made the hurt less. You took us on adventures, hosted middle-of-the-day dance parties, said yes to ice cream sundaes for dinner. In some ways, Beau is doing for now what you did then.

So even though it's wrong that you're not here, there's something right about it too.

"I didn't forget. But I tried not to remember so much because it hurt a lot." My answer was full of honesty, and I knew by the softness in Beau's eyes he believed me.

"Do you want to know a secret?" he whispered.

We were facing each other, and because of the shadow the street lamp made on his face, I noticed how thick his eyelashes were. I nodded.

"On my eighth birthday," Beau began, "I wished you would come back. Also for a new bike," he added with a grin.

This secret made my stomach flutter, and I pressed my lips together to hide my smirk, but I clearly didn't do that so well.

"What?"

"See? Maybe you were just wishing wrong is all. Stars are more

powerful than candles." I motioned up. "If you had made it here, maybe I would've come back sooner."

Beau laughed. "Yeah, maybe. But it doesn't matter now."

We turned on our backs and his eyes focused on the sea of stars above us. Our arms were flush against each other, and his fingers fluttered next to mine, as if he were contemplating holding my hand. I didn't mind that he didn't actually do it, because what he said next filled the well I had drained by missing you with a quick flood of him.

"It was worth waiting anyway."

Love,

Sienna

chapter three

SIENNA LEFT her room to make a cup of chamomile tea when she stopped at Grace's door. "What are you doing with that?"

"He was kind of dreamy," she told her mother without looking up from the yearbook. "Even *then*."

Sienna sighed and stomped over to the bed, taking the book from Grace. It had been over a week since they had gone to the game, and in just a short time, Sienna had dodged many of her daughter's questions about Beau.

At the closet, Sienna slipped the yearbook inside a box on the floor. "These don't belong to you. And it's late," she said, lifting the box and holding it against her hip.

"He was your boyfriend, right?"

Sienna looked around at what used to be her old room, focusing on the window—the one Beau had snuck in and out of what felt like hundreds of times.

"No," she lied.

"Are you sure? Henry says—"

"I was there, you weren't." She stared her daughter down until she slid back against the pillows, grabbing a book from her nightstand.

"*The Notebook?* Again?"

Grace shrugged. "Not all of us are cold-hearted shrews like

you. Some of us appreciate romance," she teased her mother as Sienna dropped the box and moved to sit on the bed.

"I'm *not* a shrew. And I read that book too, once upon a time. And I watched the movie about three hundred times with you."

"You're right, you're not a shrew." Grace's eyes pierced Sienna's over the paperback. "But you don't believe in love."

Ouch.

Sienna tilted her head. "Just because I don't believe in *this* kind of love," she said, fingering the spine, "doesn't mean I don't believe in love."

Grace raised an eyebrow.

"I love *you*," Sienna reminded her, smoothing down a cowlick of Grace's pixie cut with a smile. It reminded her of the wild ways her hair grew in as a baby.

Rolling her eyes, Grace turned a page. "That's different and you know it. When was the last time you went on a date?"

Sienna couldn't remember a proper date that involved a door being opened for her, wine, and a nice meal, but there were occasional late nights after work with Dylan Lockhart, who she had grown to tolerate more since high school, including a handful of times a year in bed.

"It's late. And a school night." She pulled the book from Grace's hands and returned it to the nightstand, her hand brushing against the coin from the game.

"Mom?" Grace peeked out from the duvet. "I love you too."

Turning off the light, Sienna shut the door, took the box to her room—what used to be her father's—and dropped it into the closet before heading to the kitchen.

"She's out?" Henry asked from the kitchen table.

Shuffling over to the freezer, Sienna pulled out a pint of ice cream before joining Henry at the table. "She'll sleep through her alarm tomorrow, I bet."

"You know what's better than ice cream? That milkshake you should've ordered the other day," her brother said, crunching on a chip.

Sienna lifted her eyes to his and brought a heavy spoonful of chocolate ice cream to her mouth.

"Sienna," Henry said with a sigh. "Beau never did anything *wrong*."

You're right, Sienna wanted to say. *He stopped doing anything.* She scraped at the carton with the spoon. "He should've come for Dad's funeral."

He should've come back for me.

Henry sat back, folding his arm. "Maybe, yeah. That would've been nice. But it was years ago. We've all lived a hundred lives since then."

Sienna couldn't argue. At thirty-three, her exhausted mind and body felt more like it was approaching her midsixties. A baby at nineteen, losing her father and buying a business in her twenties—those events aged her slowly. But Sienna could remember the moment she began to age on fast forward.

It was when she wondered, after seeing Grace change into her pajamas, if she had hurt herself on the playground at school. A fall must have caused the deep purple bruising along her back. Sienna thought she had gone hard of hearing a few days later when the doctor drawled out, "leukemia."

A hundred lives felt like an understatement.

"Dad would've been proud of him. We all know Beau was the son he never had," he joked. "Not much bragging rights about chess tournaments. State championships? Division-I scholarships? NFL? Beau was the favorite."

Sienna slid the carton across the table to Henry. "You and me are quite the pair. He didn't go around bragging about his daughter getting knocked up at nineteen."

There was a time when Sienna knew her father wasn't proud of her. Like when she flunked out of college, drank too much, and ended up pregnant after a night spent with a near stranger who had wished the baby away.

She and her father spent most of her pregnancy tiptoeing around each other in this very kitchen. But occasionally, Sienna would find a stack of white chocolate bars in the pantry or a fresh jar of spicy pickles. And on the day Grace was born, the mask of disappointment fell from her father's face, and a smile never left it.

It was a smile Sienna hadn't seen since before her mother's death.

Grace had given Sienna purpose. But she also healed a family that had been broken by grief. She filled the fourth seat at their table that had been empty after her mother died and Beau had left. Glancing at the empty chair, she could imagine her father sitting there, hunched over a plate, bringing his mouth to the fork instead of the fork to his mouth. Grace had learned how to eat from him apparently. Watching Henry, who had dug into the pint, eating the same way, Sienna smiled.

Her father and Henry were co-fathers, coaching soccer games, teaching Grace how to ride a bike, cursing as they put together presents on Christmas Eve. Her father watched Grace while Sienna worked as a bartender. *Why does she need a dad when she already has a family?* Sienna would often think to herself.

But Sienna learned at a young age that nothing was guaranteed. Parents weren't always around, and sometimes they missed the points where you needed them the most. Best friends didn't always mean best friends forever, and love didn't always mean an infinite love.

But the most painful, unfair lesson Sienna had ever learned was that children don't always outlive their parents. And she spent many years of her life holding her breath, afraid she and Grace might be an example of that lesson too.

Sienna was grateful her father was spared from watching Grace decline so rapidly. If he had been alive at the time of Grace's diagnosis, if he watched her scream through blood draws, vomit from chemotherapy, nearly die of infection twice, lose every strand of her beautiful, angelic hair, if he had seen the victorious look on her face disappear when her cancer returned, surely Sienna's father would have died of a broken heart.

"I'm beat," Henry stood from the table. "Hey, she needs her labs done before the appointment next week, right? Want me to take her after school?"

"No, I'll do it." *You've done so much already*. It took a special kind of man to do what Henry had done—to help raise his niece and support his sister through their cancer journey.

"Henry," Sienna called to her brother. "He would've been proud of you too. Trust me on that."

Later that night, as Sienna crawled into bed and listened to her brother shut his door, she felt grateful for his offer, for his attentiveness. But a deep pit swirled in her stomach as she thought about the bloodwork and the upcoming appointment, and tears pooled behind her closed eyes. She might not have been alone in the day-to-day grind with Grace, but there had been no one holding her at night when she let all her fears seep into her pillow tear by tear.

"I'm wondering if they'll invite you back to all the home games next year," Dr. Barron said, sitting behind her desk. "The Sparks have been god-awful before you showed up."

Grace grinned. "I got to keep the coin."

Dr. Barron slid the glasses from the top of her hair to her nose. "I see you came with souvenirs."

She motioned to the large shopping bag filled to the brim with Sparks mementos that Sienna and Grace agreed patients might appreciate more than the floor of Grace's room would. Grace pulled out a signed ball and tossed it to Dr. Barron, who laughed as she caught it before palming it in her hands and placing it on the bookshelf behind her.

"I'm your favorite patient now, right?"

"Well," Dr. Barron began. "You really aren't my active patient anymore. The good news is your results are still excellent, like we had hoped." She beamed at Grace, and Sienna let out the breath she had been holding. "The bad news is you're super anemic, and I'd like to see a little more weight on you at this point."

Grace did a happy dance in her chair.

"Hooray for anemia," Sienna chimed in sarcastically, trying to remain upright even though the relief that hit her body nearly made her slide out of the chair.

Dr. Barron pulled out a prescription pad. "We'll up the iron supplements. And, Mom, here's a prescription for some calorically dense food," she joked. "Other than that, we'll see you in *six* months."

Sienna swung her head. "Not three?"

Dr. Barron turned to her computer. "No need."

Grace shot up from the chair, taking the handles of the shopping bag. "Can I go now, Mom? I want to see Molly."

"I'll meet you up there." Sienna waited until Grace was well out of the office before turning to Dr. Barron. "You really don't need to see her until the summer?"

"Sienna," Dr. Barron began, "I've told you this before. You can't look for a problem that doesn't exist. That won't do you *or* Grace any favors."

Last time I wasn't looking for a problem, and there ended up being one. Sienna bounced her leg, uncomfortably recalling her daughter's last brief remission. If she had it her way, Sienna would ask Dr. Barron to run a full blood panel on Grace every week. *Is this who I am now? Wanting to drag my daughter to a lab to stick her with a needle just for my own peace of mind?*

Dr. Barron stood from her chair and moved around her desk, leaning against it. "Sienna, how long have we known each other?"

"No offense, but it's been too long," Sienna said dryly.

"We've been with each other through some high highs and

low lows," Dr. Barron said. "And what do I always tell you? Celebrate the highs—"

"So that she will too," Sienna finished with a sigh.

Dr. Barron reached out, squeezing Sienna's shoulder. "It's time you go back to being the mom of a healthy kid. And you're far too young for frown lines."

Sienna rubbed her forehead as she stood. "Can you write me a prescription for Botox so insurance covers it?"

Laughing, Dr. Barron shook her head. "I'll see you in six months. And I hope not a moment sooner, but you know the protocol."

I know it too well.

Sienna entered the hospital hallway she knew like the back of her hand. Grace had her treatments on the third floor. Urgent Care was on the first, and the ICU—where Grace ended up intubated, fighting a serious infection for ten long days—on the seventh. Oncology—where Grace had celebrated two Halloweens with all the other kids—on the twelfth. They had worn costumes over their ports, their IVs, and instead of superhero masks, many had medical ones over their mouth and nose as a preventive measure to protect whatever little of their immune systems remained.

She tried to ignore the little boy who got off the elevator with his parents—the sunken circles under his eyes, the frail bones of his wrist, the roundness of his bald head. But what Sienna couldn't ignore was the curt, distracted nod of his father, the hurriedness of his mother's steps, and the worry that flowed freely off them. But the smile on the little boy's face made Sienna smile back, and she remembered all of Grace's smirks and grins, her cheekiness popping through even her sickest of moments.

And if she could be like that back then, Sienna thought, *why can't I be like that* now?

Sienna got off the elevator, hanging a right. She jumped when a warm body knocked into her.

"Oh, thank you for all the Sparks stuff!" It was Luella, Sienna's secret favorite nurse. "You're going to make my son very happy." Luella released Sienna, patting her on the cheek. "He wants to be just like that Beau Walker. What do they call him? The flying receiver? He's loved him since he was seven years old."

Him and me both, Sienna added in thought. "I'm glad he'll like them. How have you been, Luella?"

Luella straightened her stethoscope. "Well, I'm better now that I got to see my sweet Grace. Can't believe how well she's doing. And she's grown, my goodness! She'll be catching up to her mama soon enough. You know, we love when they leave and don't have to come back. But I'll tell you a secret." Luella leaned forward and whispered, "We love to see them come back *thriving*, too."

Sienna's heart twisted. If there was anything positive that came out of Grace's cancer journey, it was that Sienna quickly learned that angels did walk on earth. They happened to be trapped in the bodies of nurses who somehow made every needle stick hurt less, who washed your daughter's hair after she threw up on it, who placed catheters and changed sheets, all while pulling laughter out of terribly sick children.

"We'll be better about visiting," she told Luella. "Who is she bothering now?"

"She's sitting with Molly. Your girl put a big smile on that one's face. She's over in isolation. Fever today."

Oh, Molly.

"I'll make sure she doesn't tire her out. Thanks, Luella."

Sienna rounded another corner and caught sight of Grace down the hall, pressing her hand on the glass that kept Molly safe from the outside world where the common cold could kill her.

Grace laughed. "No, but seriously, number seven's butt in real life is out of this world. TV doesn't do it justice."

Sienna couldn't hear Molly's response but rolled her eyes as her daughter continued.

"Do you want to go to a game next season? I told you my mom used to date Beau Walker, right? He could get us VIP treatment again. She was totally in love—"

"Grace!"

Gasping, Grace let out a giggle. "I have to go. I'll text you."

Sienna sighed with a heavy heart. *Friendship shouldn't be this way. Kids shouldn't have to live this way.*

A few minutes later, Sienna and Grace rode the elevator down to the lobby.

"How's Molly?" Sienna asked, waiting for Grace to follow after she bid farewell to the familiar security guard.

Molly and Grace met during treatment after Grace's second recurrence and grew to be fast friends. But while Grace's prognosis finally grew more positive, Molly's turned bleaker, more complicated.

"Ready to bust out of this place. And when she does, let me tell you. We've got plans."

Sienna laughed. "Oh, yeah?"

Grace nodded emphatically. "Big time. All-night movie marathon. Disney World because I've *never* been," she reminded her mother. "And neither has she."

"I promised I'd take you, and I will." *When I can afford it.* But a trip that included Molly, Sienna was unsure of. "Are you hungry? How about we grab a bite?

"I want a chicken quesadilla," Grace announced, bumping her arm against Sienna. "And *extra* guacamole."

Sienna peeked over her shoulder at the hospital as they made their way to the parking lot. If there was a way to celebrate six months of no more hospital visits, of health, and the happiness radiating off her daughter, it had to involve guacamole.

"Your wish is my command."

"Do you want the good news or the bad news?"

Sienna dropped a crate of clean glasses on the counter behind the bar. "I'm sort of on a good news kick today, so let's start with that."

Her barback smiled. "We need a new fridge."

"Frank," Sienna groaned, "I said *good* news."

Frank stared at her, unblinking.

"Well, what's the *bad* news then?"

"The fridge is broken."

So much for having a positive outlook on things. Shaking her head, Sienna knitted her brows together.

Frank stepped behind the bar, helping unload the crate. "Well, now, at least we won't have to kick it to get it going. Stubbed my damn toe last week."

Sienna slid the last glass onto the shelf. "Well, do me a favor since you're wearing boots today. Go kick it and see if you can get it going again."

She made a mental note to ask Henry—her unofficial, unpaid accountant—if she could get something and put it on layaway.

Frank frowned.

"Frank, I just finished paying the plumber to fix the bathroom, and the heater is—"

"You know," Frank interrupted. "If you shimmy it with that kick, we probably could get another few weeks out of it. Forget about all that, I'll try to fix it. The only good news is Grace's good news." He winked before lifting a stack of empty crates.

Sienna smiled and sighed, looking around Maloney's. More than the plumbing and heater needed fixing. But there was a plus side to owning the only bar in a small town. With no other place to go after work, no other spot to gather on Friday and Saturday nights, patrons didn't mind that it was more of a *dive* bar. They ignored the stripping floors, the barstools that should have been replaced the day Sienna had bought it with her half of her father's life insurance payout. At that point, buying the place she worked at seemed like an investment. Really, it was a money pit.

"So?" Dylan appeared at the bar, yanking Sienna from her thoughts. He widened his blue eyes as if he were waiting for something. "How was it?"

Sienna popped open a beer and handed it to him. "Good. For now, it's good. Six months—"

"I meant the game. Saw y'all on TV. Didn't think Gracie liked football. She's girlier than you."

"Guess you don't know her too well."

Even though Dylan Lockhart had known Sienna since high school and Grace since she was born, Sienna never gave him much of the opportunity to learn of Grace's big heart, silliness, or stubbornness. Just because Sienna gave him a chance or three in bed after too much whiskey didn't mean he deserved more than that. He wasn't a bad guy. Sienna just knew he wasn't the guy for her. But sometimes loneliness was palpable and painful.

"Did you talk with Beau?"

Sienna half shrugged, half shook her head. There had been more wondering than talking on her part. She wondered, even though he was older, larger, if he felt the same. Was the crook of his neck still the perfect hiding place for her lips? Would he exhale when she inhaled so their bodies never moved apart? Sienna wondered if Beau still felt like a missing piece—the one that brought peace to her chaos and a smile to her sadness.

"Son of a bitch can *still* run like hell," Dylan said.

"Running was never his problem," Sienna retorted before spinning around. "Do you know anything about refrigerators?"

"Yeah. They keep food cold."

Sienna sighed. "The back fridge has been giving me trouble. I need to keep it going for a few more months. Would you mind taking a look? I can afford a fifty-dollar Band-Aid, but that's about it right now."

He raised his beer. "Show me which one after I'm done with this."

"Thanks, Dylan."

Maloney's was as crowded as it usually was on Mondays, which wasn't very much. But Sienna was at the point where every five-dollar beer, every basket of $2.99 greasy fries, counted. It wasn't just business Sienna was worried about. Sienna was behind on thousands of dollars of hospital bills that had collected as she argued with her insurance company, which she was no longer sure was worth the massive amount of money she paid annually to keep.

But the good thing about owning a sinking bar was that there was *always* something to do. With her bartender at home with a brand-new baby, she was popping bottle caps and pouring drinks. Sienna was in between doing those two things when she felt the stare, direct and strong, right into her.

If she hadn't gone to the game, Sienna might have forgotten how intensely Beau looked at her. But when her cheeks flushed and she said a quiet prayer, thankful for the dim lighting, Sienna knew that wasn't true. You couldn't ever forget someone who could see right into your soul with the quickest of glances.

"Well, I'll be damned," Dylan said. "Beau Walker. The prodigal son has returned."

He was the first to call Beau's name. But he wasn't the last. One by one, the handful of customers said it, repeating it to themselves and friends and family over their phones as if they couldn't believe he was there.

Beau Walker. Beau Walker.

The continuous echo of his name forced Sienna to take hold of the counter to keep from swaying

It was bad enough that she had to be on his turf a few weeks ago. But here he was in her place of business, welcomed like the hometown hero and not the heartbreaker who never looked back.

"You aren't going to say hi?" Dylan asked, sitting back on the barstool when patrons swarmed Beau on the other end. "*Beau Walker* is here," he whispered, as if she didn't know.

"You don't say."

Dylan knitted his brows together and lifted his hat to smooth down his red hair. "Y'all used to be close."

We used to be inseparable.

"I'll catch up with him later."

Later, Sienna hoped, would be never, but as the night went on and *more* people flooded into Maloney's, she suddenly wasn't so upset that Beau had made an appearance. But an hour after his arrival, Sienna realized the excitement of his presence had made everyone lose their sense of southern hospitality, so she poured him a whiskey, then slid it over.

Beau turned and held her gaze, not saying anything. Goose bumps crept up her arm when one of his fingers brushed against her hand as he reached for the glass.

Spinning away and prepping to close out for the night, Sienna wiped down the bar, trying *not* to overhear any of Beau's conversation with Phil and Leslie Cummings, an older couple who owned Brookwood's small grocery store.

"Never thought we'd see you here again," Phil said, giving Beau a light punch on the arm. "Thought you forgot about this old place

"No," Beau said firmly. "I could never forget."

"Liar," Sienna seethed under her breath.

Leslie smiled. "Well, we miss your parents a whole lot. Never could quite find a good peach cobbler since your mother left for Florida."

"That's why I'm here actually. Season's over, so I've got some time on my hands. They want to list their house."

Oh, now *he wants to get the house ready to sell?* Sienna scoffed to herself. Beau's parents had moved to Florida a long time ago.

"Fridge sounds funny. Might be the fan." Dylan returned. "I'll swing by tomorrow after work with my tools and see what I find."

Sienna sighed, relieved. "Thank you, Dylan."

"And I was just messing with you. I'm real happy Grace is

doing well." Dylan smiled, rubbing Sienna's arm up and down before squeezing it. "I'll see you tomorrow."

Sienna's hand drifted to where Dylan's hand had been as she watched him walk out. But it wasn't the ghost of Dylan's touch Sienna was trying to brush away—it was Beau's stare burning into the same spot from feet away until the lingering customers stole his attention.

When Phil and Leslie couldn't take a hint while Sienna hovered behind the bar, fiddling with clean glasses she had stocked for tomorrow, she helped Frank wipe down the high-top tables before heading back to the kitchen to help Gina clean the fryer and take out the trash.

"Go home," Sienna told them both as she went back to the front. It was past their weeknight closing time.

Sienna halted when she realized that Phil and Leslie had finally left and Beau sat, tipping the glass to finish the rest of his drink. She watched, taking in the stubble that sprinkled his defined jaw, the flex of his throat as he swallowed down the whiskey.

"You closing, or is there time for another round?"

Sienna could only now see the exhaustion on his face, how his body had finally relaxed on the stool, shoulders slumping. Suddenly, she felt sorry for him, and even though her mind was telling her not to, Sienna walked straight to the front and locked the door, flipping the sign to read Closed and lowering the shades.

"I guess even celebrities deserve to drink in peace," she said, making her way back behind the bar for the Jack Daniels and then pouring it into his glass. "I still need to close out the register."

Gathering the few credit card receipts, Sienna opened the drawer and pulled out the cash, trying to count but growing distracted by Beau sliding his glass back and forth on the bar.

"That was Dylan Lockhart."

Sienna reached for the singles. "It was."

"He's still living around here."

"He is."

"He's still a prick. And still has a crush on you."

Sienna turned. "Excuse me?"

Beau took a drink. "You know, he was the one who stole Henry's crutch that day. He was always an immature asshole."

"Says the grown man playing tattletale."

Beau's mouth shut before it curved into a grin.

Sienna looked at the billfold in front of Beau, the one she had passed Phil and Leslie. She reached and immediately shut the leather folder as soon as she opened it.

"Give it to me," Sienna ordered.

"Give you what?"

She removed the hundred-dollar bill from the envelope and slid it across the bar. "Whatever *they* paid, give it to me." Beau looked down at the money and shrugged. "Beau—"

"I had two drinks—"

"On the house. I'm considering it a marketing expense because you sitting here, brought in almost the same amount this place makes in *one* week. Now please, take this and give me whatever they paid."

Beau's dimples disappeared beneath a frown before he shifted in his seat for his wallet. "They didn't tip you."

Sienna looked at the ten-dollar bill he had placed beside the hundred. Slowly, she leaned across the bar. Beau's Adam's apple bobbed as she moved close to whisper, "They don't have to. I own the place. And I'm telling you, you can take your money and get the hell out of my bar."

chapter four

BEAU LEANED FORWARD, trying to inhale what lingered of Sienna's scent—fresh and floral—as she stepped back, returning to the register.

"Did too much football affect your hearing?" Sienna asked. "I said get out."

"Sienna—"

"Leave, Beau."

"Sienna—"

She groaned, spinning back around. "You know what? This place doesn't take handouts. *I* don't take handouts. Especially from you."

Rubbing a hand over his face, Beau watched Sienna as she stomped around the bar and lifted chairs, placing them on top of tables. He stood to do the same.

"Beau—"

"Can we just *talk*?" Beau took a chair from her hands, lifting it. "I'm sorry about the money, alright?" Silently he added, *I just want to be doing something.* "That's great you own the place. What happened to Mr. Maloney? Did he finally realize he was a drunk and probably shouldn't be running a bar?"

"He died. Cirrhosis." Sienna placed her hands on her hips. "What do you want to talk about?"

Beau glanced around, suddenly unsure and overwhelmed. "How have you been?"

Sienna scoffed and lowered her hands, moving to the next chair.

"Alright, look, I know I've been gone awhile—"

"Sixteen years," Sienna corrected him.

Beau nodded. "I know I've been gone forever."

"And what are you doing here now exactly? You dropped a hundred dollars on milkshakes the other day and would've done the same thing here tonight. You could clearly pay someone to take care of your parents' house," Sienna paused in thought and sighed. "I'm not sure why you haven't already."

Beau tongued his cheek. When it came to the house, he told his parents not to worry after buying them a home in Florida years ago. But he never could bring himself to sell it, to sever what little connected him to Brookwood, to Sienna. But judging by her dark, angry glare piercing him, Beau wondered if it would have been better if he had sold it years ago and erased any and all connection to the place. He could have hired someone to deal with everything in his childhood home Beau didn't have the courage to face—like his brother Greg's room, where he hadn't stepped foot in since the day he died.

"Look," Sienna began, placing her hands on her hips. "Thank you for the time you spent with Grace after the game. And for the milkshakes. But if you're here because you feel guilty about leaving and never looking back, don't. Most people here would jump if an opportunity ever came up. But those of us who stay, we're doing alright." She took a deep breath. "I'm doing alright."

But I want you doing better than alright, Beau wanted to say, because there was a dullness in Sienna's eyes, dark circles enveloping them. He didn't need Grace's letter to know the truth that made his gut clench and his chest ache—Sienna had been on her own for a long time.

"I didn't sell the house because I'm a pussy, alright? I didn't want to deal with what's in there." Beau swallowed heavily, and when Sienna looked up, the smallest flash of sympathy washed across her face. Because of all people, Sienna understood what it was like to tackle grief head-on. "And I didn't want to face this. You. Hating me."

Sienna tucked a piece of hair behind her ear. "You never came back."

I did, he wanted to shout, but regardless whether he came back, he left again without her. "I'm here now," was the best Beau could offer.

"And what do you want now that you're here?"

Beau stepped forward, unable to stand the distance, and the closer he got, the lower Sienna's eyes went, focusing on the floor. He tipped her chin up. "Another chance. To make things right."

Sienna's eyes pierced his before she stepped back out of reach. "What makes you think you deserve a second chance?"

"I don't," Beau said. "But you do." *Because I used to make you happy. And you deserve to be happy.*

"Maybe I'm seeing someone."

"What makes you think I'm talking about you and me like *that*?"

I am. Kind of. Shit. I don't know. Alright, I am. I'm wondering if you still taste like the first lick of a lollipop. I'm wondering if you'll do that nervous, breathy half laugh right before I kiss you. I'm thinking about being a teenager on your roof and in your bed, wondering if you'll still feel exactly like you did back then beneath me—damn near perfect.

Sienna didn't give him an answer.

Beau swallowed. "Are you?" *Please say no.*

"Maybe it's Dylan."

Beau couldn't hold back his laughter. "It's *not* Dylan."

"I slept with him," Sienna announced. "More than once."

With balled fists, Beau took a deep breath through clenched teeth and tried to ignore the jealousy that ripped through him. *She has a kid. There already was someone else. And you were with other women.* He groaned inwardly. *But for real, Dylan Lockhart?*

Sienna tilted her head, and Beau watched her long blonde mane sweep to the side. "Does that bother you?"

"No," he lied and gritted his teeth. "But don't push it. Besides. He left. You're here with me."

"You came to *my* work," Sienna reminded him, folding her arms across her chest and cocking an eyebrow.

Beau nodded. "Yeah, I did. But not to hear about other guys—"

"Kissing me?" Sienna's tone changed and eyes narrowed. "Or doing everything else you never got the chance to do?"

"You have a kid, Sienna," Beau said. "I'm a dude, but I wasn't expecting you to be the Virgin Mary. That jig is kind of up."

"Exactly, Beau. I have a *kid,*" Sienna said. "I'm not seventeen anymore with my head in the clouds thinking the boy I loved would come back for me, and we'd ride off into the sunset on a motorcycle and live happily ever after. I'm not living in a fairy tale. I'm living in *reality*. And let me tell you something. It hasn't been easy."

When Sienna paused, Beau had to grip the table beside him to fight the urge to step closer, to hug her. *Fuck, I know,* he wanted to say, thinking of Grace, wondering how it was fair that the unimaginable was something Sienna had to see and feel. *Not easy might be the understatement of the year.*

Sienna moved to lift another chair. "But things are turning around. She's healthy."

"You don't know how happy I am to hear that. And you?" Beau asked. "What about you?" *Who's been looking out for you?*

"I told you," Sienna reminded him. "I'm doing alright."

"You're doing more than alright," Beau corrected, an image of Grace popping into his mind. He thought about the light in her eyes, the wonder and borderline mischievous look on her face. But the tone of Grace's letter had shown him that even though Grace had probably been through hell and back, she had a wonderful heart. And Beau knew that was because of Sienna. "You're doing a great job."

Sienna's eyes dropped to the floor.

Beau checked his watch. *11:52.* "Do you want to know how I know you're not seeing anyone? Or at least no one who matters?" *Like Dylan Lockhart.*

"How?"

Lifting the last chair onto the table, Beau motioned to the register behind the bar. "Are you all done with that? Get your stuff. I'll meet you out back."

He walked to the door, unlocked it, and slipped outside into the chilly January air, waiting until he could see the glow of the lights through the shades fade to black. He unlocked his truck and drove around the corner, pulled into the alley behind Maloney's, and waited with the engine running until Sienna finally appeared at the back door. She turned to lock it, half of her long blonde hair shoved into the top of her coat.

Hopping out of the truck, Beau went to the back, opening the bed. "I know there's no one who matters. Because if there were, I wouldn't be the one doing this." He motioned with his head. "Come on."

Sienna looked between Beau and his truck but stood in place.

"Suit yourself."

"What are you doing?"

Hopping into the truck bed, Beau lay down, folding his hands behind his head. "If you won't make a wish, then I will."

"Tomorrow isn't my birthday."

He could hear Sienna's boots on the ground as she hesitantly moved toward him.

"I know. Tomorrow is your mom's birthday." In between beats of the truck's engine, he heard Sienna take in a sharp breath. "You think I forgot that you told me you do this before hers too? I didn't."

He looked up at the sky, waiting for some wispy clouds to

move, and sighed before Sienna bumped into his boot hanging out of the truck bed. Pushing onto his elbows, Beau stared.

"What are you wishing for?"

With the light coming from the street at the beginning of the alley, Sienna stood backlit in front of him, illuminated. He could hardly see her face but somehow found her eyes clear as day in the darkness.

Beau cleared his throat. "The only thing I've ever really wanted. You to forgive me."

Sighing, Sienna placed her hand beside Beau's leg and climbed beside him. She turned, scooting to lower herself down, her shoulder to his. Beau could feel the heat of her body through their clothes despite the chill of the night and the nippy bitterness of their past.

"If you say it out loud, it won't come true."

Beau let his fingers brush against hers. He wanted to grab them, grab her, whisper an infinite amount of apologies against her palm so they permeated her body. With Sienna's obvious hardened shell, Beau knew his words and actions had to be deep enough to reach Sienna's heart.

"If you give me a chance, I'll make it come true," Beau said, turning so he could look at Sienna, but her eyes never left the sky. In the shadows, he studied the familiar, slight slope of her nose, the parting of her lips, where small clouds of her breath escaped, but her voice didn't make it through. "How about a game? Two truths and a lie."

He watched Sienna press her lips together for a moment before she spoke, "I'm doing alright." She took a deep breath, her voice softening, the change in tone tearing at Beau's heart. "I haven't missed you. I still make a wish every night."

I'm so fucking sorry. I'm so sorry I left you here when you needed me.

His mind flashed to the burial, where he had watched Sienna from beyond the crowd, had taken in the gentle shake of her shoulders as she simultaneously swayed Grace in her arms, running a hand over the top of her daughter's head as she clutched some pink stuffed animal. Beau's stomach turned, thinking about how he wished he had let Sienna know that if she needed him, he was behind her.

"I'm here now, Sienna."

Sienna turned her head. "The last one was the lie." She sat up and slid off the truck. "I never looked at the stars after you left, Beau. But if I had, I would've wished you never existed."

"Fuck."

With a heavy, defeated heart, Beau plopped down on his childhood bed—a twin that stopped being large enough for him in the ninth grade. The small mattress squeaked in protest under his weight.

"Penance," he voiced to no one.

Maybe there was a price to be paid for making wrong decisions. Maybe there was a price to be paid for breaking promises and hearts. And maybe, Beau was out of second chances. Maybe the third time wasn't the charm but the straw that broke the camel's back in the stream of good luck.

He had been lucky that Greg pushed him out of the way of the car.

He had been lucky that his body had healed after his motorcycle accident three years ago and he could return to the field.

But this time, Beau couldn't make his own luck, not with the coldness of Sienna's stare or the defensiveness in her body, which she had every right to bear.

"What am I doing?" he whispered into the silent room. "What the hell am I doing?"

His eyes flickered to his desk, and a framed photo caught his attention. They were several years apart, but nearly the same size—something Greg had hated. Beau imagined his brother might mirror his father in stature—six feet with broad shoulders, a decent build for a running back, but not tall enough to be the exceptional wide receiver Greg had always wished to be, the one Beau became because his brother never had the chance.

But while Greg never grew past five seven and stayed forever fifteen, Beau continued to grow taller and faster. He worked harder, imagining his brother trailing behind him while he tried to cut a minute off his mile, telling him to pick up his damn feet.

When he got his offer from Florida State, the first person Beau told wasn't Sienna or his parents—it was Greg. In this very room, he whispered to him, "We did it, man." And Beau said the same thing when he started his first collegiate game, when he became a Heisman trophy candidate, and when he led a team to a national championship.

But the continued rise to fame, even when accompanied by his loving, living parents and dead brother's spirit, was awfully lonely for one reason—the one he wished was there to celebrate all the achievements, to hear all his hidden fears, wasn't at his side. Beau could never say with one hundred percent certainty that his heart was under the bright lights of a roaring football stadium in Los Angeles when it felt like he had left it back in small-town Texas.

While he grew into a professional athlete endorsed by major sporting brands, racking up more zeros in his account than he ever could have imagined, Sienna grew into a mother. Though it stung to think that Sienna had made that dream come true with someone else, Beau reminded himself her most important wish had been manifested. And even though it brought Beau heartache, Sienna's happiness was most important.

But seeing the exhaustion on Sienna's face after the game was more painful than any tackle from a fiercely strong defensive back—it stole his breath in the worst way possible. Beau couldn't think of a person who deserved to struggle that way less than Sienna.

Beau pulled his vibrating phone from his pocket. He rolled his eyes at Chase's text.

Booked you extra agility with Barry. You've got to put in the fight if you're going to ball out big in LA.

Tonguing his cheek, Beau shook his head. *The only thing that will be big out in LA is my absence,* he told himself, silently vowing that he would end this discussion with Chase once and for all the next time they saw each other. *Sienna can remain walled up all she wants. But I need to be in Dallas—be here—just in case.*

Beau tossed the phone onto the bed before he glanced at the duffle bag of things he had brought from his condo. He unzipped it, sliding out the leather-bound book he had made years ago, and sighed. If Sienna wanted nothing to do with him, he could still give her what he always had planned—a gift as worthy as she was.

Beau closed the book after pulling out the note he had tucked into the pages—*for when you can't see the stars on a cloudy night.* He stood, moving to his desk and opening a drawer to find a pen that hadn't dried out, and added: *But rain or shine, I'll be waiting.*

the unimaginable a reality

DEAR MOM,

The other day I was putting something away in the coat closet when I saw a box at the bottom—Scrabble.

My heart dropped. We haven't had a Sunday Scrabble night since you died. It had been a weekly thing for as long as I could remember. We'd have pizza, snacks, ice cream. You'd tell Dad to stop lying when he said he needed to use the bathroom and really escaped to check the score of whatever game was on TV. There'd be words—real and imaginary—and endless challenges, which usually resulted in Henry being right.

When I picked up the game, I realized something. I couldn't remember how long it had been since you died. And at that moment, my phone vibrated from my back pocket.

"Are we still on for tonight? All the lights are on," Beau said in a hushed whisper.

Still holding the box, I swallowed heavily. "Yeah. I'm just cleaning up. My dad is sleeping."

"What's wrong?"

"I'll be up in a few." I ended the call and looked at the phone in my hand.

Mom, I haven't been counting because of Beau.

I went to Henry's room and pushed open the door. He wasn't sleeping but reading as usual.

"Hey."

"There's a thing called knocking." Henry looked up and saw the Scrabble box and went back to his book. "We don't need that anymore."

His words didn't just hurt, Mom. They sliced through me, each one a serrated knife. I wanted to scream.

"She would've—"

"No, Sienna," Henry interrupted. "She wouldn't."

I turned the box in my hands, giving it a shake, the tiles clunking against each other.

"She killed herself on a Sunday," Henry said without looking up. "Do you think she had Scrabble on her mind? Throw it out."

I left Henry's room, but I didn't throw it away. I shut my door, left the box on my bed and opened the window, pulling myself up the trellis.

Beau said nothing when I got to the roof. He slid over a plate with what looked like strawberry shortcake, but I shook my head and folded my knees to my chest, trying to gather my thoughts. I was pissed at Henry and sad for him at the same time. I was angry and *missing you, Mom. It was a mix of everything I felt for everyone all at once, and I started to shake.*

And there was Beau, scooting closer.

"You know, on Saturday mornings, my mom changes all the sheets in the house. Greg's too. Even though he hasn't slept in that bed in years."

I turned my head to look at Beau as he continued.

"My dad takes a long walk while she does it, and I don't even go near his door." Beau sighed. "There's no right way to grieve, Sienna. There's no wrong way to miss somebody. I haven't been in Greg's room since before he died, but that doesn't mean my mom shouldn't."

I nodded and let out an enormous sigh, but jumped when a motorcycle ripped down our street, grabbing his arm at the surprise of the noise.

"There's this group of bikers who hang out at Maloney's," Beau told me. "They come to my dad's shop to tune up their bikes."

"I always wanted to go on a motorcycle," I confessed. Then turning my head to the sky, I added with a smirk, "Wish list."

The wish list has become our thing. I mean, it's not an actual thing. We keep adding to it, and I don't mind that it's long or ridiculous.

"Sure about that?" Beau teased, and I realized I was still holding onto his arm so I let go and swatted him.

He folded his hands behind his head and lay back, and I tried not to notice the way his biceps bulged.

"That's on your wish list? Riding a motorcycle?"

"Have you ever seen Top Gun?"

"Who hasn't?"

"I used to watch it with my mom all the time. She had a thing for Tom Cruise."

"Who doesn't?" Beau snarked.

"Me," I admitted. "He's not my type."

There were a few beats of silence before Beau spoke. "Who's your type?"

My cheeks flushed. You.

"He's too short for me," I said, wondering if he'd get the hint. Most of the guys at school were shorter than me. But not Beau.

Beau's wingspan is endless, and his presence is big but not overly intimidating. It's more welcoming. And I won't lie, Mom. I'm finding it harder to stop myself from imagining just how it might feel if he hugged me. I bet he's like a warm blanket on the perfect fall day. Soft and safe and comforting, and something you just want to wrap yourself up in.

If my attempt to be subtle went over Beau's head or he just ignored it, I'll never know because he didn't press.

"I've been working on one for a year," he admitted. "Building it from scratch."

"No way. A motorcycle?"

Beau nodded. "At my dad's shop." He cocked his head at me, and I could see the questioning look on his face with the glow of the street lamp. "Didn't take you for a biker chick."

"I'm not." I lay back so we were side by side again. "But I bet it's the closest feeling I'll ever get to flying."

When I turned my head, I noticed just how close we were, with Beau now on his side, head propped up.

"Do you want to be a Navy pilot too?"

"No, but sometimes I think it would be nice to be weightless for a few seconds." I've felt so heavy and bogged down for the last few months—the freedom of flight is something I've been craving. I squirmed uncomfortably. "I'd settle for a ride in a convertible too. A really cool old one that still goes fast. Like the one from Ferris Bueller's Day Off. *Wind in my hair. The whole thing." I turned and smiled. "Wish list."*

Beau laughed. "I don't think a thirty-year-old car goes very fast. You could go skydiving," he offered. "Remember when we tried that?"

I laughed as well because I do. It involved climbing onto the highest tree branch we could reach and jumping to the ground holding a sheet.

"You almost broke your leg." I reached out and brushed my finger across the scar on his left forearm, also a result of that day, when he banged into an old wheelbarrow. Beau didn't flinch from my touch, but I pulled back because his skin felt like velvet even under the dusting of fine hair.

"Not gonna lie, that hurt like hell." He reached down, rubbing his ankle. "And the whole time you were so afraid we'd get in trouble, you told me to quit being a baby."

I can almost hear myself at six saying that to Beau as he hobbled around our backyard while I pulled twigs from my hair. "I think I told you to man up."

Beau laughed, sweet and deep. I snuck in more stares as he tilted his head to the sky, and I tried to picture the little boy I used to run around the neighborhood with. Once upon a time, I was the taller one and probably even outweighed him. He always beat me in running, but I rode my bike faster. I've realized over the past month that sometimes, when we talk, it feels like we're still kids, coming up with crazy plans and wild dreams. It's as if we were still sitting at my kitchen table, preparing our lemonade stand, certain that one day we'd franchise our recipe that included pouring lemon-lime Gatorade into an already over-sweetened pink lemonade mixture.

But then I catch a glimpse of him, and then I'm reminded of just how much bigger, stronger—and because I know my secrets are safe with you, Mom—how handsome he's become.

I wish I had the courage to tell Beau that he manned up quite well after all.

"Are you busy tomorrow afternoon?" he asked.

"Why?"

Beau sat. "I want to take you somewhere after I'm done with work."

"Where?"

He smiled, making a move to leave the roof. "Flying. But we'll be landing on water, so wear your swimsuit."

The next day, I was eyeing the lake from the passenger seat of his truck and asked, "Where does the flying part come in exactly?"

Beau hopped out of the truck and pointed to the marsh beside us. "We need to go through that and up the hill a bit."

"That sounds like hiking, not flying," I countered, immediately lowering my gaze when Beau pulled off the Weezer shirt he wears all the time and tossed it on the seat. I didn't want him to see that even though it was overcast, my cheeks probably looked sunburnt.

"Come on. It's not far."

I followed him out of the truck before slipping off my jean shorts and pulling my shirt over my head. Beau awkwardly looked away as I adjusted the top of my bikini. We walked into the marsh, my bare feet slipping and sliding along a small path as I tried not to stare so strongly into his back that he might feel it. But I did stare strongly, wondering what it would be like to run my fingertips along his smooth and tight skin, down the valley of his spine flanked by strength.

"Here." He stopped.

Mud and pieces of loose grass painted my bare feet and legs. When I looked up, Beau was walking over to a tree, reaching for a rope.

"I need some time for the motorcycle. And well. . . your convertible *is kind of out of reach at the moment. But this is more like flying anyway."*

I held my breath as Beau reached, hoisting himself on the rope, gripping long enough before he flew *into the lake, dropping into the murky water and then resurfacing. He swung his head to banish the soaked hair from his face.*

"Come on, Sienna. Man up," he joked, moving to float on his back. "You wish you could fly? Make *that come true. Don't wait."*

Eyeing the rope, I moved up the hill, still stumbling, until I reached the tree the thick twine hung from. Beau righted himself in the lake and began to tread water, waiting as I held the rough rope in my hands. I took a deep breath, reaching as high as I could before jumping, catching it between my feet.

And I flew. For just a few seconds, I was weightless. I was floating and free, and I felt nothing but lightness in the moments I soared through the air before my body met the water.

I couldn't see anything underneath the surface. But somehow, I found Beau through the haze without even trying. Panting, I opened my eyes, meeting Beau's brown pair. His warm breath fanned across my face, and I blinked hard, just to make sure I didn't imagine his hand lingering against my cheek after he pushed back wet, tangled hair. I knew I wasn't. Because Beau's other hand floated to my waist, and do you know what I felt, Mom? The chill of goose bumps under warm water. Like laughing while painfully grieving, the idea was almost impossible to imagine.

I thought that about flying too.

But there Beau was, painting the unimaginable as a reality. There he was, making wishes come true.

Love,

Sienna

i wish i was brave enough to ask

DEAR MOM,

I wonder if I should write you every day instead of these sporadic entries. Summer is over now. All the days were the same—work in the mornings at the diner, the lake with Beau in the afternoons, or get this, bike rides like we were kids (I can still beat him, by the way). And nights, well, they were for Beau too. He's now routine, and I don't just like our nights spent together, but I'm finding myself eager for the sun to set, and that's strange. Because after you died, I dreaded the night, yet here I am craving it.

I've been trying to look after Dad, but he's in full work mode. Sometimes he doesn't come home until almost nine. I don't know why, because practice wraps up at six. But he trudges into the house, eats whatever I left for him in the oven and goes to bed. People are still *bringing casseroles. No offense, but at this point, I think they are doing it more because they all love Dad, not because you died. With the season about to kickoff, it's clear he's the hometown hero. That sounds nice in theory, but honestly, I'm annoyed because that means me and Henry are the offspring of said hometown hero, and the school wanted to include* us *in the season opener.*

Get this, Mom. They wanted us to flip the coin.

I argued with Dad over and over. Henry didn't, so I argued on his behalf. But apart from telling me I should consider law school, Dad only said it was nonnegotiable. I was dreading the entire thing. Beau tried to make it better when I told him the news.

"You don't get it. I hate *crowds."*

Beau opened a tin of over baked cookies his mother made that were too hard for a customer but still delicious enough for us. "Just pretend everyone is naked."

He wiped crumbs from his mouth with the back of his hand. He missed one. I couldn't exactly process what he said because I was too busy focusing on the smudged chocolate right next to his bottom lip and wondering if the sweetness would taste sweeter—better—off his skin rather than straight from the cookie.

But I heard enough of his comment because I tried to picture him *naked.*

"Sienna?"

"What?"

He wiped his mouth again. "I said, picture them naked. Even Principal Wexman. Besides," he added before grabbing another cookie, "you can't mess up a coin toss."

But let me tell you something, Mom. Beau was wrong.

When the time came for me and Henry to make our way onto the field, I was relieved to find Beau there because he was a captain. He was standing tall, his hands pulling at the neck of his jersey—number sixteen—swaying side to side. I didn't know what to make of his number choice, but it made my stomach flutter a bit.

"Naked," he mouthed to me, and I looked at the old referee and grimaced.

I didn't want the moment to last more than it needed to, so when the ref handed me the coin, I flicked it off in Beau's direction, and everyone in the entire town learned you can, in fact, screw up a coin toss.

The coin almost pegged Beau in the chin, and when he jutted his head backward, it slipped easily into the opening of his jersey-covered chest protector. His eyes flew to mine, which widened in absolute horror.

The referee fiddled with his hat for a minute, looking around as if he was expecting someone to tell him what to do as Beau pulled at his jersey and equipment. But no coin fell.

The crowd grew silent, obviously confused as they waited for the call.

The ref sighed. "Take it off, son."

My cheeks must have been a fire engine shade of red when his teammates and the other school's captains laughed. And so did Henry.

"Shut up," I whispered through clenched teeth, trying to keep my eyes anywhere except on the warm tone of Beau's skin or the trail of fine brown hair below his belly button when he pulled his jersey and equipment over his head with the help of a teammate.

After what seemed like an eternity, the coin hit the turf, and I finally let out the breath I'd been holding.

"Heads it is," the referee announced, and Beau told him they wanted the ball.

I should've felt some relief that our school actually won the toss. But Mom, all *I could focus on was what was right in front of me—Beau without his shirt and how big he was, far from the kid I used to be a head taller than and chase lightning bugs with at dusk.*

Somehow, he made things worse and better when he finally put his equipment back on. "If you wanted to see me without my shirt again, all you had to do was ask."

It's dark and cooler now here on the roof, but my cheeks are warm, and there's this tingling all throughout my body. I feel *something, Mom—even when he's not right here.*

I wish I were brave enough to ask.

Love,

Sienna

chapter five

"YOU'RE UP EARLY. I thought you'd sleep in."

Sienna yawned. "Emily's coming over." Shuffling to the pantry, she grabbed a box of muffin mix from the pantry. "Can't host a guest with air."

"Not sure you should risk giving a breastfeeding mother food poisoning." Henry stood. "There's a few pancakes left."

"Very funny. No. Just caffeine," she said through another yawn, filling her mug before having a sip. "Jesus, Henry!"

"You got home late. I figured you needed an extra kick this morning."

Sienna put down the mug and went to get orange juice from the fridge, trying to eviscerate the taste. "One more kick and this would be cocaine."

"How would *you* know what cocaine is like?" Grace appeared with her hands on her hips.

Sienna rolled her eyes. "Isn't that a lot of makeup for school?"

"No."

"If you say so," Sienna said, wondering if her daughter had put on fake eyelashes.

Grace grabbed a banana. "Are you ready?" she asked Henry, who was at the sink rinsing his dish.

"How about real breakfast? Something with protein, maybe?" Sienna eyed how Grace swam in her sweater as she pranced around the kitchen, gathering notebooks and her backpack.

"I had a yogurt," Grace called from the side door. "And I took my medicine, so you don't need to nag me about that."

Sienna sighed. "Is the cafeteria open this early? Get her something, would you?"

Henry dried his hands. "She said she already ate breakfast."

"Henry—"

"Sienna," her brother began, his voice quieting. "You can just let her live, you know. She's a normal teenager. Did you ever eat breakfast?"

But she's not a normal teenager, Sienna wanted to remind Henry before she stopped herself because, at the moment, Grace *was*. She might take a lot of supplements to help rebuild her immune system. She might need to see an endocrinologist to talk about hormone therapy. She might wear a wig. But Grace was the same back-talking, non-breakfast-eating, sassy teenager Sienna had been in this very kitchen.

"I'll see if we have time to stop for a donut. Just relax, though, alright?" He paused when Grace honked the horn. "Overbearing mother never suited you, Sienna. You can take that hat off now."

Sienna folded her arms across her chest as Henry walked out the side door. She eyed the hot sludge in her mug and dumped it, walking into the pantry prepared to make a fresh pot of coffee.

Grabbing the canister, Sienna was about to turn off the light when her hand paused, hovering over the switch as a basket on the shelf caught her eye. The obnoxiously orange pill bottles had been labeled AM and PM. There were multiple thermometers, so Sienna could triple check for accuracy, as well as a large plastic bag containing extras of all medication Grace had been on. Sienna had dubbed it "the admission kit," so she had everything on hand when she knew, deep within her mom gut, that Grace would end up staying in the hospital. On the wall hung a list of numbers and information, like Grace's oncologist's name, Grace's blood type, the type of chemo she had been on, and a highlighted note that her daughter was allergic to Penicillin.

Sienna frowned. There was so much more to say about Grace. Favorite food: broccoli and ricotta pizza. Favorite color: Tickle Me Pink, like the Crayola crayon. Favorite animal: giraffe. Favorite movie: *The Notebook.* Hidden talent: double-jointed arms.

Reaching, Sienna tore the paper down from the wall, crumpling it in her hand. She tossed it into the trash.

Today she wants to live, Sienna thought, *and so do I.*

Sienna quietly squealed, holding the door so Emily could get in easier. "Welcome little Miss. Abigail!"

"Thanks for giving me a reason to get out of the house." Emily placed the car seat on the floor. "I think you can go crazy staying at home for so long."

Sienna hugged Emily. "I've missed you. You look great."

Emily was the first employee Sienna had hired after she bought Maloney's. At some points, Emily was her *only* employee, taking on everything from bartending to cleaning the bathrooms, and unofficial sister, helping Grace with her math homework and relieving Sienna at the hospital so she could shower when Henry was busy with parent-teacher conferences. Emily had been through it all with Sienna.

"Don't lie."

"Okay, tired, but still great."

"*Really* tired," Emily added before pointing to her red hair plopped into a messy bun. "Like too tired to take my hair down and put it back up. Tell me you have coffee."

Sienna pulled out a chair from the kitchen table. "I put on a fresh pot. Sit. I made muffins too, but you've been warned."

Emily laughed, taking a mug of coffee. "I'm not hungry. I eat all night while she's up doing the same."

"Oh, she's perfect." Sienna bent down, admiring the small sleeping baby. "You really forget how small they are in the beginning."

"I know. Six weeks already. Can't believe it."

"Me either. I swear, I remember Grace this size like it was yesterday."

Sienna's mind turned, recalling the blur of the early newborn days and sleepless nights she spent in bed or on the couch with a warm bundle of Grace on her chest, counting her breaths, falling in love repeatedly with her tiny fingers and toes.

"And *you* did it alone," Emily reminded her. "I do have Jamie."

"No, not alone." Sienna's eyes drifted to a photo on the fridge, one that captured Grace's first Halloween.

She had been dressed as the cowardly lion, Sienna as Dorothy, her father as the tin man—decked out head to toe including face paint—and Henry as the wicked witch of the east. She smiled at the bittersweet image.

"My village looked different, that's all."

"I saw your text. So, all is good with Grace?"

Sienna nodded, pouring herself another cup of coffee. "Yeah," she said with a heavy sigh. "For now, at least."

"Oh, Sienna. Don't." Emily reached out and grabbed her hand. "I can't imagine," she said, looking down at her baby, "but there's got to be an end to it all for you guys. And honestly, I feel like this is it. It *has* to be."

"How do you know?"

Emily shrugged. "I don't know. Maybe the stars aligned this time."

Sienna smiled. "I don't mean to be pessimistic, and trust me, I'm *not* in front of her, but it's just. . . we've been here before. I have to reprogram my brain, I guess. Remember what life was like before she got sick."

"Well, since she's on the other side of it, maybe think about doing something for yourself."

"I need a haircut," Sienna joked.

Emily gave her a small kick. "I mean something more than that. Last time you thought about going back to school."

There had been a time when Grace began her road to remission, the first time, that Sienna toyed with the idea of returning to college to study nursing, which she found ironic, considering science was the most difficult subject for her in high school. But the nurses she came across—like Luella—during Grace's many hospital stays had opened the door to it. *"Everyone can learn if they work hard enough. And you have an insider's foundation."* Luella had told her. But by the time she came close to pulling the trigger, Grace was sick again.

Sienna looked down at Abigail, who stirred. "Can I hold her?"

Emily pulled the blanket off Abigail, scrunching and stretching as her mother lifted her. "Maybe she'll let me drink my coffee while it's still hot."

Sienna laughed, reaching out to hold Abigail. "Learn to drink it fast," she joked before she cradled the small baby in her arms, rocking gently.

"Does her breathing sound funny to you?"

Sienna stilled, listening. "She's snorty. A lot of newborns snort. Small nasal passages."

"Great, so my baby is a pig."

"Stop it. She's perfect."

"It's crazy how you can love someone so much instantly," Emily agreed.

Gently running her finger down Abigail's nose, Sienna nodded. "That's because it's been in you all along. You were meant to be her mother."

Sienna had known, as soon as Grace was born, that her love

for her had always been there, waiting for the right moment to flow from her heart. That moment came when Grace took her first breath and let out a wailing, joyful cry. The only bittersweetness surrounding Grace's birth was when Sienna realized there were people who might have carried around the same love for her but would never know it. Like Sienna's mother or Grace's biological father.

His loss, she had reminded herself on that first night in the hospital. *What a gift to the world she is.*

It wasn't that Grace brought an infinite amount of unconditional love, but her daughter gave Sienna a renewed purpose, a way to turn her life around and leave behind the coasting and partying that had gotten her pregnant.

Peeking at the photo on the fridge, Sienna remembered that Grace had given purpose to more than just her. She had reignited the sparkle in her father's eye that had dimmed the day her mother had died. Everything she did—from burping to stretching and yawning—brought bragging from Henry.

Grace's arrival into the world had mended a family that death had broken and re-birthed it into something whole and living.

"Before I forget," Sienna told Emily. "That bag over there is for you. Grace didn't even wear most of it. And your check is in there too."

"You don't have to pay me for maternity leave, you know."

"Don't be stupid, Emily. Cash the check."

"Sienna—"

"I'm covering for you until you're ready to come back. Your job is waiting for you."

Sighing, Emily put her mug down. "Thank you."

"Thanks for bringing her. Holding babies just makes everything better. It's my mom's birthday," she added softly, and Emily reached out, placing a kind hand on Sienna's leg. "I'm okay. It's an off day. And everything else has just been crazy."

"Anything crazy good?" Emily lifted her brows in question.

"What do you mean?"

Emily bypassed the burned muffins and grabbed a handful of nuts. "I heard Beau Walker stopped by Maloney's."

"Of course you did."

"I heard he looks the same as he did in high school but better."

"Oh yeah?" Sienna asked. "Who told you that?"

"Dylan texted Jamie," Emily said, and they both erupted in laughter.

Rubbing the baby's back, Sienna shook her head when they both quieted. "That ship has sailed, my friend."

"Not too far, I think. I passed by his parents' house. There's a big shiny black truck in the driveway," Emily said.

"He's selling the house."

"Oh, right. I'm sure that's it," Emily trailed off, looking around the kitchen.

"Emily—"

"Maybe the stars aligned, remember?"

There were a million things Sienna could have done around the house after Emily left. She could have folded the laundry that had been sitting on the dryer for two days. She could have searched through Grace's closet for her missing green blouse, or resumed the battle with her insurance company. She could have lain in bed thinking about her mom. But Sienna didn't know how any of those things would set her on a new path. So instead, Sienna did something for herself—she went on a run.

New year, new me, she thought, passing the calendar. *Even if it's the middle of January.*

But it only took Sienna three minutes to remember that while the idea of running—the wind burning her cheeks, her body warming in the chilly air as it met that "runner's high" everyone raved about—sounded nice in theory but in actuality, she hated it.

Hardly half a mile in, Sienna turned around awkwardly, hoping no one had seen her only make it a few blocks before heading home. *Baby steps,* she told herself. *Walk first, run later. More vegetables, less chips. And ice cream.*

Nearing her house, Sienna had grown her mental list of things to do for herself. *Haircut. Go to the movies alone in the middle of the day. Take one full week off work and leave Frank in charge. Go on a date. An actual date. With a guy* not *from Brookwood. Someone who wears a suit and opens doors and orders the right wine and not whatever is on tap. Go on multiple dates with the same guy before sleeping with him.*

She was about to make it to the side door when she paused in her driveway. A box wrapped in butcher paper sat on the front step, and Sienna approached cautiously. Looking around, she found no one nearby and picked it up, her fingers gliding across the butcher paper wrapping to the cardstock with her name printed on it.

She looked around again before peeling back the tape, which bit at the skin beneath her fingernails, revealing what appeared to be a thick leather book.

"For when you can't see the stars on a cloudy night," she read aloud from the card. "But rain or shine, I'll be waiting."

She opened the book with a furrowed brow, her eyes drifting to the first page—a group of stars with one circled followed by coordinates. Biting her lip in confusion, she flipped to the next page. More stars, more coordinates, and so forth.

Slamming the book shut, Sienna tucked it under her arm and took off, down the street and across the town that had once been streaked with past laughter of childhood friends, the sneaky footprints of young lovers, and now with Sienna's present, palpable fury.

★★★★★

When she spotted Beau's truck from a block away, Sienna pictured exactly how this should go. She would knock, Beau would open, and she would begin screaming at him. *What do you want from me? Can't you just leave me alone?* She would shove the book against Beau's chest and tell him that, rain or shine, he could still shove it up his ass.

But when Beau opened the door, Sienna couldn't even catch her breath.

Beau wiped at his sweaty head before his dark eyebrows knitted together. "Hi?"

Sienna shook her head. *This is what he looks like sweating?* She knew her hair—which she hadn't washed in two days—was matted against her forehead from the run. Her cheeks had to be beet red, judging by how much they burned. Beau was breathing deeply, but not *as* deeply as Sienna, who was heaving. And him leaning against the doorway with his joggers hanging loosely on his hips did nothing to help the racing of her heart.

"Are you alright?"

"What. . ." Sienna pushed out through gasps. "What is this?" She held the book between them.

Beau scratched the back of his head. "I'll get you some water. Come in."

Sienna stayed put but leaned against the side of the door. Beau sighed before disappearing and reappearing with a glass.

"Did you run here?"

Sienna took the glass with her free hand, chugging it before handing it back to him. "I asked you a question." She raised the book again and watched Beau press his lips together tightly. "Beau, what *is* this?"

His eyes flicked back to hers. "It's something I should've given you a long time ago." He waited for Sienna to speak, but when she stayed silent, he groaned. "It's a present, Sienna. Most people say thank you."

When her breathing finally evened out, Sienna opened the book to the first page. "You bought me a star?"

Beau ran a hand across his stubbled jaw. "No, not exactly."

Okay, great, Sienna thought, relieved. *I'll be on my way then. See you never, hopefully.*

"I bought you all of them."

Sienna's breath hitched in the back of her throat, and her eyes flew to his. "You *what?*"

"Well," Beau began, "I technically didn't *buy* them. They aren't anyone's to buy, you know, legally. They're adopted, or whatever. *Indefinitely,*" he added. "And I didn't get all of them, obviously. But enough for you to have limitless wishes when the night sky is cloudy."

"Beau—"

"I *hate* you don't do that anymore," he admitted, painfully. "I hate you don't do it because of me."

"We were kids," she reminded him. "That's childish stuff. It's stupid and—"

"It's not stupid."

"And it doesn't even work."

Beau shook his head. "You got Grace. I was there when you made that wish, when you wished for a family."

There was a sadness to Beau's voice, and Sienna knew why. That wish he was talking about was forever connected to an unhappy memory.

Sienna's eyes dropped, and she tucked a wad of sweaty hair behind her ear. "A happy accident."

Her daughter was more than a happy accident. Grace was Sienna's total happiness. *She took your place when I needed her to.* After Grace was born, there wasn't room for Beau in Sienna's head, let alone in her heart. For once, it was full. And that love was unconditional, everlasting through sickness, and, now Sienna knew, through health.

"No," Beau corrected her. "She was a wish from the heart. A dream come true. All of the above."

Sienna swallowed heavily.

"I'm sorry I bombarded you last night," Beau began after a minute of silence. "Seeing you at the game, meeting Grace, well, it was a lot for too short of a moment."

Isn't that how it's always been for us? Sienna wondered. *There's never enough time.*

She recalled, as kids, how the sunset came too fast, signaling it was time to go home. As teenagers, nights on the roof were never long enough—there had been as little time to talk and laugh as friends, and as lovers, there was never enough time for the number of Beau's kisses and touches that Sienna needed to get her through to morning.

She cleared her throat. "I didn't mean what I said last night. It was nasty. I've got a lot on my plate, and you kind of caught me on an off day. I'm sorry."

"You don't need to apologize."

Standing on her toes, Sienna peeked over Beau's shoulder, seeing what looked like the living room couch turned on its side. "So, you're really getting it ready to sell?"

"Yeah." Beau ran a hand down the back of his head. "I've got a little downtime this week. Need to keep busy. The realtor wants to stage it. I'll donate what I can, send things to my parents. Family stuff, Greg's room. I haven't dealt with that yet."

Sienna's eyes flew to the porch. *Greg,* she said to herself, thinking of Beau's brother, who was almost imaginary more than anything else. She remembered a few things like his shiny red bike, his light hair—a far contrast from Beau's. But mostly, she remembered annoying and teasing him with Beau and Greg's heavy footsteps as he chased them out of his room. His voice was a distant, faint memory. But Beau's laughter beside her as they sprinted into the backyard wasn't.

A pit brewed in her stomach. Sienna shifted, feeling guilty for leaving someone alone, who once meant so much, to face the burden of packing up his dead brother's room, which he hadn't been able to step into in over twenty years.

It was a fear she always held in the back of her mind—what it might be like to pack away Grace's room after she was gone.

Panic seized her, and she swayed.

"You alright?" Beau steadied her arm. "Come and have more water."

Letting Beau lead her into the kitchen, Sienna left the book at the bottom of the stairs. She plopped down into a chair before reaching for the glass he had refilled, desperate to flush the anxious heat that had crept through her body.

"Do you need to eat something?"

Sienna focused on a loose thread dangling from her sweatshirt. "You know, I thought about your mom when Grace was sick. When she was *really* sick. She got pneumonia before her stem cell transplant and was intubated and. . . " Sienna couldn't say more.

I thought I would be her one day, walking into my dead child's room, stripping the bed, loading the wash, like she was just at a sleepover at a friend's house. Letting go of the thread, Sienna rubbed her arm at the vicious chill of sad, desperate memories swarming her.

"We didn't get it when we were younger, you and me. When Grace almost died, all I could think about was what would happen to her stuff. Clothes, toys she still played with, the most random, half-broken gizmo from a Happy Meal. It's all these little things. And they fit in boxes or in bags. But it's those things that make up who they are." Sienna took a deep breath. "I remember looking at her while she was intubated and wondered how someone that tiny could really be *so* big, you know? And to just pack it all away into a few boxes, it's not right. There's nothing right about burying your kid. I would've been like your mom. I would've clung to *everything*."

With her head still down, Sienna hadn't realized Beau had moved across the kitchen and squatted in front of her, until he reached for her hand. If it had been moments earlier, Sienna would have jumped or startled. But when the language of loss couldn't be spoken, it could be felt, and Beau felt like he did when he climbed up on the rooftop with her for the first time—understanding and safe.

"I stopped giving away things, like old ratty pajamas, shoes she grew out of. Broken barrettes. Toys with missing parts. I thought, well, one day she might not be here, and maybe I'll forget about something. Like this glittery headband with cat ears she thought made her invisible."

Sienna wanted to laugh at the memory of Grace wearing the headband, creeping around the kitchen with a bag of Skittles she had swiped, believing no one could see her. But the laugh got caught in the back of her throat, because the thought only made Sienna remember how scared she felt, thinking there might be a cap on the number of memories she had with Grace—limited instead of limitless, more sad than happy.

"They said it would take a miracle. She was *so* sick when they first found it."

"And she beat it. Maybe she was your walking miracle. You just didn't know it." With his free hand, Beau wiped a tear from her face. "I'm sorry. I hate I wasn't there for you."

I hate that I wished you were so many times. I hate that back then, I talked to you about my dead mom, and now I'm talking to you about my dying daughter. The thought brought a twitch of pain to her chest, and she remembered. Grace was at school, healthy, on minimal medication. But the fear was so real, in Sienna's mind, nothing had changed.

"Don't be." Sienna sniffled, turning her cheek into his palm—large and warm. She grew enough courage to look into his eyes. "Besides, you knew me as someone else. I used to be fun, outgoing. And now, after everything, I'm different. Be happy you got the old Sienna," she tried to joke, pulling back from Beau's hand.

"She's still in there though."

Sienna smiled sadly. "How do you know?"

"I'd recognize the girl I fell in love with when I was five years old, even if a hundred years passed and I went blind and deaf."

Just for a day, she thought, *I want to go back just for a day.*

Sienna wanted to return to the first time Beau had re-entered her life, back when he made her laugh when she wanted to cry, when he sat with her in silence when talking was too much. When he reminded her there could be small pockets of joy even while hurting, that you can make plans even when you don't know where you're going.

Sienna wanted to go back, for a day, to the moment Beau told her he loved her before he said goodbye.

I want to be the one he came back for instead of the one he left behind.

And not for a day, but for a moment there in his parents' kitchen, Sienna was that girl, staring at Beau, mesmerized by how his dark eyes, framed by thick, full lashes, glowed with golden flecks when the light hit them. How his hands, strong and broken-in, could feel impossibly soft and smooth. It was as if Beau's breath wove a spell into her, and suddenly, at thirty-three, in an outdated kitchen, she was really seventeen, blissfully unaware—but *happy*. The feeling was so strong it made her sway in her seat. But Beau's hand returning to her face held her steady.

His hand slid down, fingertips ghosting through the strands of her messy ponytail. "I wish you'd let me show you again."

After a moment of silence, Sienna sighed. "I wish I was brave enough to let you."

chapter six

BEAU'S GAZE didn't waver from Sienna's. *Please let me show you everything I've wanted to do, everything we should've done together. Give me a chance.* Beau's thumb stroked the soft skin of her cheek, which had faded from flushed red to a soft pink, the change bringing a smile to his face.

"Actually, my favorite color is your cheeks after I kiss you," Beau once told her a long time ago. At the moment, he decided the light flush was, in fact, still his favorite.

But Sienna didn't return the smile. She removed his hand from her face and stood, pushing the chair back. He followed, expecting her to walk out the front door. Instead, she made her way up the stairs, careful not to step on the book she had left at the bottom.

"Where are you going?" he asked.

With a hand on the banister, Sienna paused. "I'll take care of the linens while you work on Greg's room."

Beau shook his head. "You don't have to do that."

"I know." Sienna continued up the stairs, picking up a flattened box from the stack and a roll of tape, then disappeared from his sight.

Sighing, Beau took the stairs and went down the hall to Greg's room, opening the door slowly. He wished it would have been magically empty, the opposite of how it was—full and exactly how Beau had remembered it as a child.

It was a stark contrast from his own childhood room. Greg's room practically bled maroon, a manifestation of playing at Florida State. The bedspread, the curtains, the faded posters littering the walls—all of it was a shrine to one of the greatest houses of college football history.

Apart from a game-winning ball and some school sweatshirts from early college visits Beau had taken with his parents, there was no evidence of his football career in his room across the hall. And yet he wore the maroon jersey, the gold helmet. While Greg was six feet under and his name was whispered as if people weren't supposed to say it, thousands chanted Beau's name as teammates lifted him onto the shoulders of the biggest lineman, celebrating game-winning catches.

Beau shook his head and began pulling out clothes, neatly laying them on the bed. He would pack everything. It wasn't his place to decide what pieces of Greg needed to be kept even twenty years after he had died. And Beau didn't need one piece. Enough had already been embedded the day he had decided he would continue to live his brother's life.

Sienna knocked on the open door, and Beau turned from the desk, still filled to the brim with school supplies and yellowing homework assignments Greg had never turned in. She pulled in a few boxes and approached the bed.

"This stuff?" she asked.

"All of it."

Sienna began placing sweaters and pajamas into a box. "Is there something of his you want to keep?"

"No," he said. "I think I have enough." *Of him in me. Too much.*

For an hour, they worked in silence, filling more boxes until the closet, desk, and dresser were empty. Sienna gently peeled the posters off the wall, rolling the thinning papers up as Beau stacked the boxes neatly in the corner before plopping down on the bed they hadn't yet stripped.

"You know, I hate this kind of red." Beau patted the maroon bedspread as Sienna looked up from her place on the floor. "You were right back then, I never *hated* football. But I didn't love it the way he did. I still don't. Keep that to yourself though," he added, trying to lighten the mood.

Sienna rose from the floor, dusting her hands across her leggings before sitting beside Beau. "You had to love it a little to put in all the work."

"I guess. But I loved Greg more." Beau leaned forward, balancing on his elbows. "Maybe too much."

Beside him, Sienna shook her head. "You can't ever love someone too much."

"But you can live for them too much. Even when it's something you would do without a second thought." He turned to face her. "But at some point, kids, brothers, they live or die without you. And then what?"

A somber expression fell across Sienna's face. "I don't really know."

Beau ran his finger over the scar at his temple. "I lived for Greg every moment after this," he said, tapping it. "Except for two times."

"When?"

"When you came back in high school," Beau told her. "And when I saw you at the game."

Sienna's eyes dropped to her lap.

"I've got one more year in me," he admitted. "I wish I could say I'd play forever until I win it all for him, but I'm *tired*."

Beau was tired—tired of getting hit, of worrying about injuries, of training harder each year because the competition only got younger and faster as he grew older.

"You're an old man now," Sienna teased, bumping her shoulder against his.

"I just want to have some *fun*, you know? All these years, I've been the serious guy. I train hard as hell off-season, I play as hard as I can during the season. Rinse and repeat. It tastes awful."

Sienna raised an eyebrow. "You're telling me that million-dollar contracts and traveling, fame, notoriety, all that tastes awful?"

Beau pressed his lips together for a moment. "It tastes awfully lonely. All that stuff doesn't mean shit." He motioned to the boxes. "You can't take it with you."

Sienna's eyes drifted across the room, and she stayed silent for a moment.

"What are you thinking?" Beau asked.

"I'm thinking," she started, "that I based my whole identity on preparing myself to do this exact thing for Grace. And now that I'm starting to believe I finally won't have to, I should be happy. I *am* happy, honestly. But I never built anything beyond being a mom and taking care of the bar. I guess loneliness doesn't discriminate against the rich and poor or famous and nobodies."

"You're not a nobody."

"No." Sienna sighed. "But I'm realizing I'm just a body. Like a robot. Sometimes, it feels like I haven't lived since. . . " She paused, shaking her head.

Beau nudged her. "Since when?"

"Since we were kids. Climbing roofs. Dreaming. Wishing." Sienna looked at Beau. "That's why it's hard, Beau. You didn't just take *us* away. You took an extra part of me too. I found a little of it again when Grace was born. It's special, but it's still different."

Beau balled his fingers. It would be too easy for him to just reach out and hug Sienna, to pull her into his lap. He could give her a thousand apologies. But that wouldn't change the look on her face, which was just so sad it made his heart hurt. If he was going to replace it with a smile—one that spread ear to ear and lit up her eyes—actions were needed, not words.

But Beau said and did nothing when Sienna rose from the bed.

"I need to get going. I have to shower and do a few things before Grace gets home from school. Want me to help you take those downstairs?" She pointed to the boxes.

"I've got it. Thanks."

Beau followed Sienna as she walked out of the room. He paused in the doorway, watching as she made her way down the hall, his gut twisting tighter with every step she took farther from him. As Beau imagined what it would be like when Sienna reached the stairs and finally the front door, the nervous knot in his stomach traveled to his chest, squeezing his heart. It was hard enough for *him* to be the one who left. But watching Sienna walk away was excruciating.

This is how she felt, he imagined, and a fresh wave of guilt swept over his body, but Beau wouldn't let it drown him.

"Sienna," he called out, and just as her hand reached the banister, she turned, waiting for him to continue. Beau bit his lip nervously, pocketing his hands before spitting out, "I'm going to take you on that date you always wished we went on."

Sienna's head jolted back. "You're what?"

"Back then, when I could barely afford shit to throw in a picnic basket. You wanted to get dressed up, eat a five-course meal. You wished you felt like a princess. I'm going to make you feel like a princess."

"I was joking. And I was seventeen," she said, rolling her eyes.

"Exactly. I want you to be seventeen with me again. I want to have *fun* with you again."

"What are you talking about?"

"I'm talking about being that guy you once said made all your wishes come true."

Sienna shook her head. "Did you not hear yourself before about living someone else's dreams?"

Beau laughed.

"What's so funny?"

"You don't get it by now, do you?" he asked.

"Get what?"

That you're the dream, Sienna.

Beau shook his head. "I'll pick you up at seven thirty on Tuesday."

"I didn't say *yes*," she reminded him before pressing her lips together in thought. "And *if* I do. Hypothetically, you get *one* shot with me. This isn't a game, Beau. If you don't make the catch with me, you don't get to just line up for the next snap and another down."

Beau shook his head. "With you, it's touchdown or nothing." He bent and tore off a piece of cardboard, grabbing a marker. "Here," he said with the cap between his teeth. "This is my number. Call to cancel only if there's an actual emergency. Otherwise, I'll see you Tuesday. You can let me know if you get it after that."

He waved and walked back into Greg's room to stack boxes until her feet padded down the stairs and out the front door. The noise of Sienna leaving brought a smile to his face because Beau could feel it. *She'll be back.*

"Oh look, the prodigal player returns," Chase's voice boomed through the Bluetooth of Beau's truck, and he imagined his agent rolling his eyes.

"It was *one* missed call."

"And *three* texts," Chase reminded him.

Beau pulled out of the Goodwill parking lot, where he had dropped off all the contents of his old room. "It's off-season, Chase. Can you give me a break?"

"It's a few weeks into off-season, which means it's about time we figure out what's going to happen *next* season, Beau."

Stopping at a traffic light, Beau leaned his head against the seat. "I want to stay in Dallas. Make that happen."

"If you're really serious about retiring, can we at least go over your options—"

"No," Beau interrupted. "If Dallas doesn't want me another year, then I'm done, I'm good."

"Beau—"

"Chase, I didn't call to talk shop, alright? I need your help."

Chase sighed heavily. "Fine. You're my lowest maintenance client. What do you need? New trainer? A massage session?"

"Not football stuff. I'm set." Beau had his training schedule for off-season—weights, conditioning, agility, massages—and it kept him busy most mornings and several afternoons during the week.

"Then what?"

"A few things," Beau said as he entered the intersection. "And the only answer you need to give me is 'yes,' alright?"

"I'll say yes if you agree to sit down with me and go over all your options."

"Chase, you work for *me*."

"Exactly, and my job is to make sure you make decisions that are in your best interest."

That's exactly what I need you to do right now. My best interest is not just getting Sienna back but keeping her this time.

"Great, we're on the same page." Beau cleared his throat. "Listen, find someone who can get me into the new planetarium—"

"The what?"

When Beau hit another red light, his phone buzzed from the console. Picking it up, he pumped his fist at Sienna's text.

Fine. Tuesday night. But I have conditions.

"The planetarium at the science center. The old one closed." Beau knew that already because Dallas's old planetarium location now housed two things—the restaurant he invested in and the condos above it where he lived. "Tuesday night," Beau reiterated to Chase. "Maybe around ten."

You don't even have to name them. He typed back to Sienna.

"Why do you need to go to the planetarium on Tuesday night?"

Beau lifted his head in frustration. "Let me know when it's done, Chase." He looked down at his phone when it buzzed again.

I do. This is Luella's number. Her son Damien could use some coaching that she can't afford. They live in North Dallas. Make it happen. And get them comped tickets for next season.

Beau's phone buzzed again with Luella's contact.

Consider it done, he replied.

"Look, I know how some people get toward the end of their career and have a what-the-fuck-will-I-do kind of moment, but what, is space a new hobby or something?"

Ok. You can pick me up on Tuesday.

"No," Beau said, driving by Sienna's house on his way home. He caught sight of the side roof and smiled. "An old one."

It had taken Beau nearly forty minutes to get off the phone with Luella when he called her. He learned she was a Pisces, from North Carolina but had lived in New York for ten years—they spent a chunk of their conversation arguing over the best bagel shop—and she hated her son played football but encouraged him because he loved it so much.

On Saturday morning, when Beau got out of his car in a municipal lot in North Dallas, he was expecting to meet a kid as much as a chatty Cathy as his mother.

"Damien?" he asked, approaching a teenage boy sitting on

the bench of a picnic table. He was a fair size for a teenager—close to six feet.

The boy pulled off his hat, revealing a buzzed head, and jumped as if Beau were a drill sergeant. "Yes, sir."

Beau dropped the mesh sack of cones and balls to the ground. "How's it going, man? I'm Beau."

"I know who you are." Damien swallowed, pressing his hands into his thighs. "Sir."

Beau pressed his lips together. "Okay. . . alright."

Kid's about as tight as a stretched rubber band. If he widens his eyes more, they'll pop out of his head.

"How about a warm-up?" Beau looked beyond the picnic tables at the track surrounding the field. He could feel Damien's wide eyes focused on him. "A couple of laps?" Beau suggested.

Damien nodded. "Yes, sir."

How do I let him know to lose the 'sir' a.s.a.p.? Beau wondered.

"Alright, let's go." He walked, but Damien stayed still. "You. . . you coming?

"*With* you?"

Beau's eyes bounced between the track and Damien. "Saturday's normally my rest day. But I never say no to a workout."

"Oh, okay." Damien nearly tripped on his feet when he followed Beau to the rubber track. They barely did one lap when Beau realized Damien was slowing his pace—even his warm-up pace.

"Hold on, let's stop for a second. I'm not much of a coach. I've *never* coached, but this is pretty informal. I'm feeling like you showed up for a job interview or something."

Damien let out a laugh, to Beau's relief. "It's just. . . you're kind of my hero."

"Is that right?"

He scratched his head. The idea that Beau could be someone's hero never sat well with him. It's why he rarely interacted with fans to the same extent as some of his teammates. Heroes weren't flawed—they were perfect. But Beau—who had played dozens of what were considered perfect games over his career—found himself far from perfect at heart.

Damien nodded.

Sighing, Beau put his hands on his hips. "You shouldn't idolize me. Or anyone. I'm just another dude in the game. I've been around long enough that I can give you pointers. But if you're going to hold back on me, you won't do yourself any favors."

"Yes, sir."

"Beau. My name's Beau. You can call me Beau."

Damien released a heavy breath. "Alright. Yes, Beau."

"Your mom tells me you're pretty fast. See that court over there?" Beau pointed. "Feel like racing?"

Damien blinked. "Race *you?*"

"Yeah. All out, okay? Don't hold back. I won't." Beau took off sprinting. He might have had a two-and-a-half-second lead on Damien, but by the time Beau crossed from the grass to the pavement, Damien was on his heels.

Beau slowed to a jog, folding his hands behind his head.

"Good," he panted. "You didn't hold back."

Damien raised his head to the sky. "By that much."

Beau laughed through his heart palpitations as he slowed in the center of the court. A lone ball sat along the fence lining the court. Jogging over, Beau bounced it before passing it to Damien.

"I don't play basketball. I mean, with my friends but not like *play play*." He fingered the ball before dribbling.

"Good." Beau smiled. "Me either." Quickly, he reached out, stealing the ball and cutting around Damien, going in for a layup he missed. Passing the ball back to Damien, he readied himself for defense. "Think of me as your friend while we warm up, yeah? Then we'll go back to the field."

Twenty minutes later, after Damien not only beat Beau at basketball but also knocked him on his ass twice, they returned to the field. Damien was looser, more comfortable, and Beau could see he had a natural speed, quick feet, but slow cuts.

"We can keep working on that," Beau told him as Damien collected cones, dropping them into the bag. "You good for same time, same place next week?"

"For real?"

Beau laughed. "For real, man. But don't get your hopes up. I'll be working on my jump shot. Don't think you'll beat me twice."

the flying receiver

DEAR MOM,

You might be happy to know something. I joined the school newspaper as a photo editor, and they asked me to cover football. I don't mind going to games anymore, so long as I don't have to do the coin toss.

This week, Brookwood was down by three, and it was fourth down and long. *Too long for a field goal. Dad knew this. It had been a brutal, toe to toe game. The boys were tired, some even bloody. I was behind the bench, standing on a cooler and trying to take some shots of the huddle Dad had going on.*

"Long star. Only way. You put a hell of an arc on that." Dad grabbed the quarterback by the neck of his jersey before reaching for Beau. "And I promise you, he'll catch it. Right, Beau?"

Beau put his hands on his hips and nodded. "Give it air. I'll catch the damn ball."

"The rest of you," Dad said before sighing. "Well, just block for your life."

I snapped a few more shots and said a silent prayer, Mom. Because I understood a "long star" for Dad really meant a Hail Mary. Sometimes, football comes down to a prayer, or in this case, a shooting wideout.

I started running down the sideline before they snapped the ball.

Like everyone else, I knew where this was going. But sometimes, it's not just about a prayer or a shooting star or wishes. Sometimes you just need to be at the right place at the right time.

Beau is parallel to the turf in the photo, one arm outstretched, the ball landing in his fingers as he flew—*and I mean, flew—into the end zone.*

People called it a Sportscenter moment. The local news used my *photo when they covered the story over the weekend—"Walker the Flying Receiver" was how they captioned it. And I can't stop smiling, thinking about how it was a joint effort between the two of us.*

"Maybe football isn't so bad after all," I told Beau a few nights later on the roof as I admired a copy of my photo. Glancing at him, I noticed the weak pout on his face. "What's wrong?"

"I hate football."

My eyes widened. "Careful. That could get you capital punishment in Texas."

Beau let out a chuckle. "Would you love sprinting and being tackled all the time? Do you know why I run so fast? It's not to score. It's to avoid being hit." He sighed, his face growing serious. "This was Greg's dream, not mine."

I knitted my brow together.

"I'm able-bodied. I'm alive. *I have a chance. He didn't. It should be him, not me. But I'm here, and he's not." Beau's eyes grew dark in the glow from the streetlight. "I'm doing it for him."*

I swallowed heavily and waited for him to continue.

"He gave up his life for me."

Beau ran a finger along the scar at his temple, and my heart squeezed. I knew it was hard as hell to walk around and live life while missing someone who was such a big part of who you are. And to bear that burden and *carry a physical reminder too. . . I hurt for him.*

"That sounds an awful lot like you're living for someone else," I told him. "I can't imagine he'd want to see you do something you hate."

"Maybe I don't hate *it," he admitted. "But I'm not sure I love it the way he did."*

"Then why do you work so hard?"

Beau trains hard, Mom. He gives it his all, and I didn't understand how someone could go all out for something that wasn't really in their heart.

"I want his death to mean something," Beau admitted. "To me, to my parents, to everyone."

"It already does," I told him.

Beau remained quiet, looking at the paper. "I want to mean something," he whispered.

"You already do." Without thinking, I reached out and covered his hand with mine.

The moment our eyes met I nearly stopped breathing. Beau turned his hand beneath mine so our palms were touching. "Do I mean something to you?"

The uncertainty in his voice made my heart hurt. I don't know how I ever let myself forget that Beau once meant everything to me. I don't know how I let you make me forget, Mom.

"You always have," I admitted with a cracked voice. I looked at our hands. I hated mine was shaking as I wondered if he might link our fingers together.

Beau cleared his throat and let go. "I guess if football gets me out of here, it's not for nothing."

It wasn't for nothing. I know this. I know what a scholarship means, and I also know Beau is on a track for not just one, but one somewhere really great. It looks like Beau will go to Florida State next year. And I guess I'm happy for him if he's happy. But I have no colleges on my list in Florida. They're all in Texas. Who knew geography could be bittersweet? It's more than bittersweet, though, thinking that a year from now, we'll be settled in different places. It's actually painful to think about and I remembered the first few weeks after we moved back. There I was, climbing to the roof for more space when I really had never felt more alone in my entire life.

"You'll get out too."

What Beau doesn't know is that I'm not worried about getting out of Brookwood. I'm worried about being me without him again, like I *was when we moved away as a kid. Only this time, Mom, I won't have you to pull me out of that awful feeling.*

"That photo might land you a job at Sports Illustrated one day." He tilted his head up toward the sky. "Go on, wish it."

I rolled my eyes. "I don't want to work for Sports Illustrated."

"No. Wish to get out of here," Beau told me. "We don't belong here, Sienna. There's no life *here. It's just day after day, and a game or two of football sprinkled in. There's a whole world out there we haven't even stepped foot in."*

Beau was right, Mom. I still have never been to the ocean.

"Where is there life?" I asked.

"Just about anywhere else."

That made me laugh because I thought the same when we came back to Brookwood, missing the charm and culture of Nashville, the music, the people. But the truth is, since Beau and I started hanging out, I'm finding there's a lot of life to live here, even if it's quiet and sometimes boring. With the right person, it's not all that bad. All the other stuff—like dipping my feet into the ocean, or running through Provence's lavender fields—that's just a bonus.

I humored him, though, and focused on a star above us.

But between you and me, Mom, I wished for something else. I wished Beau felt the same about me as I felt about him—like he's the missing piece that makes bad things better, and the piece that makes good things extraordinary.

Love,

Sienna

under neon stars

DEAR MOM,

I spent most of today kind of sulking. I got a C on my History test, but that's not the only reason. Tomorrow is our birthday, so if you were still here, you'd probably tell me not to worry about the test. We'd come home from school, and you'd be cooking up a feast, making Henry's favorite, lasagna, and mine, chicken parm. We'd wait for Dad to come home so we could dig in and go to bed like it was a normal night, except you would sneak into our rooms a half hour later and bring us outside to make our birthday wishes.

"It's still raining," I told Henry on the way to the cafeteria. I glanced angrily outside, where the sky was as dark as I felt, knowing tonight, we wouldn't be able to see the night sky.

Henry nodded. "Thanks, captain obvious."

"It's supposed to keep *raining."*

"Okay."

I sighed in frustration. "It'll probably be really cloudy at night."

Henry stopped dead in his tracks. "Sienna, come on."

"What?"

He shook his head. "You can't possibly be upset about that."

"Why not?"

"Because we're turning seventeen, not seven."

"So what? I don't remember you complaining last year. Didn't you wish for a new phone?"

Henry scoffed. "That was last *year."*

"And what, suddenly you're too old for a family tradition?"

"It wasn't a family tradition, Sienna. It was a Mom *tradition. And it died with her."*

Henry didn't slap me, but he might as well have. Because tears started stinging my eyes, and my face—my entire body—burned.

Henry shook his head as he walked away. "The sooner you accept it, the better."

I was left standing at the entrance to the cafeteria as Henry walked away, mumbling. Someone bumped into me, and suddenly I was aware that I was a moment away from having a breakdown in front of the entire school. I turned on my heel, pressing my lips shut tightly so the sobs wouldn't come out until I made it down the hallway and out to the vacant courtyard, abandoned because of the bad weather.

And they poured out of me as loud as thunder.

"What's wrong?" Beau's voice came from behind me, and even though my cries were loud and the pelting rain pinged every time it hit the ground, I could hear him clearly.

"Nothing."

He touched my shoulder, and I pulled away before he sighed. "Can you come under the awning? It's pouring."

I kept my head down toward the wet pavement and moved to the side of the building. "It's raining."

"I said that already."

"And cloudy."

Beau leaned against the brick wall. "That usually comes with rain."

"Tomorrow is my birthday."

"I know."

"That means tonight, Henry and I should be lying out in the grass and wishing on a star."

Beau and I made wishes all the time. But birthday wishes, well, they have to mean something. I wiped my face angrily.

When does it stop, Mom? At what point do I not need *you as much, miss you as much? Never, right? Do you ever stop needing your mom? Did you even* think *about that? Or about Dad? He needs you too. He folds towels wrong. He can hardly cook. He always forgets to buy paper towels. When dinner is ready, he pulls your chair out like he's waiting for you to sit in it.*

"Clouds or not, stars are always around." Beau nudged my shoulder. "I promise. I'll find you one."

I skipped the rest of my classes, and Henry must have said something to Dad about it because when he got home that night, he came to my room. I pretended to be asleep. The bed shifted when Dad sat beside me.

"I wish you knew how much she loved you and would hate to see you upset."

After he left, I thought about throwing on my jacket and climbing up to the roof, but the rain continued to pound, yet in between pelts, I heard a louder tap on my window.

Flipping on the light, I saw Beau. He motioned impatiently at the glass, and I clamored out of bed to slide it up. He handed me a plastic bag before lifting himself in and falling onto the floor.

"What are you doing?" I whispered. Dad was probably asleep, but I didn't need to take any chances.

He stood, pulled off his rain jacket, which was soaked, and left it on the floor by the window before toeing off his sneakers. He reached for the bag.

"Turn that light off."

I walked around the bed and flipped the switch, staring at his shadow.

"Lie down," Beau told me, and even though he couldn't see my face, he could obviously feel my questioning stare. "Just do it." He bent, reaching for something along the wall.

I locked the door and climbed into bed.

"Close your eyes."

I did as told and could hear Beau place something on the nightstand before the bed shifted, and I could feel the warmth of his body beside mine. I held my breath.

"Open."

Cautiously, I lifted my lids, but when I saw what Beau had done, they flew open. A gasp escaped my mouth. My room was covered in hundreds of stars—on the ceiling, the walls, the curtains, against my dresser. I raised my head to look past Beau at the end table, where a small globe night-light gleamed.

"I told you I'd find you a star." Beau looked at his watch when I lay back down. "It's 11:07. You still have time."

I closed my eyes, and when I opened them, Beau was staring, his focus bouncing between my eyes and lips nearly at the same pace my heart raced.

"I wish you'd kiss me."

A frown struck Beau's face. "You aren't supposed to say it out loud."

I turned, inching closer. "Then make it a dream come true."

Honestly, it was the best first kiss I've ever had. There wasn't anything awkward about it. Our teeth didn't bump, his head went one way and mine the other. Beau's lips were soft but firm, and he tasted like a memory—sweet, light, and dreamy. I couldn't even remember being upset or angry minutes earlier. Maybe this is what you meant, Mom, when you used to say, "When it rains on your parade, dance in it." You never really know what surprises you might find in the clouds.

Under the neon stars on my ceiling, we kissed and kissed, and everything fell into place. And I'm starting to think, even though we were apart, even though we grew up, everything between us stayed exactly as it was.

As a kid, Beau always said yes to a game of tag, to riding our bikes down hills we knew were too steep. He said yes to jumping out of a tree. And now, at eighteen, Beau said yes to kissing me, and when he moved his body—warm even though damp clothes—on top of mine, I opened my eyes just for a second and narrowed in on one, tiny star hovering above us.

I had no idea how I could focus on anything other than Beau's warm lips sliding down my neck, whispering, "You don't know how many times I've dreamed about kissing you."

Somehow, I found my voice. "How many?"

"How many stars are in the sky?" he asked, tracing his words against my skin with his tongue.

"Too many to count."

His breath was at my ear. "Somewhere around that," Beau whispered, but before I closed my eyes when he kissed me again, I made my real wish.

I wished—from deep within my body sandwiched between him and the bed—that Beau would never stop.

Love,

Sienna

peanut butter and fluff

DEAR MOM,

It hit me today that you aren't going to be here for certain moments in my life. You won't be there for my high school graduation. If I make it to college, that one either. You won't be there to help me choose a prom dress. Those are big moments. Today wasn't a big moment, but it was an important one. I could've used your help breaking the news to Dad.

"I'm going on a date with Beau Walker," I announced, stepping into the kitchen. I tried to not *look at Dad when I told him, but out of the corner of my eye, I saw his mouth hanging open, his hands holding a sandwich below his chin, like I had shocked him out of the next bite.*

"Excuse me?"

"Oh, this should be good," Henry heckled

I ignored Henry. "He's picking me up in twenty minutes."

"Beau Walker?" Dad asked, dropping the sandwich and wiping mustard off his thumb with a napkin. "Like my wideout, Beau Walker."

"Like Beau Walker who I've been friends with since I was five. The same one in Henry's chemistry class. The Beau Walker who believes the only place raisins belong is in Raisin Bran—"

"Sienna—"

"And yes, Dad, your wideout. But I didn't realize you had dibs."

Henry stole some chips off Dad's plate. "Oh, this is going to be really *good."*

"Shut up, Henry," Dad and I both said at the same time.

Dad stood. "I thought you and Beau were friends."

"We are."

"Friends don't date."

Friends don't climb through each other's windows and kiss in each other's beds, either, which is what we've been doing for weeks. But Dad doesn't need to know that.

"Henry, give us a second." Dad tilted his head at the door when Henry didn't make a move. "Get lost."

Brushing crumbs from his hands, Henry left the table.

"Sienna," Dad began. "Look, I know I probably haven't been the most present father since we got here." He paused, and I knew he wanted to add, or since your mom died, *but he doesn't.*

I wanted to tell him I agreed. Dad hasn't just been not present—he hasn't been anywhere. Or at least anywhere but work. I wanted to point out the irony that he has probably spent more time with Beau between practice, film, and games than with me or Henry, but I didn't.

"I don't know if your mom. . . if she talked about boys *with you—"*

"No. Please don't." This was more embarrassing than when he asked if I needed tampons from the store.

"I like Beau. Beau is a great kid. He's got a good head on his shoulders, he's respectful. But he's still a boy.*" His cheeks puffed when he let out a big breath. "And a football player."*

I also wanted to point out that there isn't anything "boyish" about Beau. Not his height, his weight, the strength of his arms, the light brown hair on his long legs that tickles my own a few times a week.

But for both of our sakes, I let Dad keep thinking Beau was still the boy I used to make mud castles and eat worms with.

"And boys—even good ones, Sienna—they only have one *thing on their mind."*

Here's where Dad was wrong again, Mom. Without telling you too much detail, because I need to maintain some self-respect and boundaries, I tried to move things further with Beau. But he wants it to be special and says that not a lot between us is. We hang out on the roof. I time his forty-yard dashes. We eat lunch in the cafeteria. But he's also wrong. Because every moment with Beau is special for me, even if it's day-to-day, even if it's ordinary. But he's right. Because if all those moments are special, the most special of them all shouldn't be in my bed with the door locked, trying to keep quiet.

"Dad." I tried to save him the embarrassment. "We talked. Me and Mom. Save your talk for Henry when he needs it in ten years."

"I heard *that!"*

Dad stayed quiet for a minute. "I don't want to see you get hurt, that's all. You've hurt enough."

I didn't tell him I'm still hurting, but Beau—his presence, his listening—helps me feel better.

"Beau wouldn't hurt me."

Pressing his lips together, Dad smiled sadly, and I didn't like it. It was like he knew something I didn't, like he'd be counting the days until he could tell me "I told you so."

"I'm going to get ready." I left the kitchen and pushed Henry's shoulder annoyingly when I bumped into him, and I could hear the two of them talking from down the hall.

"Did you know anything about this?" Dad asked.

"They hang out a lot," Henry offered. "He's cool, I guess. There could be worse. Like Dylan Lockhart. He's a real douchebag."

In my room, I rolled on lip balm and changed into a blouse, straightening the light blue fabric. I'd never been happier to hear the doorbell ring. Dad huffed as he trudged to the door. I giggled, imagining the conversation happening on the front steps. But Beau is a good guy. And Dad, well, he's a softy. I don't have to tell you that, Mom.

I gave them another few minutes and grabbed a sweater on my way out. Beau's eyes flashed with relief when he saw me over Dad's shoulder. I ignored Henry smirking and slid past Dad.

"Ready?"

Beau looked to Dad, as if he was still waiting for permission, but I took his hand and led him away.

"Hey," Dad called out. We both turned to face him. "You take care of my daughter now."

"Yes, sir," Beau replied. "It's a promise."

Dad held out a finger. "And you always treat her right, you hear me?"

I was about to roll my eyes but then saw they gave each other gentle nods, and the moment changed.

"And have her back by curfew, Walker. Or you'll be sprinting on Monday."

Now I rolled my eyes. "Come on."

Beau opened his truck door, and I hope Dad saw it for bonus points.

"Was he so bad?"

Beau shut his door and started the engine.

"Are you shaking?" I asked when I saw his hands tremble against the steering wheel.

"No."

"You totally are." I laughed. "It'll be fine. Just don't break my heart." Please, please, don't. I took his hand and held it in my lap, feeling his sweaty palm, and I laughed. "I wish you were that nervous to ask me out in the first place."

Finally, Beau laughed, his body losing its tension.

"What?" I asked.

"It's the same but different with you and your dad," Beau tells me. "He makes me nervous. But you don't."

"How do I make you feel?"

Beau slowed well before a stop sign, and I made a note to add safe driver to the justification list later for Dad. A smile spread across his face, wide and bright. It was like when we were kids.

He's the same, but different too, Mom.

"I'll only admit this to you. And if you tell anyone, it's over. I've got an image to protect."

"Tell me."

Beau glanced around the intersection, which was free of cars. He leaned over and pressed his lips to mine. "You give me butterflies. Always have. I just didn't know what to call them when I was little."

And honestly, Mom, that was the best part of the entire date. It wasn't the picnic basket Beau packed with all my favorite foods—like *appetizers of Saltines with cheddar cheese and entrees of peanut butter and fluff sandwiches with sour cream and onion Pringles on the side. That one admission was my favorite part. Oh, and maybe the Chipwich ice creams Beau packed, which basically melted in the cooler by the time we got around to eating them. But I didn't mind. I learned they taste better right off Beau's lips.*

"What's so funny?"

I didn't realize I had been smiling. "This is the best first date ever."

"Yeah?" Beau asked, pushing up from me. "Picnic in the grass?"

I nodded. "We have time for the fancy stuff."

Beau tilted his head to the side. "Is that what you want?"

Running my hands along his chest, I smiled. "I guess I'd like to see you in a suit one time. But open collar, no tie."

"What else?"

I slid my hands over his broad shoulders to the back of his neck and wound them in his hair. "Fancy restaurant, five-course meal." I don't really care about a fancy dinner, but I say it anyway because this life with him in it feels like a movie. "Make me feel like a princess."

Beau's eyes fluttered shut when I scratched at his scalp, and it's sort of my favorite look—the way his dark lashes move against his skin as he bites his lip.

"What else?"

I didn't really have anything else, but as I saw twilight taking over the sky above us, I blurted out the only thing I could think of. "Planetarium."

Beau laughed. "Why?"

I pulled his face to mine and whispered against his mouth, "I want you to kiss me under all *the stars. Real and fake."*

The way he smiled against my lips became my favorite one of his smiles.

I only peeked at the sky for half a second before I returned my gaze to his. And while we looked at each other, that's when I made my wish. Because I saw the stars in Beau's eyes.

Love,

Sienna

chapter seven

SIENNA WAS three outfit changes and one coat of mascara deep when Grace appeared at the door.

"Whoa."

"Have you seen those black strappy heels?" Sienna asked. At five foot ten, Sienna didn't need the height. *But I could use the confidence.*

"*What* are you wearing?"

Whipping her head around to face Grace, Sienna chewed on the inside of her cheek and looked down at the form fitting, black velvet dress. She tugged the long sleeves down. "That bad? Too low cut?"

Grace pursed her lips together in thought. "You're not a cool mom—"

"I don't need the *Mean Girls*—"

"You're a *hot* mom." Grace folded her arms across her chest. "But won't this dress be a waste at Maloney's? I mean, that Dylan guy wears flannel shirts and work boots." Grace sat on the bed. "That dress deserves a guy in a suit."

"What do you know about Dylan?"

Grace rolled her eyes. "Did you really think last year I believed he just stopped by for pancakes at seven in the morning? I had chemo brain, not naive brain."

"I'm not seeing Dylan tonight." Sienna turned and stuck her hand deeper into the closet. "Just dinner with a friend."

A friend who makes my heart race, my brain foggy, and my thighs clench together.

"That isn't a dress for a friend, either."

"Have you seen my shoes?" Sienna asked with a huff. She could hear Grace rise from the bed and leave the room, only to come back a moment later, dropping something on the floor. "These don't even fit you," Sienna said, finding the heels.

Grace shrugged. "I'm practicing."

"For what?"

"Prom. I think Justin is going to ask me." She twirled the ends of her wig.

Prom, Sienna sighed. Brookwood was such a small town that the annual dance was for all high school students—including freshman like Grace.

Sienna grabbed the shoes. "You have a few months." She slipped the strap into the buckle. "I put a lasagna in the oven. I told Henry—"

"So, this friend," Grace began, "does it happen to be Beau Walker?"

Sienna's eyes pierced her daughter's. "What do *you* know about Beau Walker?"

"Lots of things. He's six four, two hundred and twenty-five pounds. A Scorpio. Used to be the—"

"Do me a favor and go check on that lasagna," Sienna said, motioning at the door. She stood, tugging down the dress, and moved to the mirror beside the closet. *Acceptable. Appropriate. Kind of. Maybe a little short.* She still didn't know where Beau was planning to take her.

"Mom?"

Sienna held her own gaze in the mirror. "I'm having dinner with Beau Walker."

"Shut up." There was an excited curiosity in her daughter's

eyes Sienna could practically feel through the reflection. "For real?"

"For very real."

"Beau Walker. Like *'oh, he wasn't ever my boyfriend,'* wide receiver Beau Walker?"

"The one and only."

A gasp came from her daughter. "No way," she whispered.

Sienna raised an eyebrow at her daughter through the mirror. "Is it really so hard to believe?"

"Huh?" Grace asked her mom. "No, it's not that. Henry!" she squealed, dashing from the room. "Henry! You're *never* going to believe it!"

I don't blame either of you. I wouldn't either. Sienna ran a hand through her hair. *Now or never*. She slipped her phone into her purse and grabbed a jacket. Even over the clanking of her heels against the hallway's wood floor, she could hear Grace and Henry in the kitchen.

"I bet he's bringing flowers. *And* a limo."

"Five bucks says flowers but no limo. Definitely no chocolates, but I'll bet candlelight dinner." Henry paused. "If he has game, a string quartet."

"Ten bucks says *both* of you watch too many Lifetime movies." Sienna glared at Henry. "Don't let the Lasagna burn," she said, pouring herself a glass of water.

Henry playfully threw the box at his sister. "Don't act like you actually made it and there isn't another in the freezer."

Grace picked the box up from the floor and scrunched her face. "It's *spinach*." She dropped the box into the recycling bin and looked at Henry. "When they leave, let's order a pizza."

"And wings," Henry added.

Sienna was about to tell both of them off when the doorbell rang, and Grace bolted from the kitchen.

"I'll get it!" she yelled before returning to whisper, "make him wait. Guys like that."

Henry shook his head in objection. "No, no, we don't."

Grace rolled her eyes and left the room. Sienna looked down at her empty glass and sighed before opening the cabinet and pouring herself a shot of whiskey.

"Oh, come on." Henry rose from his chair, taking the glass from Sienna. "You can't get drunk *now*. What if he shows up with a horse-drawn carriage and you puke on the way to his castle? But for real. You told me you were having dinner with a friend."

"It is dinner with a friend."

"I'm your brother but I'm saying this as a guy." Henry pointed at his sister. "This dress is not the kind you wear for drinks with a friend, let alone Beau Walker."

Sienna placed her hands on her hips. "Okay, I'll go put on my overalls then," she huffed. "And you know his name is Beau. Why do we have to refer to famous people by their full names?" Sienna rolled her eyes. "He's just in town for a few days." *I think*. "We're catching up."

"And then where is he going? Mars?"

She snatched the glass from Henry. "Can you check on your niece and make sure she isn't bombarding *Beau Walker*?" Tipping the whiskey into her mouth, Sienna put the glass in the sink and then reached for her purse, popping a few mints into her mouth to mask the liquid courage she wished she hadn't needed.

It's only dinner, she reminded herself before sighing, *with a side of sweaty palms and a knotted stomach.*

Sienna slipped on her coat, walking to the front door. She bit her lip at Beau in his sleek dark-gray suit and crisp white shirt with an open collar, knowing dinner would also come with a side of heart palpitations.

His dark-brown eyes gripped hers, so strongly, Sienna squirmed in her heels and nearly tripped.

"Where are the flowers?" Grace asked.

Beau fought to look away from Sienna. "I. . . "

Grace placed her hands on her hips. "The flowers?"

"Grace, knock it off," Sienna seethed under her breath. "Dinner, homework, bed."

"You set?" Beau asked, and when Sienna nodded, he motioned his head.

"Have her back by curfew, Walker," Henry teased.

Grace snickered beside her uncle. "Yeah! Or you'll sprint!"

"I'm sorry." Sienna offered Beau an apologetic smile as they made their way down the steps. "I hope she didn't give you a hard time." She tried not to lose her balance when Beau placed his hand on her lower back, sending tingles along her spine.

"She could've gone harder on me, considering what you're wearing. I wouldn't have minded." Beau's eyes darkened. "Not at all."

Sienna bit her lip.

They reached his car, something black, low, and sleek, a far contrast to the large pickup he had the other day. Sienna was thankful he was the one who opened the door. She was afraid to leave any smudges on the shiny metal.

She watched Beau through the windshield as his long, thick legs glided along the pavement. Everything about him was effortless and working in his favor—the stubble from not shaving, the way the hair at the top of his head sat soft and barely done.

Beau's hair reminded Sienna of a time when it was her hand that made it unkept after hours and hours of kissing and winding her fingers through the tresses, her nails scraping Beau's scalp, making him kiss her harder. Beau closed his door, and Sienna ran her thumb across her bottom lip, which felt plumper, softer as if it had grown in size. *Muscle memory*, she thought, trying to focus on the "memory" part. There had been so many, and suddenly Beau's closeness in the car, his smell—woodsy and leathery—the view of her home, of the roof they had lain on in the quiet of so many past nights overwhelmed her.

"You okay?"

Sienna nodded over enthusiastically, slipping off her coat. "Yeah, just a little warm." She looked back at the house, but not at the roof this time, at the living room window where she could see Grace peeking through the curtains.

Beau pulled onto the street.

"Where are we going?" Sienna asked.

His focus remained on the road, but she could see the wide grin spread across his face.

"Back in time."

Sienna wasn't sure what Beau meant by "back in time" because it only took her eight minutes to realize they were heading to Dallas.

"Do you have something against ties?" Beau asked as he pulled onto the highway.

"No, not personally," Sienna told him while thinking, *but I do love an open collar.* "Why?" She watched as Beau removed one hand from the steering wheel, reached into his pocket, and tossed a long black piece of material at her.

"Grace ordered me to take it off."

Sienna giggled, winding the tie in her hands.

"She also said I should've brought you flowers."

"You don't have to bring me flowers."

Beau shrugged beside her. "I think it's kind of awkward. I hand you a flower arrangement, and you stand there before putting it down. If you like the girl enough to bring her flowers, you don't want to wait a minute for the date to start." He cocked a grin at Sienna.

"Even worse, a bouquet wrapped in paper that I would have to trim and find a vase for."

A quick chuckle escaped his chest. "What do you think, I'm a dog bringing you a stick? I'd never." Sienna watched his face slide into a clever smirk.

"What?" she asked.

"I hope you like them," Beau said.

"Like what?"

He turned quickly to look at her. "Nothing. Just let me know if you do." Sienna was about to ask again, but Beau continued, "Grace seems like a lot of fun."

"And a lot of work," Sienna added. "But she's pretty great. Especially considering everything."

"But she's good now, yeah? Full on remission?"

"Not exactly full," Sienna corrected him. "That comes after five years." *I hope we make it to that part.* "But she's good. No evidence of disease."

For now, she nearly added, but Sienna lost her voice when Beau reached for her hand, clasping it with his on his thigh. She studied it for a minute, the way his thumb slipped from her grip to brush gently back and forth before squeezing and letting go. The slight movement provided an enormous amount of reassurance, as if Beau were saying all the things she had needed to hear over the course of the last tumultuous years.

It's going to be okay.

"Thank you for what you did for Damien. Honestly, I thought you could call in a favor." She broke their hold and pulled her phone from her purse to flash a photo Luella had sent of Beau and Damien after their workout. "I didn't mean *you* had to coach him."

Beau shrugged. "He's a good kid. Quick feet. He's got drive, just needs some fine-tuning."

"Luella said it was a dream come true for him." Sienna put her phone away. "It must be nice to have that kind of impact on someone. I mean, an hour of your day gave him a memory he'll keep for a lifetime."

Beau's hand left the steering wheel to rub across his jaw. "I guess."

"She means the world to me—Luella. She's taken care of Grace for some time." Sienna sighed. "People like her, who willingly work with sick kids. . . they deserve the world. So, thank you."

"Sick kids deserve it too," Beau said with a nod. "I mean, you can't say no to a sick kid, can you?"

"Not very easily." Sienna leaned her head toward the window. "You know, we *might* be on the other side of it, but I think about Grace's friend Molly. They got diagnosed around the same time. They used to be inseparable. But Molly's case, it got complicated. She's prepping for another stem cell transplant. But they're making plans to go to Disney World through a glass wall." Sienna sighed. "Life isn't fair sometimes. When you have a kid with cancer, you're between a rock and a hard place of wanting to do more and you can't. I'd like to do more for those kids one day."

"Have you taken Grace?"

"To Disney? No." Sienna shook her head. "It was always too expensive, or she was too sick. I couldn't exactly put her on a plane when she had no immune system, and the drive would've been too hard on her. Maybe I can swing it next year. And she'd want to take Molly, but we'd have to wait until she was clear for travel. We'll see how summer goes."

"But now things are a little less risky, right? She told me she was going to see Simon Gorges in concert."

"She did?"

Beau chewed on his lip. "Uh, yeah. When I picked you up, she mentioned something about it."

"Oh," Sienna said. "Yeah, Henry got her tickets."

"Good. She deserves to have a little fun," Beau reminded her. "And so does her mom."

"Il Cielo? We've never been here." *Definitely not.* From the sleek branding of the sign to the dim light she could see through the window, Sienna knew this restaurant was already out of her league. "Maybe you're thinking of someone else."

Sienna eyed Beau as he made his way to her door, waving off the valet who had moved to open it. The way he walked—smoothly and purposefully—made her unable to look away, and Sienna wondered how many other women had watched him from this very same seat, had let him open the door. She frowned inwardly.

His bed was probably never empty.

She jumped when he opened her door and held out a hand. "Do you trust me?"

Do you actually know *me?* Sienna wondered as she glanced at the restaurant behind him. Fancy food—fancy *anything*—wasn't exactly her type. She would have been happy with pizza and garlic knots.

But there was something in Beau's eyes that made Sienna want to trust him. It was a confidence that only could have been embedded over a lifetime. A long time ago, if Sienna had asked Beau to jump, he would, with no question, not even *how high?* He would jump out of trees as kids, off the roof as teenagers—whatever she wanted—risking broken bones and her father's wrath.

And all he's asking for me now is to take his hand, she thought to herself.

But the truth was, Beau didn't have to ask. As strong and stubborn as she tried to be since Beau returned after a long, painful hiatus, Sienna would be lying if she had said she didn't like that he was around.

"What does that mean? Il Cielo?"

"The sky," Beau said, opening the door.

Stepping into the restaurant, Sienna felt like she was among the stars, with the tiniest twinkling lights recessed into the ceiling and candles scattered on the tables.

"Mr. Walker," the maître d' greeted Beau with the slightest nod. Beau didn't stop, only gave a small wave hello.

"This way," he told Sienna. A few patrons lifted their heads at them, letting out a whisper or two of *Beau Walker* as they made their way through the dimly lit restaurant. Sienna could feel eyes on her and tried to avoid all of them as Beau led her by the hand to a corner booth.

"I hope you're hungry," he said, sliding next to her.

The nerves in her stomach had morphed into barely there flutters by the time they had arrived in Dallas, and Sienna realized she had been too anxious to eat much of anything all day.

"I am," she told him, still looking around. *And I might need a pizza after this.* Everything about Il Cielo screamed two-bite portions.

A server approached, but Beau didn't take his eyes off Sienna. "Drink?"

God yes. "Um. A vodka martini, please."

Beau ordered a beer. "Fancy tonight, huh?"

"If I'm being honest, I'm not much of a martini girl."

He raised an eyebrow. "Then why did you order one?"

Shrugging, Sienna pulled down the length of her dress when she felt his gaze on her bare thigh. "To fit the part," she admitted, motioning around with her hand.

"For me, you fit." He blew out a breath and looked to the side. "You fit perfectly." Beau waved down a waiter. "George, forget those drinks. Bring us a bottle of Jack Daniels, two glasses, please. Rocks?" he asked, facing Sienna.

"Never." The smirk on her face disappeared when her stomach growled.

"And George? Let's get the food out."

"Very good, sir," George said. "I'll bring out the first course."

Sienna's stomach grumbled again.

Beau laughed. "You know what? Bring it all at once. I'm starving."

Sienna blushed, her eyes dropping to her lap. "Sorry. I didn't really have lunch." *Or breakfast.* "I was too nervous to eat."

"Why?" Beau asked, narrowing his brow.

Pursing her lips together, Sienna ignored his question. "Do you come here a lot?"

George returned with sparkling water, whiskey, and glasses. Beau waved him off and reached for the bottle. "You could say that."

"What does that mean?"

Beau poured the alcohol. "I live in the condos above the place." He held his glass, waiting for Sienna.

She raised hers to his and took a sip. "I guess if you live in a high-rise condominium, a forty-dollar chocolate mousse is the equivalent of the three-dollar shake at the diner."

Beau held his glass at his mouth, staring for a minute. "I don't come here for the food," he said. "Not that often, at least. And for the record, the chocolate mousse is great, but the apple tart is what you want to order. But I'm more of a burger and fries kind of guy. You should know that."

I do, Sienna thought, recalling dozens of diner meals, dipping French fries into thick, sweet milkshakes—Beau's strawberry, Sienna's chocolate.

"Then why did you bring me here?"

She didn't want to tell Beau that whatever single oyster was about to come her way on a small plate wasn't her style either. But just as she should know, so should he. *Maybe this is another example of how far apart we've grown. How little we actually know each other now.*

"I told you I'd take you to the planetarium one day, didn't I?"

Sienna narrowed her eyes. She looked around the restaurant. "This isn't the planetarium."

"When I signed with Dallas, I walked around the city one day."

Humming in confusion, Sienna pretended to follow along. "Okay."

Beau took another sip of his drink. "I thought I was coming to the planetarium, but they closed it a long time ago. I found this place instead. *Il Cielo.*" He paused. "The sky. And then I noticed there were condos for sale, and I was in a short-term rental on the other side of the city and—"

"What does that mean, Beau?"

Placing his glass on the table, Beau sighed. "The name seemed fitting, considering I always wanted to bring you there. If I hadn't been such an idiot, I would've taken you *here* while it still *was* the planetarium."

Sienna's throat bobbled with a heavy swallow.

"That's what you said, right? Back on our first official date? You don't need anything fancy. Only a trip to the planetarium." His eyes softened.

"So you took me here because it used to be the planetarium?"

Beau nodded. "I promised I would."

Sienna pressed her lips together. "And why did you buy an apartment here too?"

"I wanted a stake in the space. If things had gone differently, if I had done things differently…I like to think it would've been our place. I was looking for pieces of you everywhere."

Sienna's eyes fell.

Beau shifted beside her. "You don't believe me."

"I don't really know what to believe," she said, shaking her head.

"Do you believe me when I say I remember everything?" Beau asked, and when Sienna stayed quiet, he continued. "You told me you wanted me to kiss you under all the stars. Real and fake. That was on your wish list."

"I might've said something like that."

Her mind swirled to the evening of their first date. She could remember Beau's sweaty palms after facing her father, the sigh of relief he let out when they drove off in his truck for a picnic in the meadow outside of town. They ate sandwiches and ice cream that the cooler couldn't keep frozen. They kissed for so long that neither realized they had rolled off the blanket and into the dirt.

Sienna looked down, expecting to find the grass stain left on the blue blouse she had worn that day instead of the dress she currently had on. The memory was so strong that when her eyes raised to Beau, it was almost as if she was looking at him sixteen years ago. He was clean-shaven then with longer hair and no crow's feet flanking his eyes. She was thinner and lighter in many ways. They had driven his loud, dusty truck, the well-worn seats a far contrast from the sleek sports car he had picked her up in tonight.

Sienna inched closer, lost in the moment's nostalgia where everything was right, when she didn't shy away with hesitation from Beau's touch and instead sought it out, fighting for one last kiss, one more shared breath, a last moment of his delicious weight on top of her.

Her eyes flickered from his lips to the recessed lighting of the ceiling. But while it was tastefully done, dim and warm, the bulbs weren't stars.

"Just wait," Beau whispered, as if he could read her mind.

chapter eight

BEAU NEEDED to remind himself to wait as well. As much as he wanted to wine and dine Sienna, to make her feel every way she deserved, all Beau could think of was lying down nose to nose with her, counting the lightest freckles that painted her cheeks, wondering if more had grown since they had last been in that position. He wanted to trace his finger from the top of her hairline, down her sloped nose, into the valley of her Cupid's bow, and over her full lips.

They were nearly that close, Sienna having turned her body to his, her bare knee pressing into his leg. Beau was a ball of tension as he strained to hold back, but the rigid knot loosened—and he nearly jumped—when Sienna reached for his hand, resting it on her bare thigh.

Her whisper tickled Beau's lips. "I lied before."

"About what?"

"I wasn't nervous," she admitted. "You made me remember what butterflies felt like."

"I want to make you remember what everything feels like." He abandoned Sienna's hand only to tug her bottom lip free from her teeth. "I want you to remember how the world looks when you're happy."

But under the glow of Il Cielo, seeing the soft smile dancing across Sienna's face after her admission, a tough realization struck Beau. The smile only went so high, flaring her cheeks and going no further, as if there was something inside Sienna—who had known too much grief and too much tragedy—keeping it from reaching her eyes.

Their locked gaze broke when the waitstaff approached the table. Sienna looked questioningly at the array of covered plates placed in front of them and, at the last one, a silver box.

"Thanks, George. I've got it from here."

"This," Sienna began, running a finger over the metal box, "is freezing."

Beau pushed the box away. "That's dessert." He reached for the lids covering the plates, pulling them off. "Let's start with these." He focused on the table but tried to catch a glimpse of Sienna from the corner of his eye.

Slowly, she reached out, picking up half of a sandwich from the large plate, inspecting it curiously. Beau turned his head a little more, watching her place it back down and pick up a chip.

"Peanut butter and Fluff." Beau cleared his throat. "With a side of—"

"Did you bring me to a five-star restaurant to feed me Pringles?" Sienna asked, and Beau's face fell in defeat.

Yeah, Sienna, I did. Pringles on a silver platter.

The confidence Beau had built up, thinking it was a good idea to replay and upgrade their first date, waned until Sienna brought her hand to her mouth. She popped the entire chip in before bursting into laughter that reached her eyes and touched Beau's heart.

Beau had downed two sandwiches and nearly half a can of Pringles when Sienna paused, tilting her head in question.

She reached for a small crumble of cheese next to what remained of the nearly florescent processed yellow they had scarfed down. "What's this?" she asked.

"Well, I upgraded the cheese plate a bit." Beau took the tiny crumble from her. "This," he began, "is a truffled gouda."

Sienna leaned her head back and let out a laugh. "At what point did you become a dairy snob? You used to shoot Cheez Whiz straight into your mouth."

"I still do that," Beau admitted cheekily, popping the gouda into his mouth. He was about to continue but paused to savor the richness. Reaching over the saltines for another cube, he held one in front of her mouth. "Try this and tell me it's not what heaven tastes like."

Sienna narrowed her green eyes at Beau's hand before moving them to his own, holding his gaze as she took the cube into her mouth, her lips grazing the tip of his finger. When her lids drifted shut, and Sienna's tongue swiped her bottom lip, Beau moved the hand still floating in front of her face and poured himself more whiskey.

"I'll get us a driver," he told her, tipping the glass back and welcoming the delight of the burn. *Because I might need another one of these.*

Beau didn't know where to look—at Sienna, whose cheeks were flushing pink, at the table where her arm leaned, long, slender fingers fiddling with a fork. If he looked down, Beau would find the warm, smooth skin of her thigh flanking his.

He took another drink.

"I can't believe you did this," Sienna said quietly with a small laugh, peeking over her shoulder at the waitstaff on standby. "They probably think you're nuts."

"Let them." *I mean, they work for me,* Beau added in thought but refrained from telling Sienna he owned the restaurant just yet.

"So, your neighborhood joint is a five-star restaurant that you have cater grocery store meals. Or your downstairs joint, I guess. You *really* live upstairs?" Sienna asked through thick lashes.

"I do. But don't ask me to take you up there tonight. I'm not sure I'd be as much of the gentleman I'm trying hard to be right now."

As she tilted her head, Sienna's hair fell to the side, curtaining half of her face. There was a darkening to her eyes. "Not much has changed. I spent a lot of time trying to get you to be less of a gentleman."

"You came pretty close to succeeding. You could try the patience of a saint."

When Sienna's mouth flattened into a coy smirk, Beau trailed his vision down to the creamy skin of her neck, wondering if she still tasted the same. It was a battle to keep himself from leaning forward into the dip of her collarbone and finding out.

He cleared his throat. "But you're right. I'm holding off until it's the moment you deserve."

Sienna's smirk disappeared. "That's what you said back then."

"I know. It's still true." Beau reached out, holding her chin when he could sense she was going to look away. "You wanted to do a lot of things. Like this fancy date, the—"

"At the end of it all, back then, I wanted to spend time with you."

"And now?" Beau asked. "What do you want now?"

"I want to be happy."

I want to make you happy.

"I'm afraid, Beau. Of you. Of how I feel with you, even after all this time apart, even after *everything* that's happened since you've been gone." Sienna sighed. "I'm one tragedy away from a breakdown. I don't know how I've kept it together for so long." She shook her head. "It's like I've been living only to get past all the hard bits. Mom dying. Dad dying. Grace's cancer. Sometimes it feels like *my* life hasn't even started yet. And here I am finally at that point, and you show up and. . . "

Beau prodded her. "And what, Sienna?"

"My heart is back there." She pointed to the crust he had left of one sandwich. "It's rolling around with you in the grass and sneaking you through my window. My head is telling me if I leave it there, I'll get hurt. Like the last time."

Tonguing his cheek, Beau sighed. He hadn't planned for the night to be heavy or painful. He didn't need reminders of how much he hurt Sienna—that had been written on her face when he first saw her again after the game, in the way she carefully and curiously eyed him, like he was a stranger instead of her best friend, her first love. It was in the hesitancy of her voice, her touch.

She has every right. I fucked up, Beau thought angrily, frustrated. But then he remembered what he was asking Sienna for wasn't forgiveness.

He shifted and folded his left leg over his knee, pulling his suit as far up as it could go and nudging his sock down. "I had an accident a few years ago, off-season. Broken tibia. Surgery. A metal plate. Months of physical therapy. But do you know what else I got?" He waited, and Sienna shook her head. "A second chance to finish that dream I started the day I left you. A second chance to make all that time away mean something."

Sienna fought his hold to look away, but Beau held her in place while his other hand moved to tap his left temple. "Eighteen stitches. A grade three concussion. A dead brother."

Eyes softening, Sienna reached for his hand. "I know."

"Do you know what else I got? A second chance at *life*," Beau said. "So when you showed back up in high school, I was there to fall in love with you."

Beau watched Sienna try to fight the tremble that took her mouth. His hand slid from her chin to her cheek, cupping it gently, trying to erase the emotion.

"And you now, all these years later. . . " Beau wasn't able to stop himself. He pressed his thumb against her mouth. "I'd be an idiot to think it means I'm forgiven, that we can pick up right where we left off. But do you know what you here gives me?"

Sienna shook her head, and Beau sighed as his finger rubbed against the smooth length of her lip from the movement.

"Hope, Sienna. That there's a piece of you that wishes as much as I do you'll be able to give me another chance. I have to hope that this is the time I prove, even though I was wrong to leave, I was still right about one thing."

Taking a shaky breath, Sienna brought her hand up, holding onto his wrist. The smallest turn of her head into his palm brought waves of both anguish and happiness through Beau's body.

"What were you right about?"

Beau moved, his fingers tracing her face, over the freckles that reminded him of constellations. He picked his favorite—one just below her right eye and made a wish.

"It's always been you." He could feel Sienna's breath hitch. "I can tell you I'm sorry a million times. Words aren't enough. Please give me a chance to *show* you."

After ten seconds, Beau was prepared to plead his case more. *This fancy restaurant I own? It's fancier with you in it. These sandwiches are good, but they taste better with you eating next to me. This life I've built is big, it's exciting, but the only thing that would make it exceptional is you in it,* he mentally rehearsed.

Sienna pulled back. "You know, I need to, uh, use the bathroom. Excuse me."

"Yeah, sure." Beau cleared his throat as she slid from the booth, and he watched as she made her way through the restaurant, only she didn't head to the bathrooms. Sienna went outside.

Beau released a heavy breath. "Fuck." He ran a hand over his face before pulling out his phone.

Find out what I need to do to close Disney World for a day.

Chase responded immediately to his text.

Disney World? It would be cheaper to build your own amusement park.

Beau didn't care about money. Not when it came to Sienna and what she cared about—sick children.

I didn't ask you for a cheaper option. Find out.

Beau pocketed his phone, ignoring how it vibrated again in his jacket. He passed his half-empty glass between his hands, focusing on the amber liquor, trying to ignore how his heart raced faster with each second she was away from the table.

Too much too quick, Beau told himself. But he had little time to waste. *And even if I had the time, I don't want to wait. I don't want to wait anymore to be with her.*

"Okay," Sienna said, sliding back into the booth. Her cheeks were flushed, bitten by the cool winter night.

"I thought you left."

Sienna shook her head. "I just needed a moment. Some space." She took a deep, calming breath. "Show me."

Her words brought a smile to his face before his brain could even register what she said. He grasped Sienna's hand.

"We'll take dessert to go, come on."

"Don't we need to get the check?"

Cooler under his arm, he pressed against her back, ushering her toward the front of the restaurant. "Why? I own the place."

"Where are we going?" Sienna asked, matching his stride as her heels beat against the sidewalk.

"Short walk. Are you cold?" Beau watched as she ran a hand up and down her bare arm before she folded her arms across her chest. "Where's your coat?"

He had been so infatuated with Sienna's body in that dress

that he hadn't noticed the jacket she had been wearing when he picked her up was nowhere to be seen.

"I left it in the car."

He moved to the side, placing the box on the ground. "Here," Beau said, taking off his suit jacket. Sienna smiled gratefully as he stepped behind her, slipping it over her shoulders. He lifted her hair, letting his fingers comb through the silky strands before he picked up the box and extended a hand. "Come on."

"So you bought the restaurant too?" Sienna asked from beside him.

"I told you," he said, running a thumb over her knuckles. "I wanted a stake in the place. I didn't want to risk losing it. Plus," he added, "my accountant told me to diversify my investments."

Beau kept his head down, avoiding the odd gaze from others walking in the opposite direction. There was a side of being *Beau Walker* that Beau didn't always like but was forced to appreciate. When he felt a group's gaze burn into his back after they passed, Beau pulled Sienna to his side, protectively.

"Sorry," he whispered, even though he didn't feel bad the situation brought her closer.

They hurried a few more blocks before crossing the street and heading down a back alley.

Looking skeptically at their surroundings, Sienna popped an eyebrow, and her head snapped forward when a door opened.

"All set, Mr. Walker." A woman appeared, motioning them in. "Take your time."

Beau thanked her before stepping inside, leading Sienna through the dim corridor until they reached the lobby. Their feet echoed in the large, open space absent of anyone else.

"Where are we?" Sienna tugged his hand, but Beau said nothing and continued through the Science Center. "Do you own this place to?

"It's not for sale. Don't think I didn't check."

Pulling open a door, Beau motioned with his head. "Il Cielo

was where the old planetarium was. But it's still not a planetarium."

He waited, watching Sienna bite her lip in question before she peeked into the dark room, hesitantly walking inside. He leaned against the wall, watching her small steps as shadows flanked her silhouette. The deeper she went into the auditorium, the more her body came into view. When Sienna stopped and looked up at the illuminated ceiling, her hair cascaded down her back, over Beau's suit jacket.

"Wish list?" he asked.

The ceiling—the sky—didn't just light up. Sienna did too, and Beau pushed off the wall, his mouth stretching with a grin of delight when she lifted her hands to the air and twirled.

"Wish list," came her voice, light and airy, when she stopped circling, not letting her head fall from the ceiling.

"How about dessert?" Beau asked, approaching.

Sienna finally turned back to him, staring at the package he held out. She slipped off his jacket, dropping it to a chair. "Back then, those melted," she said about the ice cream before taking it.

Beau nodded, swallowing heavily, as he recalled licking the ice cream that dripped down her chin to her neck.

"I've stepped up my logistics game a bit," he rebutted, placing the box on the floor and pushing it to the side with his foot. "Dry ice. But damn. You don't know how hard it is to find Chipwiches these days."

Sienna ripped open the package, holding the treat to the lit ceiling to examine the chocolate chips lacing the vanilla ice cream between two soft cookies. She stepped closer, offering him the first bite.

After an evening of Sienna's body pressed to his side, of her fingers wound between his own, Beau could no longer not touch her. He grabbed her wrist, holding it as he bit into the ice cream before gently guiding Sienna's hand back to her as she did the same. Beau's next bite was different—he could feel where her mouth had warmed the cookie, softened the ice cream, and a tingle swirled down his chest to his toes now curled inside his dress shoes.

They finished it in silence, until there was nothing but cookie crumb left on Sienna's fingers, which she licked off before wiping a smudge of ice cream from Beau's mouth. He immediately pushed his tongue forward, swiping his lips to get a taste of her. Sienna let her finger linger.

"Are you going to make a wish now?" Beau's words kissed her skin delicately, a far contrast from how hard his heart was thumping.

Eyes focused on his mouth, Sienna shook her head.

Beau frowned.

"No wish. But I'll tell you a secret."

Her fingers traced his lips, the shape, the length, the tiniest space between them, catching the quick breaths Beau let out, struggling to find his voice. "What's that?"

Green eyes found his beneath the dim light. "My favorite time star gazing with you never was on the roof."

Beau swallowed heavily when she dropped her hand.

"We weren't even outside," Sienna whispered, moving closer.

Beau's hands found her waist, his fingers spreading, palms pressing into her hips. The silent sigh that left Sienna's mouth floated over to his own, and he let himself drink it in, knowing that as soon as he swallowed it down, he would need another hit.

"We were in my bed."

Beau would never forget—he could never forget—the way Sienna's soft lips moved against his the first time, how achingly familiar she felt beneath him even though they had never been in that position before. It was something new and old at the same time—a welcome home as if both of them had left, or maybe, Beau had wondered, *as if it were meant to be this way all along.*

Beau wet his lips at the memory. Sienna had only stopped kissing him that night to tell him a second wish.

"Dancing in the rain," Sienna panted.

Beau had to force his eyes open, fighting the spell she had put him under. "What?"

"I want to dance in the rain with you," she told him. "I love the rain now."

He raised an eyebrow. "The rain ruined your birthday." When Sienna smiled, Beau wanted to lean forward and taste the grin.

"No. The rain was the best part."

Beau wouldn't let her stop him then. "Wish list," he said, capturing her mouth again.

"You made two wishes that night."

Sienna's nose grazed his when she nodded.

Chewing on the inside of his cheek, Beau shook his head when she pushed closer. "Say it. Wish it," he whispered, the beat of his pulse pounding in his ears.

Tell me to kiss you, Beau thought. *Beg me to.*

The desire for nostalgia angered his body—his hands on her waist, which wanted to grip Sienna harder, his mouth, which wanted to kiss her and never stop. But Beau needed to hear that even though they were different, some things remained the same.

"Which one?" Sienna asked.

"Well, there's no rain on the forecast. The first one. Wish it," he demanded again with a growl, fighting his body's impatience.

Sienna tilted her head back, her eyes narrowing in curiosity, but she didn't ask Beau *why* he wanted and needed to hear her say it. Instead, she broke their gaze and glanced down at their bodies a breath apart.

"Wishes are for kids."

"Wishes are for *us*."

Ignoring him, her hands slid up his stomach, drawing goose bumps beneath his shirt. It was only another way his body was screaming and fighting to get to hers.

"Wishes are for kids," Sienna repeated before her eyes finally found his again as her tongue peeked between her lips quickly. "And there's nothing childish about what I want right now."

Fuck it. Beau hardly finished the thought before he pulled Sienna in, sealing the gap between their bodies. Their mouths moved against each other as if they were battling all that was between them—love, happiness, and disappointment. *Fight for it, Sienna,* Beau thought as she fed a delicious groan into his mouth. *Fight for this with me.*

His thoughts silenced, every sense focusing in on Sienna, overwhelmed that they kissed and moved together as if they had never been apart. She nipped at his bottom lip in the way that drove him crazy, and Beau kissed her fiercely, deeply as she kept up until he cupped her chin to slow it down, to drown in her sweetness.

Beau could have sworn that they were teenagers, that the stars glowing above them didn't come from a professional installation, but from a night-light he had purchased at Walmart for five bucks just to see her smile.

But they were no longer teenagers who had to keep quiet behind a locked door as they explored each other's bodies, searching for the smallest spot that brought the most gratifying kind of noise. Sienna's hands clutched and clawed at his shirt, pressing harder against him. Beau's hands glided to her lower back, to the perfect swell he gripped headily. But when Sienna's mouth found his neck, the intensity and desperation with which she nipped and kissed his skin struck Beau with a heavy dose of gravity, bringing him out of the sky and onto the ground of the auditorium. Sienna was kissing him like time was running out on the clock.

It was as if with each press of her mouth, with the fierce flexing and gripping of her hands, Sienna was trying to steal pieces of him, savor them, like they would soon be a memory she might need to revisit one day.

I'll be here, he promised. *For good this time.*

Beau's hand went to her cheek, directing her mouth back to

his and pressed his lips to hers, holding the kiss steady before he pulled away. Sienna's eyes were still shut as her face fell forward in search of his. His hand held her in place with only a breath between.

"I was wrong before."

Sienna's lids fluttered from their half-mast position in a daze. Her chest heaved, and Beau couldn't stop himself from letting his hand leave her face to run down her neck and chest, over the swell of her breast before resting on her heart.

Shivering beneath his touch, Sienna asked, "About what?"

"About the gouda."

She leaned into his palm when he returned a hand back to her face. Beau pressed a small, confident kiss to her mouth.

"The best taste in the world is you after eating a Chipwich." When a small smile crept across her mouth, Beau traced it with his tongue. "Back then and now."

And because Beau knew in his bones that second and third chances didn't happen every day, for good measure, he silently added *and always.*

i wish it will always be this way

DEAR MOM,

For the second time in my life, my breath was taken away from me.

You were around for the first. It was that time Beau and I jumped out of the tree, and when he did, landing on his ankle funny. We were little, so you might think I was afraid we would get in trouble. But really, I didn't care about that at all. I was afraid because he was hurt.

The second time was at this week's game.

I was on the end zone sideline when it happened—the moment Beau caught the ball—when he fumbled it after a defensive back hit him so hard, I could hear the breath sucked out of him too. They went helmet to helmet. What an awful sound. Just writing it makes me shiver.

Beau didn't move for two minutes and eight seconds. I know, Mom, because I counted. It took seven seconds of him lying there for the refs to blow the whistle, another eleven for the trainer and Dad to jog out to him. And then it took 110 seconds for him to sit and be helped off the field.

I swear I couldn't breathe the entire 128 seconds.

I gave everyone space but hung close by as Beau sat in front of the trainer asking him questions.

Do you know where you are?

What day is it?

What's eight plus eight?

Beau answered slowly, his voice dragging a bit. I knew, even without seeing his eyes, he had a concussion.

And I knew he was terrified.

During halftime, I found Henry in the stands and shoved my camera at him. "Hold this."

I wandered nervously to the locker room, waiting. It took another eight minutes, nearly all the break, but Dad and the trainers came out, and then some players.

"Is Beau alright?" I asked DJ, the team quarterback, who was half walking, half stretching.

"He's good."

"What does that mean?"

"It means I'm good," Beau said, walking up behind us, followed by more players.

I wanted to give him a bear hug, Mom. My hands, my arms, my whole body fought to fling myself around him. I looked into his eyes, which were a little glossy, but normal, and that brought me some relief.

Beau tipped his head toward the side of the locker room. I turned, looking over my shoulder at the jumbotron, and saw a few minutes were left of halftime before slipping through the herd of players gathered outside, hoping no one would notice.

I didn't know where Beau went, but he found me when I walked around the corner, yanking me tightly against him. His helmet fell to the ground when he wrapped his arms around me. I brought my hand to the back of his head when he started to shake.

"You're not alright."

"Head hits freak me out."

Of course, they do. They freak everyone out, Mom. But Beau once hit his head so hard on the pavement that it knocked him out, and he woke up in a hospital with eighteen stitches, a concussion, and a dead brother.

"You don't have to play." I squeezed him. "Tell my dad—"

Beau shook his head against mine. "FSU scouts are here, I have to play." His breath was warm against my skin when he said that, and it upset me. Because whatever Beau was feeling—in his head, in his heart

—was scary and valid and more than enough reason to sit out the rest of the game.

"I just needed a second," he whispered against my skin.

When his grip tightened, I knew what he needed was a second with me, and I got it in that moment, Mom. Sometimes when you're scared or hurting so much that it breaks you down, just a hug from someone you love makes it okay enough to face your fears and finish the game.

You were that for me before, on the first day of school, at the kitchen table when I practiced a presentation I was nervous about giving the next day. You held my hand when I was scared and hugged me when I cried.

But now you're gone, and I want you to know, I found someone to be that for me. Or I found him again. Because, as kids, we encouraged each other. We listened to each other when we were sad. We shared candy bars and happiness, the blame when we dug up your flowers trying to see if we really could make it to China. Now we share kisses and wishes, cakes his mom makes that taste delicious but aren't perfect enough on the outside for customers, yet are perfect for us. And now we share our fears. But maybe, we always have.

When Beau let go of my hand before picking up his helmet and returning to the field with the team, I wondered how long I've really loved him, and that feeling struck me so hard I could barely take any more photos. But after the final whistle, I snapped a photo of Dad and Beau during Dad's brief moment of celebrating the win before worrying about the next game.

But the best moment came after, when Dad was yanked away by other players and staff, and Beau walked up to me. He had this funny look on his face, like he was trying to say something but wasn't sure how *to say it.*

"Will you be my girlfriend?"

I nearly jolted back, and then I felt silly. Because if I wasn't his girlfriend already, what was I?

We stood a few feet apart, and he was looking at me all dazed and confused. He was looking at me like he had stars in his eyes.

And then I smiled and nodded. But I didn't want to keep it quiet anymore. Our relationship had always been silent, a blur of whispers in an effort not to get caught. I wanted the entire world—or at least all of Brookwood—to know that the boy with the shaggy brown hair and matching eyes, with the scar on his head that carried the burden of the past and the weight of the future, was mine.

So I jumped and wrapped my arms around him, and I let him lift me up. Even though it's been a whole day, it still feels like my feet haven't touched the ground yet.

I wish it will always be this way.

Love,

Sienna

my shooting wideout

DEAR MOM,

I read the first entry I wrote in this diary or journal or whatever we're calling it. And it's crazy in five months how *much things have changed. But if it's been five months since I've started writing you, it means it's been at least six months since you've been gone.*

That's how different it is now—I used to count hours, days, weeks, months. And the sixth month milestone, I totally missed.

That should tell you something, and I hope you don't take it in a bad way. Mom, I'm happy.

When I first realized it, I felt guilty. Because if I'm happy, does that mean I miss you less? Need you less? That's not possible. But with every hour, day, week, or month that I don't count, I'm realizing you can miss someone painfully and find happiness at the same time. I'm trying not to let guilt steal time I should use to make memories.

And me and Beau, we have a lot of memories to make before he goes off to Florida State, where he's officially accepted a scholarship. The wish list is never-ending. We keep adding to it, stupid things like going to the rodeo, and more important things like figuring out how much we need to save to go to Provence, so we can take the trip to the lavender farms you and I never went on. We figured we'd start small with a trip to the ocean this summer.

But first on the list, hopefully, *involves the motorcycle Beau's been building, which he finally let me see yesterday. He had such a proud smile on his face when yanked the sheet off. I didn't want to break his heart and tell him it's kind of a mess.*

"What do you think?"

It took me a minute to figure out which was the front and which was the back.

"Super cool. But. . . "

"But what?"

"Does it work?"

Beau laughed, throwing the sheet onto a chair in the corner. "Not very well since it doesn't have an engine. Or a back wheel." He stepped aside, rolling a cart of tools over to the bike. "But do you know what it was when I started? This." He tapped the handlebars.

"Where did everything else come from?" I asked.

Shrugging, Beau slid a stool over to me so I could sit. "Here and there. Scraps. I weld them together."

I looked at a bin in the corner full of metal bits and then back at the bike. "Impressive."

It was. Because Beau made something out of nothing, and I thought that was pretty cool. I looked over at the blow torch and masks on the table.

"And this has taken a year so far?"

Facing away, Beau opened some drawers of tools. "What? No. Just a few months."

I scrunched my face in thought because even though, by this point, there are too many nights Beau and I have spent on the roof for me to keep track, without a doubt, I remember him telling me about the motorcycle.

"But you said you started last summer."

Beau straightened. He remained facing away for a minute before turning to me as he fiddled with the wrench in his hand. "Do you know the game two truths and a lie?"

"I might not be as smart as Henry, but I think I can figure it out," I told him, leaning back against a workbench.

"Okay," he began, "I'll start. Dole Whips are my favorite dessert. I

hate lamb chops, and I might have started building this the day after you told me you always wanted to go on a motorcycle."

Even though he had lied, Beau's admission made me burn with happiness.

"You hate pineapple."

Beau put the wrench down and walked over to me. "That's correct."

I gave him a playful kick to the shin. "You didn't have to lie to impress me."

"It's not about impressing you." Beau nudged my legs open so he could stand between them.

"What's it about then?"

He stayed quiet for a minute as his eyes danced across my face. The intensity of his stare made me squirm against the bench.

Reaching out, I lifted his chin. "What is it?"

"I wanted to make that wish come true for you. Be your prince charming or whatever."

My eyes found the frame on the wall behind him, the one that held my *picture that Beau's Dad had hung up proudly. I scanned the headline from over his shoulder.*

WALKER THE FLYING RECEIVER SECURES BROOKWOOD VICTORY.

"You're something better than prince charming."

Beau's mouth slid into a curious smirk. "Oh yeah? What's better than that?"

I felt silly admitting that these days—and these past few months—Beau has become the thing I wish on. But I told him anyway.

"My shooting wideout."

Love,

Sienna

chapter nine

I COULD USE **your help if you're not busy. Then I want to take you to lunch.**

Sienna rolled her eyes before responding to Beau's text.

I'd like to bring you lunch. See you in an hour.

She dropped the phone onto the couch, resuming folding the laundry. Holding a pair of socks in the air, Sienna looked around, unsure of what the noise was. It took three more pairs of socks to realize she had been humming *and* smiling, even while looking at an enormous mountain of unfolded clothes.

It was a smile—Sienna hated to admit—that had lingered more on than off since Beau dropped her off at home a few days ago, when she had opened the door and crept into the house to find a beautiful flower arrangement of white peonies—her favorite—on the table. According to Grace, they had been delivered about ten minutes after Sienna and Beau had left.

Thank you. It hasn't even started yet but it's already been the best second first date of my life—B.

Even with the exhaustive upkeep of Maloney's and the stress that radiated from the pile of overdue hospital bills, the smile Beau put on her face was a welcome distraction.

Sienna put away the laundry and went to the diner, picking up burgers and the works, and headed to Beau's parents' house, where he was getting out of his truck as she pulled in. She had barely turned off the engine before Beau was opening her door, offering his hand. Sienna reached for the takeout bag and placed it in his hand, sliding out of the car.

Beau held up the plastic bag and peeked in.

"Better not be Oysters or something," he said.

Sienna shut the door. "I hope you didn't get your snobby, foodie heart up. The cheese on the burgers is heavily processed, long shelf-life cheddar with color never seen in nature."

"My favorite." Beau cracked a grin, swinging a bare arm around her and pulling her in for a kiss.

Before her brain could register what was happening, Sienna was already leaning in for a second. And a third. There were too many kisses to make up for.

"Hi," he said.

"Hi." With his arm around her, they walked to the front steps. "What do you have going on today?"

Beau unlocked the door, waiting for her to step in. "That." He nodded at cans of paint, brushes, and rollers at the foot of the steps.

"Do I get workman's compensation, by the way? I nearly threw out my back the other day moving boxes."

She unzipped her hoodie and draped it over the banister, tugging her T-shirt down and entering the kitchen to open the blinds above the sink. She jumped when Beau's hands—large and warm—held her shoulders.

"Did you?"

Turning the water on, Sienna lathered her hands. "I did. And it still hurts," she joked. "I might sue you." Peeking over her shoulder, she found him smirking.

Beau kneaded under her neck, his touch sprouting a chill that sashayed down to Sienna's hands.

"If I make it feel better, would you still sue me?"

Only if you stop touching me right now.

His breath fanning across her skin made the small hairs on

the back of Sienna's neck rise at attention. Warm water still pouring over her skin from the faucet, Sienna lifted a shaking hand to shut it off. Beau slid his hands from her shoulders down her back, leaving a trail of tingles under the fabric of her T-shirt and a deep, warm ache blooming through her body. She closed her mouth tightly, so he might not hear how heavily she was breathing.

"What about your neck?" His lips were at her ear. "Does it hurt too?"

"Now that you mention it. . . " Beau brushed her ponytail to the side, smiling into her skin, and Sienna gave up trying to reach for a paper towel and gripped the sink with wet, slippery hands.

Sienna hummed, but she felt Beau's slick grin tighten, and he pulled his lip between his teeth when she told him, "You could kiss it and make it better."

Beau let out a whisper of a groan, one Sienna felt vibrate from his chest against her back. "God damn, Sienna." The low growl of Beau's voice made Sienna clench her thighs together. "What else? I'm willing to settle out of court. I'd make it worth it too."

Her head rolled back, laying on his shoulder, and Beau inhaled her greedily. All Sienna wanted was to settle the damages in bed.

"Lower?"

Gulping, Sienna nodded as his fingers crept to the bottom of her white T-shirt. He lifted it, rubbing the dip of her back softly.

"Here?" he asked. His lips continued to rain small kisses into the valley of her collarbone.

Here? Here is where I die.

Sienna shivered as Beau's hand slid from her back, along her side, until it was flush against her stomach, and he pulled her back to him. One of her hands fled the sink, reaching to wind her fingers in the short hair at the back of his head when Beau circled his hips.

"Fix me," she managed to whisper as he pressed harder into her ass. *With your mouth, with your body. With every part of you.* A whimper left her mouth when Beau's hand swept up her middle. *Because I'm still kind of broken.*

The kiss in the planetarium had been too much and not enough all at once. Beau's mouth, his breath, his tongue dancing with hers, the way his hands danced with ease across her body made Sienna's head dizzy and her body burn. The buzz within her cranked the wheels, and she was the one who kissed harder, who untucked Beau's dress shirt in search of his skin. When his hand flew to her wrist, pulling it back, she whimpered into his mouth as he slowed down his kisses. He quickly pulled away, led her to a chair, and tugged her onto his lap. They spent the rest of the evening there—her legs dangling over the side of the chair with Beau nuzzling her neck, as if her skin was more fascinating than the large display of stars on the ceiling.

Beau growled into her ear, "I'll fix it, I promise." His tongue traced his words, and Sienna's eyes sprang open between pants.

Forgiveness was one thing. But now, alone and no longer semi-breaking and entering, the war between her mind and body sobered her enough to lean forward and seek distance from the lustful cloud Beau had swept her in. Her movement only pressed her ass harder into him, and Sienna grew further torn between her doubtful mind and her body screaming for more.

"Beau."

He mumbled incoherently against her skin, the verse of a love-drunk song he was begging her to sing along to.

"Beau." Sienna held her breath, fingers painfully bending into the sink, and Beau's kisses and movements halted with his hand palming her breast, his thumb no longer circling.

"I'm sorry," Beau said with a heavy sigh, stepping back.

Sienna took a deep breath. "I need. . . I need a little time." She couldn't say the other words that were brewing within her. *There's no protecting my heart and coming back from that with you.*

After Beau had left for Florida State, Sienna needed no time with anyone the moment she realized that physical intimacy with a guy in her English class filled the hole Beau left in her heart fairly easily. It didn't matter that Sienna didn't know his last name, his favorite color or food, or that she lost her virginity on a creaky dorm room bed with the fitted sheet only covering two corners of the mattress. All that mattered was that someone was *there*.

And here Beau was, not just trying to fill that hole but fill it with happiness and cement it shut so Sienna would have something beautiful to carry with her the rest of her life. But Beau had dug that hole himself, burrowing pain and heartbreak all the way into her soul.

Twisting to face him, she tucked a loose strand behind her ear and let her fingers run down the path Beau's lips had left down her neck where her skin still burned. "I'm not trying to punish you."

"I wasn't thinking." He let out a small laugh. "Actually, I have been thinking. Only about you since the other night, and I'm getting ahead of myself. You need time. You don't need to explain more than that." Beau ran a hand over his jaw. "This is a redo, not a pick right back up. You should be wooed before all that, anyway."

Sienna laughed.

"What?" Beau asked with a curious grin.

"You're the only person who's ever wooed me." She watched the smile fall from Beau's face, and it was like a punch to her gut. "This might be old, but it's still new for me."

And I don't know how much of a piece of my heart I can give you now. You took so much of it already. And I forgive you, I swear, she told Beau in her head. *But that doesn't mean I've forgotten.*

She slid past him, taking the food out. "I got you curly fries. The diner still makes the best ones."

★★★★★

The ease between Sienna and Beau had settled into uncomfortable silence after they finished lunch and moved to the living room. Sienna packed stacks of books into boxes as Beau placed painter's tape along the trim.

"What will you do with these?"

Beau looked over his shoulder. "I guess I'll drop them at the library. My parents probably wouldn't mind."

"I'll wrap the photos," Sienna said, pointing to a higher shelf of the bookcase packed with frames.

She stood on her toes, pulling each one down. There were a few family shots, but nearly all the frames were school portraits of Beau and Greg. Sienna smiled, wiping the dust away on one of Beau, which had to be from first grade, with shaggy brown hair and a snaggle tooth. He had a scrape on his chin, and Sienna recalled the time he got it, falling off his bike after chasing her.

The smile turned into a frown when she realized Beau had double the number of framed photos Greg had. Sienna's heart squeezed for Beau's parents as she wiped the dust from each frame, packing Greg's away with extra care. But a laugh erupted from Sienna's chest when she picked up one of the last frames.

"You wore this shirt like *every* day."

She held up the frame for Beau, showing him the photo from senior year. He didn't look much different from now. Sienna realized Beau had unfairly been spared from awkward teenage years.

"I still love Weezer," Beau said, pushing up from the floor. "And I loved that shirt. But I don't know what happened to it." He scratched the back of his head.

Sienna pressed her lips together and smirked.

"What?" he asked.

"I have it."

Beau narrowed his eyes. *"Thief."*

Sienna shook her head in objection. "You *gave* it to me. That day at the lake, the first time we went."

She remembered Beau taking it off, how her cheeks warmed at the sight of him bare chested as she followed him to the rope. When they had returned to his car, Sienna had accidentally sat on her tank top with her wet swimsuit and Beau had given her his shirt to wear as he drove shirtless.

"I forgot to give it back, is all."

"Do you really still have it?"

She nodded.

"Do you wear it?"

Sienna shook her head and Beau looked away, seemingly disappointed. She might not have worn the shirt in over ten years, but she knew where it was, how soft it still felt folded in the bottom drawer of her dresser.

"There's still one more up here," Beau said, reaching.

Absentmindedly, Sienna put her hand out to take the frame from him, but when it remained floating in the air, she turned, expecting another shot of Beau and Greg maybe one from a family vacation, a birthday. Behind the glass she found Beau, but not Greg. Instead, she saw her father with his arm wrapped tightly around Beau in his football gear. Immediately, Sienna recalled the memory, the game when Beau had gotten hit so hard it stole his breath and hers from yards away.

"He really loved you," Sienna said, taking the frame cautiously, placing it glass side down, and wrapping it. "And he would've been very proud."

Beau turned, leaning against the bookshelf. "I wouldn't have gotten anywhere without him."

His comment made Sienna's ears burn. Furiously, she reached for the tape.

"You probably would've been just fine without him," she huffed angrily. "And me."

"Sienna—"

"No." Sienna placed the frame in the box with the others. "You know what? I don't need time. It's not about time. It's not even about hurt. I'm *angry,*" she told Beau. "Because you got yourself where you are. But he pushed you in the right direction. He rooted for you. He watched every stupid college game you ever played in—"

"Sienna—"

"And you couldn't even come. For *one* day, you could've shown up and done the right thing. Pay your respects to the man who helped mold you into who you are today. Top wide receiver, wideout, whatever the hell it is you call yourself. And. . . " She trailed off, her chest heaving.

"And what?"

"Me," Sienna's voice cracked, and she blinked repeatedly to keep the tears at the back of her eyes. "You could've made sure I was okay. I wasn't. You promised you would come back for me." She shook her head. "I didn't need you to save me then, Beau. All I needed was my *friend,* the same one who helped me during the first worst time of my life when my Mom died. I buried her when I was 17. I had to bury my father when I was—"

"Grace put a toy on your dad's coffin. It was pink and sparkly. Like a flamingo, I think. That's what it was, yeah? One of those pink birds?"

Sienna's breath hitched.

"I was there, alright? I missed the funeral and went to the burial and was in the back. I saw you." Beau shook his head. "And Grace. She had blonde hair like yours then. She kept putting her hand on your cheek and tapping it, like she was trying to cheer you up."

The tears Sienna had blinked away returned with a vengeance as she tried to find her voice.

"Why didn't you say anything?"

Beau put his hands on his hips. "I saw Grace, and I thought there was someone else. I thought you didn't need me. I thought you got that wish of the happily ever after, of being a mom like yours with someone else. I know you said you needed a friend, Sienna. This is going to sound awful, but I couldn't be your friend back then. It's not your fault, but I was young and seeing you and the thought of someone else." Beau paused, grimacing. "It hurt. Even though I left, and you had every right, the idea of you with someone else hurt in a way I could never explain."

Sienna watched how Beau's hands fisted quickly at his sides before he gave them a gentle shake to loosen his grasp.

"I'm sorry. I wish I had been stronger, more mature. I wish I went and stood behind you that day so you knew you had someone." Defeat seized Beau's face.

I wish you had too, Sienna thought.

"Say something, please." Beau glanced nervously at her face.

Sienna didn't know what to say. Her mind was too busy wondering how different life could have been if Beau had been braver. She remembered the dark days following her father's funeral, when she was only strong enough to smile around Grace despite feeling like she was dying inside, swallowed by the realization that even though she had Henry, Sienna was on her own. As she stood in his parent's nearly empty living room, Sienna's heart ached over the years that followed—treading the deep waters of mothering a seriously sick child, trying to comprehend diagnoses, treatments, and lab results when she only had a high school degree and had barely passed biology.

She thought of all the tears she had suppressed—for minutes, hours, and days—until she would have a moment in her bed to let them go, a flood of pent-up fear, stress, and loneliness leaking into her pillow, only to resume filling the tank the next morning. Quiet nights never stopped being difficult because the night had always been theirs. Sienna struggled with the way her heart yearned for Beau—his arms, his laugh, his presence—against the way her head reminded her he had better places to be than holding her.

"What about now?" Sienna asked quietly.

"What do you mean?"

"Could you be my friend now? If this doesn't work. Could you be my friend if I was with someone else?"

Beau didn't hesitate and shook his head. "I'm not going back to how it was for all those years. No way."

"What do you mean?"

"Us with other people."

Trying to ignore the sting in her chest, Sienna nodded. "I met Grace's Dad at a bar. I was drunk. So drunk that I thought his name was Alex when it was Andrew." She watched the flex of Beau's jaw when he clenched his teeth. "He asked me to get an abortion. He gave me a hundred and sixty bucks for my trouble." She let out a heavy, burdened breath. "He wasn't my only one-night stand. There were others before him. Except for Dylan, they were *all* one-night stands."

When Beau's ears reddened, she scoffed. "You don't get to be angry—"

"Thinking about a douchebag trying to dodge his responsibility after taking advantage of you…" Beau paused, looking off to the side. "Thinking of someone else touching you doesn't exactly make me want to break into tap dance, Sienna."

"Don't pretend you were celibate this whole time."

"I was with other women because I thought I was lonely. But I never felt *better*, no matter who it was. Because I never was *lonely*, Sienna. I was only missing you. So do me a favor and save the friend garbage. Don't force me into a situation where I'm the guy with a brunette in my bed pretending she's a blonde. And not just any blonde. Your kind of blonde—sunshine kind of blonde, which is my second favorite color."

Sienna looked down at her sneakers and began to rock. "It was the same for me," she admitted, struck with guilt, recalling the way she would shut her eyes tightly under the guise of pleasure when really, Sienna was imagining Beau beneath her, his hands sliding across her body, the way he filled her.

"Can you forgive me? For the funeral?" Beau asked hesitantly, absent of the confident tone his voice usually seeped with.

Instinctively, Sienna checked her watch. She needed to pick Grace up from school.

There's still time.

"You know what? Grace got sick not long after. I wouldn't have been able to give you any part of me the way you wanted." Beau opened his mouth to speak, but Sienna continued, "Your career was taking off and I couldn't have been by your side through any of it. But now, well, Grace's biggest problem is what to wear to prom, which is months away, and I think now it could be different for you and me. Maybe we needed to wait for the right time."

Beau stayed silent for a minute before he reached into the box, taking out the frame on top and unwrapping it. "Do you remember what I asked you after this game?"

"You asked me to be your girlfriend. You did have a concussion, though. So I'm not sure if you really meant it."

The corner of Beau's mouth tipped up. "I'm clearheaded now. Well, mostly. Whatever perfume you're wearing is driving me crazy."

"I'm not wearing perfume."

Beau rolled his eyes and groaned. "Then I'm the same lovesick teenage boy in a grown man's body." He sat the photo back on the shelf and stood in front of Sienna, placing one hand on each side of her body as she leaned back against the bookcase. "I want to do this right this time. All of it. I'm trying."

"Where does feeling me up in your parents' old kitchen fall on the 'right' scale?"

"I didn't say I was perfect."

"No kidding," Sienna mumbled.

"Let's try again." Beau reached out, wrapping a lock of her hair around his finger before releasing it. "Sienna Clarke, will you be my girlfriend?"

"Fine," she offered with faux ambivalence, pressing her lips tightly together to hide the smile.

Beau's eyes widened. "Fine? That's all I get? I broke into the planetarium for you the other night."

"Is it breaking and entering when they open the door and tell you to take your time? You're hardly a convict. You're the franchise wide receiver on the Dallas Sparks."

Cocking an eyebrow, Beau smirked. "Call me what you want, Sienna. As long as it's not single."

She couldn't keep the serious face any longer and smiled, overwhelmed with nostalgic giddiness as Beau continued to play with her hair.

"What's the first?" she asked.

"What?"

"Your first favorite color. You said the second was my hair." She looked at Beau with curiosity as he leaned closer, capturing her mouth in a kiss so deep that Sienna felt it in her toes.

Beau pulled back. "The color of your cheeks after I kiss you. Wait." He paused, pressing his lips to hers again with a perfect balance of pressure and softness. "There it is. I couldn't really see it in the dark the other night."

Sienna swayed against the bookcase.

Beau cupped her face and whispered, "I'm not letting you be the thing I wish for ever again. Fuck wishes, Sienna. *You* are the dream come true."

chapter ten

"HE'S ALIVE!"

Beau lowered the bar onto the rig and ducked behind it, trying to hide his annoyed groan. "I texted you last night."

Chase looked around the vacant gym of Beau's apartment building, out of place in his three-piece suit. "Yes, about *Disney World*. Again." Chase rolled his eyes.

"Did you figure out how to close it?" Beau reached for the towel on a nearby bench, wiping sweat from the back of his head.

"Yeah, sure. Consider it closed. You know, you could hire an assistant for this stuff."

"I could," Beau began, "but you've taken enough of my money over the years. So do what you do and make some calls. Call that Golden Penny Foundation woman. Get her on board."

"Beau, its *Disney World,* not the planetarium." Chase placed his hands on his hips. "What's all this about?"

Shrugging, Beau moved to the dumbbells. "You said stuff with the GPF is good press. I only want to take a few sick kids to Disney who wouldn't have the chance to go."

"Oh, yeah?" Chase narrowed his eyes. "I know you're more of a silent donor in terms of charities. This kind of high-profile shit isn't really your thing."

"I didn't say I want *press* about it."

Chase laughed. "Right. It will totally go unnoticed that the Dallas Sparks' top wide receiver shut down Disney World"—he paused, holding his hand out—"Nevermind. I came to talk shop. Speaking of Dallas, they'll take you. One more year. And you're getting a fair amount, too."

Beau reached for a dumbbell and clicked his tongue. "Good. One more year on a mediocre team sounds about right for my final bow."

"But LA will also take you back. They're drawing up papers."

His eyes immediately flew to Chase's. "I told you already, I'm not going to LA."

"I've been on the phone with their head coach and offensive coordinator *all* week. They're *hungry*, Beau."

This past season, the LA Bulls fell in the last round of playoffs, losing their chance to bring a championship parade to southern California. Beau knew from his previous tenure how much that must sting—almost as much as when they lost the Super Bowl the final season he played with them before his motorcycle accident.

"You built that team way back. They're ready to see things through."

"You're not serious." He placed the weight back on the rack and turned to face Chase.

Chase was leaning against a treadmill. "Serious as cancer."

Beau frowned.

"It's one year. And it's big. If you're going to go out, go out with a *very* lucrative bang. And maybe a championship ring."

Greg's face flashed in Beau's head. He could picture his brother, forever fifteen, pumping his fist. *"This is it," he would tell Beau. "This is what we've been waiting for."*

"Are you listening?" Chase's question pulled Beau from his thoughts.

"What?"

Chase groaned. "If this is the end of the road for you and me, let's make it a fucking *great* one."

"I need to think about it."

If it were possible for Chase's blue eyes to fly out of his head and smack Beau in the face, they would have.

"You need to *think* about it?"

Beau shrugged at his agent, who he had signed with before he had even graduated from Florida State. Chase was only two years older than Beau, but what he had lacked in age and experience in sports management back then, he made up in persistence and nagging. And Beau would be lying if he said his career wouldn't have been as lucrative if Chase wasn't the one driving it forward.

"How long do I have?" Beau asked.

"Officially, a few weeks. But they'll be bringing in some young receivers, and you know how they are—*hungry*. So how about I book you some extra sessions with Charlie, hm?" Chase asked, referring to the agility trainer Beau already met with three times a week. "Let's keep those feet light. Worst thing, you lose several million dollars and a chance at a Super Bowl if you stay in Dallas. But, hey, at least you'll be in tip-top shape, right?"

Beau nodded. "I never say no to more workouts." *But I'm damn well saying no to signing with LA.*

Moving teams meant he would need to be ready for minicamps, which started in the Spring. But the time Beau needed had to do with Sienna and not the Bulls. They had fallen into a routine—casual day dates that involved hanging out while Grace was in school. Some nights he stayed in Brookwood, in his parents' empty home, sleeping on his too-small twin bed after hanging around Maloney's and helping Sienna clean up.

But Beau had too many plans to make up for, and with this contract looming, not enough time.

"I'll take care of Charlie. Be ready tomorrow morning." Chase pulled out his phone, typing. "I'll send you the numbers so you can *think* about it," he scoffed before shaking his head, not a strand of his swooped blonde hair moving out of place as he turned to leave.

"Chase?"

Chase turned at the door, looking at Beau, defeated.

"I'll think about it harder if you work on Disney World."

His agent looked at the ceiling with a groan. "Fine. I'll call the Golden Penny Foundation and see if they'll help facilitate. I'll let you know tonight."

When the door closed behind Chase, Beau leaned forward, releasing a heavy exhale. His head throbbed like it often did when he had Greg on his mind. He furiously rubbed at the scar on his temple to both soothe and try to erase it at the same time. His shoulders ached, not from the heavy load he had squatted, but from the weight he had been carrying—goals determined by grief and guilt, a life lived for someone who had given up their own for Beau's.

Beau clenched his jaw, trying to turn his concentration back to his workout instead of dreams of Super Bowl rings and celebrations that had never been his to begin with. But his heart interrupted, and even though he and Sienna didn't have plans that day, he needed to see her. He left the empty gym, took the elevator up to his apartment, and grabbed his phone that was plugged in on his nightstand.

Can I take you out later?

He placed the phone back down and opened the drawer, seeing Grace's letter, which he hadn't read since she had given it to him. The words twisted his gut and pulled at his chest. The letter was something Beau preferred to pretend didn't exist, yet he couldn't throw it away.

Grace is at a friend's now, but I'll need to be back for Scrabble night.

Beau bounced his knee and stopped when he remembered number twelve on the list.

Do you want to fly with me?

★★★★★

Two hours later, Beau rang the doorbell of Sienna's house.

Henry opened the door and stepped back in surprise. "What are you doing here?"

"I'm here to pick up your sister."

"Well, I know you aren't here to pick *me* up. I'm asking why you're using the door. I thought you would've gone back to climbing through the window by now."

"Very funny," Beau said, stepping inside. "I didn't think you knew that?"

"Oh, please. You two weren't that stealth. I was being a good person. If I ratted her out, my dad would've taken a baseball bat to your kneecaps." Henry pointed to the bag Beau held. "Is that a present for me? I hope it's my color." Beau rolled his eyes, and Henry gave him a pat on the shoulder. "She's in her room."

Beau nodded and walked down the hallway to Sienna's closed door. He knocked, but there was no answer.

"I told you Grace is at a friend's house," Sienna's voice bloomed from behind him, and Beau jumped. "That hasn't been my room for a while."

Beau turned, stepping across the hall. "Was this. . . " he paused, glancing around at the neatly made bed, the soft white duvet. The bedroom was delicate and fresh—exactly like Sienna. "I guess I never had a good reason to go into your dad's room."

Sienna laughed, reaching for something on the dresser. "I hope you didn't." She tilted her face up for a kiss—one that Beau ended too quickly, judging by the look on Sienna's face. "What's wrong?"

I don't want to choose between you and football again.

"Beau?"

His hand rose to his head, to the thumping on the side, but

before Beau could run his finger along the scar, Sienna took his hand.

She's here. He's not.

"What's going on?"

She's right here. Talking. Looking gorgeous. Warm. Alive.

Beau circled his eyes around the room, as if he expected to find his brother somewhere—leaning against Sienna's dresser, plopped on the corner chair with one leg folded over the other, looking at him impatiently, waiting for Beau's answer. Greg's presence would haunt him every time he had to make a career decision—contracts, coaches, endorsements, a ghost of the past distracting him from everything going on in the present—whether it was the TV, Chase, or his parents over the phone.

But this time, Beau heard Sienna say his name again, and when he blinked hard, she came into view, and he stepped forward, clinging to her.

There was the smallest jump of Sienna's shoulders in surprise, but she quickly wrapped her arms around him.

"Are you okay?"

Beau nodded into her neck, relaxing as she drew lazy circles over his back. "I am now." And even though he was, Beau let Sienna hold him for a moment longer before pulling back. "Here. Put this on." He offered her the bag.

"What's that?"

"*Not* a present for Henry."

Sienna pressed her lips together, the look on her face telling Beau she was borderline annoyed.

"What?" he asked.

"Easy on the presents."

"I haven't bought you anything," Beau countered.

Sienna narrowed her eyes. "You bought me a *galaxy*," she reminded him, motioning at the nightstand where the leather book sat.

"You think pretty highly of yourself," he teased. "It wasn't a galaxy, just a handful of stars in our solar system. Besides, this is less of a present and more of a uniform."

"Since when does Neiman Marcus sell jock straps and jerseys?"

Beau laughed. "I could keep going all night with you like this, but we're going to lose the light."

"The light?"

Beau shoved the bag at Sienna and sat on her bed as she reached into it. "Biker chick uniform."

The bag fell to the floor as Sienna held the black, leather jacket in her hands, turning it back and forth. "So that was your bike in the stadium?" she asked, and Beau hummed affirmatively in response, recalling the wave of nostalgia that broke across Sienna's face that day. "You *really* ride a motorcycle?"

"Not normally. I was going to take you out on my sparkly pink huffy but one of the training wheels got a flat."

Sienna held the jacket against her chest.

"Wish list, right?"

She pressed her lips together, taking a breath. "Wish list." Her smile beamed right into Beau, bringing one to his own face. "Let me use the bathroom."

When she stepped through the door, Beau pulled out his phone that continued to vibrate with messages from Chase.

You know the Super Bowl is priceless.

Priceless, Beau scoffed to himself. *Of course it's priceless.*

Through the bathroom door, Sienna hummed over the running water as she washed her hands. His eyes looked to the hallway, where he saw Sienna's old room, and realized he had never entered it through the door. Beau flipped his palm up, remembering the feel of the window track pressed against it as he would hoist himself in and through, never landing gracefully. The thud of his body always drew a whispered giggle from Sienna, and he would shush her by pressing his lips to hers.

Beau could have always entered the room with a little more stealth. But that small laugh she released was a sound he looked forward to each day. It was only after giving it up that he learned small ordinary moments with the right person—where there was no confetti, no celebratory music, no trophy—could be priceless as well, so much so that he carried them with him for more than fifteen years.

LA is dead for me. Move Dallas forward, I'll sign next week.

Hitting send, Beau waited for the text to go through before turning off his phone, knowing his agent would call him immediately. *What Chase doesn't understand is I've got a lot of priceless memories already.* He stood, placing his phone on the dresser beside a photo of Sienna and Grace—they both had shaved heads and even though the photo saddened him, the sentiment was swept aside and instead he was captured with pride over the pair's strength and perseverance. When Sienna came out of the bathroom, he was tracing both of their nearly identical faces.

"Ready?" she asked, slipping on the jacket.

Beau nodded and took her hand.

She motioned to the phone on the dresser. "You don't need that?"

"Definitely not. I'll get it when I drop you off." Gently, he tugged her hand, leading Sienna out of the room. "Let's go fly a bike, baby."

Motorcycles were fun, fast, and riveting. The truth was, however, they also hadn't ever really been Beau's thing. The roar of the engine, the vibrations between his thighs, the world whizzing by fast and quiet never gave Beau any kind of high. Motorcycles had brought him frustration. They also gave him a snapped tibia, surgery, countless hours of physical therapy, and a season off the turf because the injury had been so severe.

But the moment he had learned riding a motorcycle was on Sienna's wish list, Beau was determined to give her that moment, so determined that he tried—and failed—to build one when he was younger. And when he could afford a bike, Beau pushed through, just in case he would find himself in this exact moment, with Sienna behind him, arms around his waist, her thighs caging the bottom of his body.

By the time they made it out of Brookwood, flying down a smooth, long winding road flanked by tall yellowing grass waiting for a spring refresh, he never wanted to get off the bike again if she was along for the ride.

Between the helmets, Beau couldn't hear Sienna. But with her chest to his back, he caught the hitch of each excited breath, the way her fingers would quickly dig harder into his waist as he accelerated. It was an indescribable feeling, living through her excitement.

They rode for over an hour as dusk began streaking the horizon with hues of ethereal pink and orange. There wasn't anything special about that sunset, Beau realized. But like the bike itself, with Sienna, it was different.

Beau was about to slow the bike and pull over when Sienna's grip on his waist loosened finger by finger, and he knew what was coming next.

When Sienna only had one hand on Beau, he reached down, squeezing her thigh, sensing her hesitancy. *Go on. I've got you,* he said with his touch as he looked ahead at the open, smooth road. Beau's small assurance was all Sienna needed. Squeezing her thighs tighter against him, she leaned back and let go.

Even though he hadn't been able to hear much over the roaring engine for the entire ride, in that moment, Beau heard Sienna. Her laughter sounded through her helmet and his, through padding and plastic, straight into Beau's heart, bouncing around each chamber, changing his heartbeat.

When her hands returned to his waist, Beau slowed, bringing the bike to a stop on the side of the quiet road. As soon as he put the kickstand down, Sienna bounced off, half stumbling into the grass. She pulled the helmet from her head and placed it on the ground, shaking her messy blonde tresses free. Beau removed his helmet and watched as she raised her hands toward the sky and spun, as if she hadn't stopped flying, as if her feet were off the ground, head in the clouds—and she was free.

Halting, Sienna faced him, her chest heaving, a smile painted on her face. Her hair glowed in the changing light, circling her in a halo. He was about to swing one leg over the bike when Sienna stalked purposefully to him.

Before he could move, she reached him and swung a leg over the motorcycle, landing in his lap. Beau had to plant his feet firmly on the ground, gripping his toes through his boots to keep the bike—and them—upright when Sienna pressed her lips fiercely to his, clutching the back of his neck.

The humming and buzzing of the engine egged Beau on and he slid his hands down Sienna's back to her ass, kneading as he pushed up into her while trying to maintain his balance. The intensity of her kiss was a far contrast to the calm, serenity of the ride and left Beau craving more—more of her mouth, her body, the way she made his world spin even though they were standing straight.

On the quiet road sandwiched between the overgrown meadows, under the setting sun, Sienna pushed and ground against him. Her thighs clenched as she panted into Beau's mouth, seemingly desperate for the same thing he had been waiting for since he was a teenager—the closest connection.

He released one hand's grasp on her jeans and slid it beneath Sienna's shirt, his fingers dancing and creeping up warm skin to cup her through her bra.

And even though more than a decade had passed, the feel of Sienna in his hands, the weight of her on his throbbing lap, Beau *felt* eighteen—ravenous as he ran his lips, tongue, and teeth down Sienna's neck, desperate when she rolled her hips as if she was captive with an ache only he could soothe.

A moan floated from her mouth—soft and airy as it dusted against his hair. But on the vacant road nearing nightfall, it was *loud*, a sobering reminder of where they were.

When Sienna wound her hands through his hair to pull Beau's face to hers, he fought it. "Wait," he panted straight into her mouth as she battled harder.

"Are you really going to stop me?" Her tongue traced the whisper she left against his ear.

No, Beau told himself when he couldn't find his voice, and he let Sienna continue to writhe in his lap. *Please, please don't stop*. But when her hand moved between them to his belt buckle, Beau grabbed it firmly.

"Yes," he admitted with a heavy swallow, leaning back to look at her.

"Why?" Sienna bit her lip, both question and frustration evident on her face, and Beau quickly reached out, pulling it free with his thumb.

"Because," he said, trying to stifle the groan in his throat when Sienna sank her teeth into his finger. "Because for what I have planned, we need time." Beau paused, glancing around. "And space."

"I see nothing but wide-open, Texan spaces."

"Not here." Beau stood his ground but couldn't help leaning closer, pressing a kiss to Sienna's still-racing pulse. "Big bed." He kissed her neck again. "Soft sheets." Beau's lips lingered, and he left another kiss for good measure and smiled at the flex of her throat when he pulled away. "And *plenty* of time. It's Scrabble night."

"Can we do it again?"

"What? The kiss or the ride?"

"Both. But I was talking about the bike. Do I need to ask for a kiss at this point?"

"Never." He shifted on the bike seat. "Was it everything you dreamed it would be?"

The only thing more beautiful than the sunset surrounding them was the smile on Sienna's face.

"More," she admitted with a sigh. "And with that sun . . . it was magical, Beau."

"If I could buy you a sunset, I would." He sighed. "But next time, I'll keep going West, so you have a second one on Pacific Standard Time."

He pulled up behind a car parked in front of Sienna's house as Grace scrambled out of the vehicle and shut the door, making her way to the steps. Sienna squeezed his shoulder, pulling off her helmet.

"Don't go yet." She swung her leg off the bike and stood on the pavement, heading toward the car in front of them.

Beau turned off the engine and removed his helmet. Running a hand through his hair, he felt a stare—Grace's stare—burning into him from the front of the house. He waved, and she dropped her bag on the steps, heading toward him.

Grace's brown eyes bounced between Beau and the bike. "Number twelve?"

Beau let out a small laugh. "Yeah, kid. Number twelve. But you know, I didn't need that list."

"My mom says men are usually forgetful. Uncle Henry *never* remembers to turn the lights off after he leaves a room. Plus, *you* play football. I'm sure you've had some concussions." Immediately Grace clamped her mouth shut.

"Well," Beau began. "I would say 'you don't even know,' but maybe you do." He ran his finger over his scar.

I'm sure Sienna told her.

He flashed Grace a small smile. "Thanks for being so

thoughtful with the reminder, then," he said, trying to lighten the mood.

"And that letter. . . it stays between us, right?" Grace's serious tone brought an immediate nod from Beau.

"I'll take it to the grave."

He didn't know what difference it would make to tell Sienna. Before Grace had even given him the letter—before the coin even hit the ground—Beau was ready to lie on the floor at her feet with apologies and prepared for the fight of his life to win her back.

Grace turned her head toward the car, where her friend was staring out the back windshield, wide-eyed and mouth open.

"So." Grace hummed. "You like my mom?"

"I—"

"How much do you like her?" Grace asked, raising an eyebrow.

Gaze floating over to Sienna, Beau's eyes might have doubled down on her long legs. But it was Sienna's laugh that held all his focus.

"A lot," Beau admitted to Grace. *More than you know.*

"Enough to stick around?"

His head shot back to her. "What do you mean?" This had been the first time Beau had been alone with Grace. It finally dawned on him that maybe he should be asking some questions. "All those things on your list, did your mom tell you about them?"

Grace evaded his question and posed hers once more. "Enough to stick around?" she repeated.

Beau pursed his lips together. *She knows.*

Grace quickly looked to her right and Beau could hear Sienna's footsteps as the car drove off. She cleared her throat. "Because it's Scrabble night, and Uncle Henry cheats. The three of us could form an alliance. Let's hog all the vowels," she said as Sienna approached, her face laden with confusion.

Beau looked back at Grace, understanding. "I'm not sure if your Mom told you this, but I hate losing."

"Why do you play for the Dallas Sparks then?" Grace quickly retorted, and Beau laughed when Sienna gasped.

"Grace—"

He swung a leg off the bike and held a fist out to Grace, ignoring the twitch of Sienna's stare when she gave him a hand pound. "Let's do it." Following Grace, he peeked over his shoulder. "You coming, Sienna?"

Beau had left a victorious—meaning Henry lost—Scrabble night and was at a red light a town away from Brookwood when he realized he had forgotten his phone he had left in Sienna's room before the bike ride. Making a right at the intersection, Beau headed back to her house, trying not to feel too guilty for the loud engine roaring through the sleepy, small-town streets.

Sienna's house was dark apart from the front door light. Hopping off the bike, he chewed on his lip in the middle of the walkway, unsure if he should ring the bell or knock and risk waking Grace and Henry.

Fuck it. He laughed and cut across the grass to the driveway, making his way to the side of the house, reminding himself that Sienna's bedroom was no longer the first window to his right but the one farther down. He tapped on the glass lightly and anxiously.

"Sienna," Beau whispered, tapping again, sighing with relief when a light turned on in her room.

"What are you doing?" her muffled voice asked through the glass.

"Neighborhood watch," he said sarcastically, trying to keep his voice down. "Do you mind?"

Bouncing anxiously, Beau watched Sienna turn the latch and slide the window and screen up before he pressed his hands into the tracking and hoisted himself through the opening.

"I don't remember the windows being this small," he huffed as his boot got stuck in the tracking when his palms held his weight on the floor. Yanking his foot free, Beau slipped, losing his balance, and clamoring loudly into her room.

But Beau didn't mind that he banged his knee or that his hands hurt from the metal window slide. The muddled giggle Sienna let out made it worth it.

"I have a door, you know," she whispered against his lips before they both straightened. "And a phone."

Beau adjusted his jacket. "I forgot mine."

"Oh." Sienna grabbed Beau's cell and handed it to him. "I didn't realize."

Pocketing his phone, Beau reached out, tugging at Sienna's pajama top. "Nice shirt, thief."

She looked down, smoothing the bottom of his old Weezer shirt. "I told you, I forgot to give it back."

"You also said you didn't wear it."

Sienna played with the bottom hem. "Well, these days I'm doing a lot of stuff I once said I wouldn't do again." Her mouth morphed into a soft smile. "I've become a little bit of a hypocrite."

Her admission seized Beau with such strong happiness that it banished the surprise that had originally painted his face.

Beau's gaze traveled down the well-faded shirt, past the soft shorts peeking out from beneath, down her bare legs.

He licked his lips. "I'll have to add 'being a hypocrite' to the list of my favorite things about you." When he swept his eyes back up her body, Beau could see her throat bob with a heavy swallow.

"Did you just come back for your phone?"

Beau cupped Sienna's cheek and tilted her head up. "What do you think?" He pressed his lips to hers, moving closer when

Sienna sighed into his mouth. "But I can't stay for more than a goodnight kiss."

Another minute of this though, Beau thought, leaning his forehead to Sienna's and closing his eyes when hers fluttered shut.

Sienna slid her hands from Beau's waist to his back, slipping beneath his jacket and shirt. "You could though," she said against his mouth. "Grace is asleep." Her fingertips fluttered along the waistband of his jeans. "Henry probably too."

"Do you think I waited all this time to hear you scream my name while you bite into a pillow?" He shook his head, dragging his lips across Sienna's jaw to her ear. "I didn't."

Sienna pulled back. "You're awfully confident."

Beau bit his lip, sliding his hand from her face, down her neck, and to the valley between her uncaged breasts, lingering. Sienna's chest stilled beneath his touch, and she whimpered when he dropped his hand.

"When you can run away for a sleepover at my place, I'm happy to show you how confident I am. Go back to sleep." He motioned at the half-slept-in covers. "And Sienna? Dream of me, alright?"

She sauntered over to the window and kissed him before he climbed through. "I was halfway there when you knocked."

Beau dropped to the ground and watched her slide the window shut, pressing her hand to the glass for a moment before stepping away. He stood there until the room went dark and made his way to the front of the house. Licking his lips, he grinned over Sienna's faintly mint taste lingering.

Beau jumped when he found Henry at the edge of the driveway, where he had dragged the trash cans to the curb. Trying to ignore Henry's laughter, Beau kept his head down, heading to his bike.

"Some things never change."

Grabbing his helmet, Beau mounted his bike. *Yeah,* he wanted to tease Henry. *Like how much I'm still in love with your sister.*

love you no matter what

DEAR MOM,

My first Valentine's Day with a real *valentine didn't exactly go as planned. Beau was going to take me to dinner—just at the diner, nothing fancy. We haven't gone on a real date, like dinner and the movies. I don't mind, but Beau does. He was insisting all week. His closeted romantic side is actually kind of cute.*

Since we were only going to the diner, I couldn't exactly go all out with the outfit and makeup, but that's not really my thing anyway. I wore a simple blue dress and a pair of short brown boots. I knew Beau wasn't going to show up in a suit, and that's fine, even though I wish he would one day. But no tie though. I like the look of an open collar.

I was walking back to my room after trying to fix my hair in the bathroom when Dad spooked me. We bumped into each other, but then he kept staring.

"What?"

Dad placed his hands on his hips.

"What?" I asked again. The dress wasn't that *short or even low cut, but I was getting ready to lecture him on men policing women's outfits when he spoke.*

"I just can't believe how much you look like your mother."

I looked down. I know I look like you—tall and blonde, green eyes. I have your nose, and thankfully, not *Dad's.*

The air between us grew a little heavy, and Dad cleared his throat. "You're pretty dressed up for Sunday Scrabble."

My stomach dropped. Because I had mentioned to Dad that we should start playing again, but I completely forgot what this Sunday was.

"It's Valentine's Day."

"Oh," he said as if he had forgotten.

And then I realized that maybe he didn't forget. Maybe he just didn't want to remember. Because this was the first Valentine's Day he would spend without you—his forever Valentine.

"You're right. Beau taking you out?"

I nodded.

Dad leaned against the wall of the hallway. "He's a good kid. He's treating you right?"

I rolled my eyes because I didn't want to get into the sex talk again *—and quite frankly, it's a moot point. Even when I push him, Beau won't budge.*

"I don't . . . he should treat you right,*" Dad told me. "It's not only about that stuff. I see he makes you happy—"*

"He does."

Dad nodded. "I see the difference, Sienna. But don't make all your happiness all about him. You're too young for that."

I raised an eyebrow. "What do you mean?"

I know I'm young, Mom, obviously. But it's hard not to make all my happiness about Beau when he was the one who didn't just turn the light on when I was living in a dark room—he merely stepped into it, and suddenly I saw that I didn't want to be in the pitch-black anymore.

Dad straightened. "You make your happiness all about your kids, *not your boyfriend." He gave my shoulder a squeeze as he walked by. "One day, you'll understand that."*

I turned, watching him walk into his room, and went quickly to the kitchen to get a glass of water. The doorbell rang, and I knew it was Beau. But it also was the moment I saw that Dad had already put Scrabble on the kitchen table.

"Henry let me in." I didn't look away from the box. "Sienna?"

Mom, I wish somehow you knew that I was so *happy, even on hard days, like the day we moved from Nashville. You never let a sad day be an actual sad day. There were only sad moments, and you made sure to sprinkle happier ones throughout. I wish I had known when you were struggling. I'm so sorry I didn't give you more reasons to smile. I'm sorry for the Scrabble nights I missed because I wanted to be with my friends. I'm sorry I didn't know just* how *hard it was for you. I wouldn't have let you worry about my happiness for one second longer. I would've tried to give you some of it.*

"Sienna, what happened?"

My eyes focused on the light blue button-down shirt he wore tucked into dark jeans. It wasn't a suit, but that was fine. I knew we had time for that—plenty of time for suits and fancy dinners at restaurants with names of food I won't be able to pronounce. We'll have more Valentine's Days, even if they look different in college. How do I know this, Mom?

Because even though we were in the kitchen, in my mind, Beau and I were back in the locker room. And I was swept up the moment my heart recognized a stranger before my head—the guy who offered a sympathetic smile even though I had just punched him in the face, the boy who rode bikes with me from dawn until dusk, who stole cookies his mother baked and gave me the ones with the most chocolate chips.

And there's more, Mom. Beau reached up to catch my tears before they fell from my eyes because he knows how much I hate crying, and he said the right thing at the perfect moment.

"Do you want to stay in?"

I nodded into his hand. Because between him and the game, and remembering the way Dad trudged off to his room, all I wanted to do was spend time with my first Valentine, who happened to have a very hurting heart, and my current Valentine.

So, I collected myself, kicked off my boots, and went to Dad's room. "We messed up the dinner reservations." I lied. "Beau's going to stay for Scrabble night. I'll order a pizza."

We played a long, grueling game that night. Henry won, of course.

We ate pizza and chocolate ice cream with freezer burn on it. It wasn't fancy. It wasn't romantic. But it was fun. And it wasn't lost on anyone that we played Scrabble with four players when we thought we might forever be a family of three. And Beau's presence was comforting and easy, but I know that's because he had already been part of my family.

And because Beau is Beau, Mom, he didn't let Valentine's Day go without, even if our plans didn't go the way he had hoped.

"Roof or room?" Beau asked quietly when I walked him out later that night.

I hummed, thinking. "Room."

"No wishes tonight?"

I shook my head. "I have everything I already need," I told him. "But maybe not everything I want."

"What if I want the roof?" he challenged, pocketing his hands.

Folding my arms over my chest, I rolled my eyes with a laugh. "We need to start flipping a coin. Do you have a quarter?"

"No, but I made something we can use." I was about to ask what when he reached into his pocket. "Heads or tails?"

I tried to get a look at what he was holding—clearly, a coin of sort, round and flat, something bigger than a silver dollar, but Beau fisted his hand around it.

"Heads or tails?" he asked again.

"Tails."

Without looking away from me, Beau flipped the coin. It was heavy and didn't go too high, and it thumped loudly when it hit the front step.

"You win."

I couldn't help but smile, even though I was confused. "How do you know? You didn't even look."

"Because," Beau said, picking the coin up. "You should know. Heads or tails. . . I love you no matter what."

He placed the coin in my hand. The message welded into it—the same on both sides—was small, but the tiniest words sure can pack a lot of weight.

I love you.

I didn't tell Beau this, Mom, but when I hugged him and whispered into his ear that I loved him too, I looked up and found the perfect star. And I wished he would be my forever valentine.

Love,

Sienna

chapter eleven

SIENNA HAD BEEN in the billing department of Texas Children's Hospital for almost an hour. Countless calls with her insurance company arguing over the outstanding balance left her at a loss.

She had been flipping through the file of bills when Beau texted.

I ordered a new Scrabble set. I'm pretty sure yours is missing two *t*'s.

Sienna realized he had secured a seemingly open invitation to the weekly gathering—but she wasn't mad about it. Not one bit.

Would those two *t*'s have made a difference last week? You lost by 42 points.

Immediately, Beau called her.

"Henry cheats."

Sienna sighed. "Qat *is* a word."

"Words that start with *q* need a *u* after."

"Didn't you see it in the dictionary when you challenged him?" Sienna asked.

"I also bought a new dictionary. Whatever you guys have was published twenty years ago."

She laughed. "Alright. Let's see how things turn out this weekend."

"What are you doing?" Beau asked.

Sighing, Sienna looked at her watch, wondering if she would make it back to Brookwood by the time Grace was out of school. She had promised to take her shopping for a prom dress, even though the dance was still months away.

Sienna eyed the typing receptionist. "Preparing for battle."

"What?"

She sighed. "I've got these bills to work out with my insurance company, and they aren't working out so well. And they're overdue." Sienna grimaced. "*Way* overdue."

There was a pause over the call. "I can help—"

"No," Sienna interrupted. "No, absolutely not. It will work out. I need the hospital to be clearer on some things, that's all. I'm here now waiting to speak to someone. I just want this headache to be over."

"Sienna, if you need money—"

"I don't," she said confidently.

Even though she was short twelve thousand dollars, Sienna knew in her heart she would never accept Beau's offer to help financially. *I've done it all on my own so far. I can close this chapter too,* she thought.

"Alright," Beau said, not pushing it. "Listen, if you're at Texas Children's, you're not far from me. How about I take you for a late lunch? I just got back from my trainer. I'll hop in the shower—"

"I need to get back home. I need to pick up a friend on the way, and we promised to take Grace shopping. I'm sorry."

"Right, of course."

Sienna tried to decipher a hint of hurt in Beau's voice but found nothing but clear understanding. And Sienna gnawed on the inside of her cheek in both appreciation and frustration. Balancing motherhood, work, *and* a relationship was something she never had to worry about too much. She learned quickly that one ball had to drop—it never could or would be Grace. But in the weeks since they had decided to give their relationship a shot, Sienna realized it was often Beau who got dropped first.

"Maybe you can come to Maloney's tonight?" Sienna still hadn't hired another bartender. "It will be quiet."

Beau was silent for a minute. "You know, I uh . . . I told Damien I'd meet him before school tomorrow. 6:00 AM in North Dallas. I'll need to hit the hay early. That kid can nearly outrun me," he said.

"You're still working with him?"

"He's a good kid. I've got some time, you know? Why not." Beau shrugged it off as if offering training to a high school student he hardly knew wasn't a big deal.

But it made Sienna's heart swell. Her father had met Beau on the field many early mornings.

A door opened, and Sienna's eyes flew to the receptionist. "You can go in," she told her.

Standing, Sienna grabbed the folder. "I have to go. I'll call you when I'm done." She swung her purse over her shoulder and walked into the office.

"How are you, Sienna?"

"Not too bad," she told Lauren Hall.

Sienna was on a first-name basis with all the accountants at Texas Children's Hospital. She sat in the chair opposite Lauren's desk.

"Sorry to keep you waiting. What do you have for me today?"

Opening the folder in her lap, Sienna pulled out several dozen papers—*one* single hospital bill. "I'm having an issue with part of this claim." She handed Lauren the papers, pointing. "I've been going back and forth with my insurance . . . I know I'm overdue here. But I don't know why insurance is refusing to pay for the diagnostic testing that led to treat a problem they *will* cover."

Sienna anxiously bounced her knee as Lauren flipped through the bill.

"They might negotiate down."

"How far down? That's like twelve grand."

Lauren shifted in her seat, looking at her computer. "Well, not to zero. But we can see if we can get them to cover a percentage of the cost. Maybe fifteen."

"That's it?"

Lauren turned away from her monitor. "Sienna. Your insurance company—"

"I know, I know they've covered a lot. But so have I."

There was the deductible, additional therapies, and one type of medication the insurance flat-out refused to cover and offered no reimbursement. Not to mention nonmedical expenses—tanks and tanks of gas to drive to the hospital and subsequent appointments, therapies, and tutors for Grace when Sienna couldn't handle helping her not get behind in sixth-grade science.

"Sometimes a push helps things. I'll talk to Dr. Barron's office and get a write-up, and I'll go back to your insurance. In the meantime, to keep this from going to collections, I'll put a hold on your account with a payment plan."

Sienna's heart sank. "I already have *two* more bills I'm paying off."

Lauren offered a small smile. "That doesn't matter. And I'll put the first payment sixty days from today. That gives insurance a little time. If they don't cover it all, we'll adjust the payment accordingly, alright? I promise." Lauren paused, stacking the papers. "We'll work *with* you."

While Sienna appreciated Lauren's offer, she couldn't help but leave the office with the same amount of debt over her head and the feeling that everyone was working *against* her.

Twelve thousand dollars, she thought angrily, imagining where all that money could go. *Fixing the leak in the basement. A new fridge you don't have to kick to keep working at Maloney's. Grace's college fund*. Disappointment seized her knowing the amount in Grace's account—four hundred and fifteen bucks.

Sienna's body burned despite the chilly February air, and she pulled off her jacket—the leather one Beau had given her. Her fingers slid across the smooth black leather, and for a brief second, Sienna wondered if she could sell it—it had to be the most expensive thing she owned. But doing something like that was just as difficult as accepting Beau's offer of money, which Sienna knew he had a lot of.

His lifestyle might have been all casual athlete up front, but Sienna saw the sprinkles of wealth. Beyond his fancy car, the motorcycle, and brand-new truck, there was his dress watch—a Rolex—the perfectly clean white Nike sneakers he wore that let her know he probably had several pairs. The same sneakers Sienna found herself staring at as her head lowered in defeat.

"Hey." Beau tilted her head up, but she fought against his finger pressing gently on her chin. "You okay?"

Hair curtaining her face, she shook her head

"Sienna?"

"No," she said quietly.

Beau's hand found hers, and she let him hold it. Her body swayed, nearly unsure of the contact. Was she supposed to squeeze his hand back? Was she supposed to hug him? There hadn't been anyone holding her hand, a thumb running reassuringly along her knuckles. There had never been a hug only a breath away.

But there is now, Sienna thought before the self-pity struck her. *And I can't even enjoy it because I'm so angry.*

"Let's go," Beau tugged her, and that's when Sienna felt it—stares from patients, staff, and security guards stalling as they walked past them.

Beau Walker.

Sienna let Beau lead her across the path and into the large parking structure, where there were more stares, more double takes. They reached the elevator and got in. Sienna didn't stop

Beau from pushing level three when she was parked on the first floor. They were somewhere between floors two and three when Beau pressed a button, and the elevator came to a sudden halt. It should have startled Sienna. But instead, the moment of privacy a few yards in the air allowed her to release the heavy, burdened breath she had been holding since she left the accounting office.

"I'm not okay. I'm *pissed off,*" she spat. "Because how is it fair that my insurance company is refusing thousands of dollars of tests but paying for the treatment of the results?" Her ears warmed. "That money should be *for* Grace's future. She has one now."

Beau leaned his shoulder against the back of the elevator, waiting for her to continue.

"I won't take your money. I'm going to get the bill as low as I can, and I'm going to pay it." Sienna finally looked up at him. "Every *single* cent."

"I know you won't take my money. And I know you will pay it off. If I didn't think you could—or that you'd kill me—I would've gone in already and handled it for you."

"Then why did you come?"

Beau pushed off from the elevator wall and hugged her, resting his chin against her head.

It took a minute, but Sienna's arms slowly wrapped around his waist as she pressed her face into his sweatshirt, breathing him in. *This is what it means when someone shows up for you.*

"I know you want to handle it alone." Beau's voice dusted a subtle promise of support into her hair. "But you don't have to be alone while you're doing that anymore."

"Wowza." Emily's hand hovered above Abigail's back, mid-burp.

"That's a lot of sparkles," Sienna said when Grace came out from behind the curtain.

Abigail began to fuss, and Emily resumed patting her back. "Don't be a party pooper, Sienna."

"For *you*, maybe." Grace gave Sienna an up-and-down look through the reflection of the mirror.

"Are sequins back in fashion?" Sienna asked Emily, balancing her coffee cup on her jean-covered legs.

"They never left, Mom."

"Well, even if it's extra sparkly, you look beautiful in it," she told her daughter, who was fluffing her wig.

Emily nodded in agreement before adding, "*Beyond* beautiful."

The sparkly green dress illuminated Grace's intensely dark eyes and the newly returned pink flush to her cheeks. Sienna relished the smiles and giggles coming from Grace as she twirled around in front of the mirror, trying to savor the milestone that, a few years ago, Sienna wasn't so sure she would ever share with her daughter. The thin strap of the dress showed the small scar close to Grace's shoulder where a port had once been buried. But the contrast of the scar and Grace prancing around in the sequined dress, looking at herself from all angles, drew a smile from deep inside Sienna's heart.

"What?" Grace asked.

Sienna shook her head. Flashbacks of Grace wearing a Cinderella costume for Halloween—when she had made Henry go as her prince charming—came to mind. *Weren't you just three and eating toothpaste?*

"I hope *Justin* thinks I'm beautiful."

Emily raised her eyebrows. "Did the kid ask you yet?"

"No," Grace said. "But he will."

"You could go with your friends. Does everyone go with a date?"

Grace shrugged. "Most people go with dates. Did you have a date?" she raised her eyebrow at her mother.

"I never went to prom," Sienna said, taking another swig of her coffee.

"Why not?"

Sienna shrugged. "I just didn't. But I'm glad you're going and that you're so excited."

Prom had remained an unchecked item on Sienna's wish list —a rather *sore* unchecked item.

"Beau should've taken you."

Sienna's eyes flew to her daughter's. "He left school early." *And took my fragile teenage heart with him.*

Grace rolled her eyes. "He *still* should've taken you."

Emily stood, swaying the baby side to side. "*Agreed.*"

The memory and the extra-large coffee Sienna had downed without eating any lunch soured her stomach. But because this was meant to be a special moment for Grace, Sienna would ignore the haunting bitter past she could forgive but not truly forget.

"Can you take a picture?" Grace asked. "I want to show it to my friends."

Sienna pulled out her phone as Grace posed.

"Oh, and by the way, I'm going to sleep at Lilah's house Saturday for Valentine's Day. We're having a romance-movie marathon."

"Oh yeah?" Sienna asked. "What are you guys going to watch?"

"*Obviously,*" Grace began with a dramatic tone, "*The Notebook. A Walk To Remember. The Titanic.*"

Sienna laughed. "Grace, all of those are sad. Tragic actually. A thousand people died on the Titanic."

Grace waved her off. "Endings are *always* sad. And they're sadder when the middle is so good and happy."

"Is that how it works?" Sienna asked Emily with a laugh.

Emily buckled Abigail into the car seat on top of the stroller. "I think you should defer to the romance expert. The first book she read on her own was by Danielle Steel, right?" She straightened. "I'll go push this one around a bit and meet you out front."

Sienna stood to make space for Emily to push the stroller out. "It's fine if you want to sleep at Lilah's if her mom is okay with it."

Grace stared at her mother with narrowed eyebrows through the mirror.

"What?"

"Mom, I said it's *Valentine's Day*."

"Yes, and you're planning on—"

"That's what *I'm* doing because I'm single," Grace relented with a dramatic groan. "But *you're* not. What does Beau have planned?"

"I have to work that night."

Grace tapped her foot. "Can't Frank help?'

"Since when do you care about Maloney's?" Sienna asked.

"I don't care about Maloney's. I mean, sure I do because it's your job and everything, but . . . ugh."

"What?" Sienna asked with a laugh. "I know you're young and in love with the idea of being in love, but some people have to work *even* on Valentine's Day."

Grace turned abruptly. "Do you *love* Beau?"

"What—"

"I think he loves you."

Sienna stood from the chair. "Are you taking that or what?" She walked over to Grace. Her eyes glanced quickly at the price tag. *At this point, I'm so deep in the hole, $110 doesn't make a difference and her happiness is worth every penny.* "You do have two months to decide. But we can return it if you change your mind."

Grace gave herself one more up-and-down in the mirror. "Do you really think Justin would like it?"

"I don't care what Justin thinks," Sienna said from behind her. "How do *you* feel in it?"

Grace's brown eyes met hers in the mirror. "Like a princess."

Sienna nodded, overwhelmed by a hint of protectiveness. *I wish your prince charming* does *take you to prom.*

"Fine. Qat *is* a word." Beau closed the Scrabble dictionary on the bar, placing his elbow on top of it.

"Told you. And you probably could've Googled it." Sienna said with a smirk before turning away from Beau and piling new napkins into the holder. She watched Beau sit back and open the dictionary again. "What are you doing?"

Beau looked up from the thick book for a moment before returning his eyes to the page. "Studying."

"You can't study while we play. That's cheating." She moved back across from him, shifting her tiles around and eyeing the board. "j-o-c-k," she said, placing her last letter down on a triple-word spot.

Beau narrowed his eyes. "Are you making fun of me?"

"You can't leave a triple open around a Clarke. Too easy," Sienna teased playfully with a wink.

"A triple what? Whiskey?" Dylan's voice boomed. "Oh." His eyes narrowed in on Beau. "Well, hey there, Beau Walker."

"How's it going, Lockhart?"

Dylan puffed his cheeks. "Hell of a day. Didn't expect to see *you* here."

Beau smiled at Sienna. "And here I am."

Sienna's eyes bounced between Beau and Dylan like a Ping-Pong ball. *Oh, no.* She grabbed a Bud Light and popped the cap, handing it to Dylan, who immediately took a long swig.

"You look pretty today," he said, and Sienna could see Beau roll his eyes. "Do something different with your hair?"

Sienna lifted a strand of hair that was essentially one long split end. "Um, no?"

"Mmm. Well, it looks nice."

"Thanks, Dylan."

"Yeah," Dylan said, taking another long drink before putting the bottle down. "Gotta take a piss."

Sienna exhaled when Dylan left the bar and made his way through the back, giving Frank a high five, thankful for the break in the tension.

"You look real pretty today," Beau mocked.

"Stop it."

"You." He held up a finger, pointing. "Look *gorgeous* every day."

Sienna rolled her eyes. "You're supposed to say that. You're my boyfriend."

Beau picked up a few tiles off the holder, stacking them in his hand. "Exactly. Don't you think he should know that?"

"Dylan?"

"Yes, Dylan. And everyone else in this place."

Sienna looked around. It was the usual weekday crowd. "What do you want me to do? Walk around wearing your jersey?"

"If that's *all* you were wearing, yeah, that would do it." Pursing his lips in thought, Beau grinned. "Wish list."

"You talk a big game, considering you've denied me twice."

Sienna's mind flashed to the night when Beau had climbed through her window and swept her up in a tornado of hormonal nostalgia, leaving her still in it when he jumped back out to the yard.

Sienna watched how Beau's jaw clenched. "Call me crazy for wanting to treat you *right*. How you should be treated."

Collecting loose receipts, Sienna glared at him over his shoulder. "At this point, I'm wondering if you've joined a monastery and taken a vow of celibacy." She thought Beau might laugh at her joke but turned and found him staring, eyes darkened.

"Do you want to know a secret?" he asked, beckoning her with his finger. "The things I want—I've dreamed of doing with *you,*" Beau said when she leaned across the bar. "They'd get me a one-way ticket to hell if you asked a monk."

"Is that a promise?" Sienna caught Beau's finger between her teeth, smiling as she bit down.

Beau pulled his hand free, stifling a breathy laugh. "You're trouble."

"You don't even know, Walker," she flirted but quickly rolled her eyes when Dylan returned from the bathroom, calling her name.

"You got a leaky sink back there."

Raising her head to the ceiling, Sienna groaned. "No way."

"I'll show ya." Dylan beckoned her with his head.

She left Beau at the bar, feeling his stare beaming into her back with every step she took.

At the bathroom, Sienna pushed open the door, heading to the sink. "I don't see anything." She squinted, looking for traces of water on the floor.

"That's because it isn't leaking."

"Dylan—"

"Walker? Seriously?"

Funny, Sienna thought. *He thinks the same about you.* "It's not your business."

"Come on, Sienna. Did he come back on his white horse to save you?" Dylan laughed at his own joke, his face growing red.

No. His motorcycle.

Moving toward the door, Sienna didn't want to give Dylan any more of her time, but her body came to a halt when he grabbed her arm.

"Sienna, if you think he's going to come here and whisk you off, he won't. Fool you once, shame on him. Fool you twice, well . . . don't get your hopes up, is all I'm saying. And people like Beau Walker don't stick around Brookwood long."

People like Beau Walker, she said to herself, wondering if Dylan or anyone at Maloney's really knew who Beau was—a cocktail of a tortured but loving, selfless soul. He wasn't perfect, Sienna knew that better than anyone. But Beau was a man who made eye contact while apologizing, who revisited his mistakes to fix them, no matter how hard that might be.

She thought of him sitting at the bar with his backward baseball hat, licking his thumb every time he flipped through a page of the Scrabble dictionary, and she wanted to instantly be across from him, polishing glasses and learning new words that broke all spelling rules. Sienna wanted to be anywhere except in the bathroom where Dylan had moved closer, so close she would have bet he could hear her heartbeat racing nervously.

"You and me," Dylan said giving her arm a squeeze. "*We* stick around. *We* have a good thing going. Don't turn it down because Prince Charming came riding back in on his white horse."

"We?" Sienna asked, raising an eyebrow. "What we *had*? Quarterly sex after we've had way too much to drink? We're *friends* who crossed lines. I'm sure you can find someone else to push boundaries with." Her eyes floated to Dylan's hold on her arm—firm but still gentle. "You're a nice guy, Dylan. You've been a good friend. But don't be the kind of guy who doesn't take no for an answer, alright?"

Defeat crept across Dylan's face, and he let go of Sienna's arm. "He'll be playing out in California in a few months. Saw ESPN talkin' about it," Dylan said. "He taking you with him? Gracie?"

Sienna shook her head and walked out of the bathroom, ignoring whatever nonsense Dylan was spewing. She stopped in the kitchen and lifted a heavy crate of clean glasses, taking them with her.

"Need a new sink?" Beau asked when she placed the glasses down, and Sienna quickly shook her head. "What?" he asked, and even though Sienna didn't say anything and avoided eye contact, Beau stood.

"No, don't," she reached across, placing her hand on his, squeezing. "He's not worth it."

"You're right, he's not," Beau said, keeping his eyes focused in the direction of the bathrooms. "But you are."

Sienna squeezed Beau's hand. "Please sit down." Beau remained standing until Sienna sighed, and he returned to the bar stool. "It's over. I handled it. We never were together. . . We were just kind of each other's person for a while, that's all."

When Sienna saw Beau's Adam's apple bob and his lips flatten into a long, thin line, she knew he didn't like that explanation. "You're upset? About me and Dylan?"

"I don't have a right to be," Beau said, flipping through the dictionary.

Sienna reached out, shutting the book. "I hate that there are women in this world who have been with you the way I've dreamed about since I was seventeen," she began, placing her hand on his. "But you know you've always had me in a way Dylan, or anyone, ever could."

With his eyes still focused on the dictionary, Beau's full lips reappeared in the shape of a smile.

"And I'm happy you're back," Sienna said, trying to coax away his remaining jealous unease.

He raised his eyes to hers. "As your boyfriend? Or as your person?"

"You know you're more than both of those things."

It was easy for the words to slip out of her mouth when they were full of such veracity. Because Beau wasn't just her friend, her boyfriend, her person. *You're my everything,* Sienna wished to tell him but felt the need to hold back, as if the words would forever give him the upper hand.

But Sienna silenced that train of thought when Beau pushed the Scrabble board to her. "What about your valentine?"

Confused, Sienna looked at the board.

"You cheated," Sienna said, seeing "valentine" spelled out where several other words had been. But she couldn't keep the smile off her face and pushed the board to the side, standing on her toes and pulling Beau in for a kiss.

She could never say no to anything Beau asked to be in her life. Because everything meant the good and bad. He could be the boy who broke her heart and the man who returned to piece it back together. Beau could be this year's Valentine and hopefully the next one and the next one, until before they knew it, Sienna would find that Beau had been her forever Valentine all along. He could gift her a clear, starry sky on a rainy night. But Sienna could only hope, from deep within her, he wouldn't be the one to bring the storm clouds too.

chapter twelve

"FOR FUCK'S SAKE, BEAU," Chase exclaimed with his head in the fridge. "It's *Disney World*!"

Beau pressed his palm down onto the marble countertop. "I'm not asking for a week-long comped vacation with Donald Duck, Chase. I want a few hours with no crowds for some sick kids, and I'll *pay*. What exactly did the Golden Penny people say?"

Chase turned from the fridge with a beer in his hand. "Not to get your hopes up. She should be calling any minute."

Beau pushed off the counter and folded his hands behind his head. "I don't need their money or anything. I only want their muscle."

Chase shook his head. "Look, she said there are a lot of moving parts. If she had more—"

"I don't have more time," Beau insisted. "I need an answer today. Or by tomorrow at the latest." *So that I can come up with a plan B for a Valentine's Day present.*

"Beau, you don't even have kids. I mean, if you do, and this is something we need to get ahead of—"

"Would you shut up?"

Chase ran a hand over his face. "Alright, look, I know this

past year you've sort of been . . . on edge. You came off a bad injury. You played for a lackluster team—which *was* your choosing, by the way."

The intercom beeped, and Beau moved to the hall to answer it.

"Mr. Walker? It's Joe from downstairs. I've got some men here with a . . . " The doorman paused. "Well, they say it's an ice cream machine. And boxes—a lot of boxes—of Dole Whip mix."

"Awesome. Thanks, man. Send them up."

"Dole Whip?" Chase asked from the kitchen. When Beau returned, he found him leaning against the counter with his arms folded across his chest, his face twisted in confusion. "Dole Whip. Disneyland. What exactly did I miss?"

"Not for me," Beau said. "I hate pineapple."

"Beau, what—"

Chase was cut off by the doorbell, and Beau practically pranced back into the hallway, greeting the two delivery men and Joe. "This also came for you, sir."

"Thanks, Joe." He took the box and stepped aside for the men to enter. "I cleared out some space in the pantry. There's water, electric. Should be everything you need."

"Don't tell me that's Cinderella's long-lost high heel in there." Chase pointed to the box.

Before Beau could answer, Chase's phone rang from his pocket.

"Don't get your hopes up," he reminded Beau, opening the call. "How are you, Janet? I've got Beau with me."

"Oh, wonderful. You'll save me an extra phone call then."

"Fuck," Beau mouthed at Chase.

His agent gave a lame shrug and whispered, "I told you so."

"To share the good news. We've got Magic Kingdom."

Beau's eyes widened.

"Beau, I know from Chase, you had your heart set on renting out *all* of Disney World, but we need to be realistic. They can't shut it all down for one day. But what we can do is rent a *portion* of the park after hours."

Beau pressed his lips tightly together, shifting them side to side. He had never been to Disney World and knew nothing about it. "Is that enough?"

Janet laughed. "It's *more* than enough. As of now, GPF has one hundred eighty-four kids with Disney as their wish."

"Great. So how do we—"

"But," Janet interrupted, "you're looking at maybe fifty or fifty-five who might actually be able to attend."

Leaning forward on the counter, Beau shook his head. "Why's that?"

Janet was quiet for a moment before she cleared her throat over the phone. "Beau, The GPF doesn't discriminate in terms of *who* can make wishes and *when*. We only do our job to reach the most kids." She sighed. "There are many on this list, but either they won't be fit for travel by June, or we've received notice they're on hospice."

Jesus. The air was sucked from Beau's lungs, and he looked at Chase, who ran a hand over his face.

"But what you're offering . . . it's more than the foundation could carry on its own right now. What you're willing to do, well, it's a very big gift that will put a lot of smiles on a lot of kids' faces."

"Alright," Chase said, folding his arms across his chest. "What's the next step?"

Beau slid onto a bar stool, listening to Janet go over logistics, confirm dates and hotel blocks. "We can see about discounts for—"

"It doesn't matter. I'm covering everything," Beau pledged, ignoring the deep breath Chase took beside him. "Travel, accommodation. Whatever they want at the park."

Chase's eyes bulged.

"Let me go over all of this with my team. We have contacts at hotels and airlines. Sometimes we're able to get trips comped.

The only thing we need to address immediately—given we want to do this in June—is the deposit for the park rental."

"Chase will put you in touch with my accountant. He'll take care of it."

Immediately, Chase hit mute on the phone. "I *will*, but I don't *want* to."

"Wonderful," Janet's voice chimed. "So, we'll start with the logistics and numbers on our side. And then we can touch base once the date is locked in."

Beau unmuted the call. "Sounds great. If there's anything else you need from me in the meantime, don't hesitate to ask."

"I'm sorry it's taken so long for me to know that you feel so connected to GPF's cause. Had I known earlier, I would've reached out for your help a long time ago," Janet said. "You're going to help make many kids smile a little harder with this, Beau. Kids like Grace Clarke. I'm sure you remember her from your season's closer."

Beau felt Chase's eyes narrow in on him, but he ignored the hard stare. "I'm not looking for any recognition. I just think it's a cause we can all get behind. More smiles, the better."

A pang of selfishness hit him because Beau would have done this for *one* smile in particular—and that smile didn't belong to a child. But if his quest to prove his love for Sienna also happened to prove dreams do come true to a handful of sick kids, Beau figured the motivation behind the idea didn't matter in the end.

They ended the call with Janet, and Beau immediately stepped into the pantry, eyeing the men setting up the machine in the corner.

"Needs a good two hours to get to temperature once we finish setting it up," one of them said.

"All good, man. I won't really need it until tomorrow night." He went back into the kitchen, grabbing two beers from the fridge and opening them, but Chase didn't raise his bottle to Beau's cheers.

"The Clarke girl. Coin toss girl," Chase said. "Or that Clarke girl's *mother.* Jesus, Beau. This is why you've been spending time out in the boonies?"

Beau scoffed. "What's it to you? I'm doing my part. I'm training. I'm going to camp—"

"You're tossing a multi-million-dollar contract and a competitive season, that's what you're actually doing," he exclaimed. "Beau, we're a team. If there's something else going on that's affecting your decisions, then you need to let me know about it."

Beau paused with the bottle at his mouth. "I told you over a month ago, I don't want to go to LA."

"Yeah," Chase said. "You did. But maybe you need to think about *why* you need to think about it in the first place. I really don't know what you've been up to these days. But if you're about to make a life-changing decision based on someone else and her *kid*, well, that's something we should talk about."

I'm standing in the luxury condo I own, paying you your cut, being in the position to close Disney World *because I based all my decisions on someone else,* he thought and Greg came to his mind. *I was just thinking about the wrong person before, that's all.* He shook his head with a laugh and grabbed the package before opening a drawer for the scissors.

"I'm glad you think this is funny. Maybe you can get a job playing Goofy at Magic Kingdom when you retire."

"Goofy? You must be kidding." Beau opened the box, digging through paper. He pulled out the sparkly pink and gold Mickey Mouse ears and put them on his head. "Call me Walt Disney."

The next day in the same kitchen, Beau tossed the plastic containers and wiped down the counter after making a mess of the food he had brought up from Il Cielo. He had turned down the restaurant's offer to send the food up on dishes. If he couldn't cook, he could at least do *something* himself to prepare for Valentine's Day—even if that meant not so gracefully plating fettuccini and lighting candles.

The candles were unlit when the doorbell rang. Beau quickly put the plates into the oven to keep warm and rinsed his hands before rushing to the door.

"You're early. I didn't light the candles yet."

"I know. I was expecting more traffic," Sienna said, tucking a piece of hair behind her ear.

Beau liked that even on Valentine's Day, Sienna didn't look much different apart from a little more eye makeup.

"Happy Valentine's Day," she spoke quietly, dusting her lips against his.

He rubbed his nose against Sienna's, drawing a breathy laugh from her. "Come in. Let me take your coat," Beau said, offering to hang up her trench as he stepped in, but Sienna moved past him. "It's not much."

Sienna rolled her eyes at him over her shoulder.

"I mean, it's small. But it's only me."

The condo might have been in a luxury building with a gym and a swimming pool, but Beau took one of the smaller units—a two bedroom, two-and-a-half bath on the eighteenth floor.

"Didn't make sense for me to have something bigger. I'm on the road a lot, don't need a lot of space. It's got a killer view though."

He watched Sienna run a finger across the length of the marble island as they entered the kitchen, taking in the way her hips swayed.

He bit his lip. *Maybe not as good as* this *view.*

Deeper into the living room, Sienna stopped in front of the floor-to-ceiling window. Beau swallowed heavily watching her silhouette in contrast with the twinkling lights of downtown Dallas—the curve of her waist where the coat was cinched, the fullness of her hips beneath. His pulse raced, and his fingers twitched greedily at his sides.

"It's the nicest place I've ever been in," Sienna admitted, still facing away and looking out the window. "What?" she peeked over her shoulder, clearly curious about his silence.

"It's better than I imagined, that's all."

"What is?"

Beau cleared his throat. "You. Here."

Sienna shook her head, hair cascading down her back when she raised her head and laughed. "How long have you been waiting to use that one?" she asked, turning around.

Beau chewed on his bottom lip. "Since the day I bought the place."

The apartment was dimly lit. Beau couldn't make out the shade of Sienna's eyes, but he could *feel* them darken.

"Can I ask you a question?" She took a deep breath when he nodded. "Did you really imagine me here?"

"All the time." Beau took a deep breath. "And in the house I had in LA, the apartment in New York. I imagined you everywhere."

In ways you couldn't even dream about.

Sienna broke the hold her eyes had on his and looked around in question. Beau didn't have much in the apartment. He had the interior designer keep it minimal. Apart from floating shelves that housed a few awards and game balls, there was little of *him* in the space, as if he had been hoping and wishing that somehow, one day, there might be more of *them*.

Beau shifted on his bare feet. He could tell from Sienna's body language, the way her hands twisted together as she looked around the apartment, that she was thinking the same thing—*we wasted so much time.*

"But, we would've needed a bigger space. For Grace. And Henry," he added playfully, trying to lighten the mood. "Didn't he ever think to move out?"

"No. I needed him. You don't do that to family."

Beau's heart sank to his stomach.

"I want to know how you would've done it, you know, if you stayed after the funeral. If you found out about Grace and knew that it was only *us* and there was no one else. Because she's here. And there's only *you*. And even though she's older, I can't have a man in and out—"

"I would've learned to love her. And I think it wouldn't have taken that long." His mind flew back to the day of Jack's burial, recalling Grace's nearly white hair, her full cheeks, the way she smiled at Sienna as if she knew her mother needed it. "I would've loved her because she's a part of you. All the best parts, I think."

And in some strange way, I'm indebted to her now.

"But Henry, he could get lost," he joked, and finally, Sienna laughed for a moment before she grew quiet again, turning back to the window.

"You can see the stars. Some, at least. The ones farther, on the outskirts of the city."

Sienna stepped out of her heels and pushed them aside, her bare feet gliding across the rug. She spun around, and Beau swore the movement littered the air with her scent, intoxicating him enough that he didn't even realize he had moved closer to her.

"The brightest one is actually in reach." His voice was raspy, strained as he skimmed his fingertips along Sienna's side. A hum of delight escaped his mouth.

"What did you imagine in here exactly?" Sienna looked down at his hand on her waist. "Cooking together?"

Beau spread his fingers. "Not really. I'm awful in the kitchen."

Sienna smiled and stepped closer, his feet now caging hers, and placed her hand on his chest, smoothing the fabric of his T-shirt.

"Did you imagine us lying on this couch and watching TV?"

Her eyes flickered to the sofa at their side, but Beau's

remained on Sienna, focused only on what was right in front of him, no longer a memory or a figment of his imagination.

He reached for the tie of her jacket, but Sienna stopped him, running her smooth hands over his forearms as his other hand held her covered waist. "Tell me."

"Sometimes. Just you and me," he croaked. "Lazy days. Hanging out."

There was a slight sway as Sienna's grip left his forearms, her fingers flexing now against Beau's stomach. "What else? Us playing Scrabble?"

Beau didn't want to laugh, but a chuckle escaped—a chuckle Sienna swallowed down with her mouth when she covered his. Instinctively, Beau pressed his hand flat to her lower back, pulling her against him. Sienna also gulped down the next sound he released—a groan straight to the back of her throat.

"Did you think about what it could've been like?" she asked, her voice a sweet whisper.

Beau leaned forward to kiss her, but she tilted her head back, waiting for his answer.

"All the time."

"Tell me," she demanded. "What was the first time like?" When Sienna rocked her hips, Beau immediately slid his hands to the tie to loosen it. "Where were we?" When Beau didn't—and couldn't—answer, she stepped back, fighting his hold. "Tell me."

"Bed," he breathed out, grunting when she shoved him down onto the sofa now behind him.

Sienna smirked. "So, not the couch?"

Practically heaving, Beau shook his head. "Are you punishing me with the coat? Take it off and come here." He was desperate for close contact.

"Tell me more," she said, sweeping her long blonde hair to the side. "I want to know how you imagined it." She unfastened the top button under the collar and then the one beneath it. "What was I wearing?"

Beau swallowed heavily over his pounding pulse and shook

his head. "You were ready to ride me on a motorcycle in the middle of a street, and now we have a moment to ourselves, you're making me work for it? Quit fucking around and get your ass over here." He watched her pouty mouth morph into a proud grin and shifted, adjusting himself. *Before I bust out of my pants,* he thought.

Sienna stepped between his legs but didn't sink into Beau's lap. She leaned forward, taking the bottom of his T-shirt, and pulled it over his head, tossing it to the side before straightening. Beau's hands pressed into his jean-clad thighs, the pants now tighter, and he gripped the carpet with his toes when Sienna stepped out of reach.

Sienna tilted her head. "What was I wearing, Beau?"

"Nothing," he grunted through clenched teeth.

"I couldn't think about what to get you for Valentine's Day," Sienna said, untying the belt and fumbling with the buttons. "What do you get the guy who has it all?"

Of course she's naked, Beau thought, gnawing on the inside of his cheek and bracing himself for the moment he had been waiting for.

But instead of a smooth, bare stomach and full breasts, Beau found familiar shiny white fabric that hit her upper thigh. He trailed his eyes to the star on her chest, continuing up to her shoulders where he saw his number—sixteen—embroidered on both shoulders.

"Wish list?" she asked with a tiny grin.

Beau released the flesh of his cheek and ran his tongue over his lip. "Wish list."

She nudged his thighs further open with her knee and bent, reaching for his belt buckle. "You probably weren't wearing jeans, am I right?"

A bead of sweat formed on Beau's brow, watching as Sienna loosened his belt and popped open the button of his pants. Involuntarily, his hips lifted as Sienna tugged them off his legs. Unable to take it anymore, Beau forcefully grabbed Sienna's waist, then slid his hands under his jersey, where he found her bare ass and a thin band of underwear. He gripped her hard, yanking her to his lap, bringing a surprised giggle from her mouth before she quieted, dragging her lips along Beau's jaw.

She whispered in his ear, "Were we like this?"

The gentle circling of Sienna's hips made Beau's hands slide along her velvety skin, and when her movement changed, still slow but even more deliciously deliberate, Beau let out a soft moan into her neck.

"Sometimes," he admitted, tugging the jersey aside so his tongue had space to taste the dip of her collarbone. He tried to stifle the groan that Sienna drew moving against his length.

Sienna brought her hands behind Beau's head, adding pressure, making each kiss firmer to match the force of her hips.

"Sometimes?" Her voice was hoarse, as if she had been screaming with the same intensity that filled the room. "What about the rest of the times?"

Beau tilted his head up to look at her. Sienna's eyes were fluttering shut, her teeth sinking into her bottom lip.

You don't even know, Beau thought, wondering how many times he had wished to be in this exact position and more—innocent teenage fantasies that grew more mature and intense, more graphic. But some things stayed the same, like how Beau imagined Sienna's skin would taste—candied and creamy—or *how* warm and hot she would feel sliding against him as she was now.

Sienna was everything Beau had dreamed about and more.

"Tell me," Sienna said, the decade-plus of wanting and longing breaking her voice.

She mewled when Beau's mouth pressed firmly to her chest, dampening the fabric covering the peak of her nipple. "Tell me," she repeated.

Beau was hell-bent on ignoring her. *Leave me. Let me just be where I've always wanted to be.* But Sienna's next whimper of his name, coupled with her fingers in his hair, winding and pulling

—fighting her own body and his—made Beau give in. Sienna said his name, not with just a need for pleasure but a need to *know* that she was the thing that had occupied his mind, body, and soul.

"Not only here."

The whimper Sienna let out turned into a gasp when Beau rose from the couch, taking her with him. Her legs squeezed his waist, and she yelped when he slammed her against the wall.

"Here," Beau panted into her neck, nipping at the skin. Sienna's chest beat against his with heavy breathing when he pinned her wrists above her head with one of his hands. "I'd fuck you here." Beau's free hand traveled down Sienna's body, gripping her ass as he rocked his hips up, making her gasp.

"You'd scream my name *here*," he growled against Sienna's ear. His fingers found the fabric of her underwear. "I'd rip these off *here*."

"Do it," Sienna challenged with her words and body as she grinded harder into him.

Beau shook his head and kissed her, swallowing her moan. Sienna leaned into him with every part of her—mouth to mouth, her center, warm and wet through the flimsy underwear against his. But Beau pulled his head back just enough to run his tongue along the inside of her parted lips.

"No." He shook his head, fighting every urge to pull Sienna's underwear to the side and sink deeply into her. "You asked for the rest of the times."

A groan of objection floated from Sienna's body when Beau dropped his grip on her wrists and backed up to let her body slide down. But he spun her so her back was to his chest, her ass to his lap. With a firm grip on her waist, he pushed Sienna to the window until her body pressed flush against the glass.

"Here," he growled, moving Sienna's hair to the side and pulling so she would look up. The straining beneath Beau's boxer briefs throbbed painfully when his teeth found her earlobe, biting the sensitive flesh before running his tongue over it. "I'd make you see more stars than these."

Pressing one hand between Sienna's shoulder blades, he pushed her forward, overwhelmed seeing his name embroidered on her back. He traced the blue letters while his other hand crept around her waist, cupping her through the lace underwear. Their breaths panted in sync until Sienna's hitched in the back of her throat when Beau slipped a finger beneath the lace and inside of her.

"Mine," he said, leaning his head against his name on her back as she moved against his hand. "Fuck," he groaned.

Sienna reached back, winding her fingers into his hair when his hand abandoned her back, slipping beneath his jersey and finding the smooth skin of her stomach before greedily letting her breast fill his palm.

"Do it, Beau," Sienna panted, but when he added another finger her challenge turned into a plea. "Please."

Beau couldn't ignore the need in Sienna's voice. He lifted his head, watching her hand slam against the window for more leverage. Her fingers spread along the glass, lining up with the brightest stars in the sky.

"Wish it," Beau ordered. His hand left her chest and traveled up her neck to turn Sienna's head to the side, trying to see as much of her as possible. "Like you did that night. *Wish* it," he growled. "Exactly how you did. Because if you don't, I'm about to take you here against the window and that's not how this starts."

"Why not?" Sienna panted with a whine as her pulse pounded beneath his thumb with the same force he was holding back from using on her.

Beau fought to still his fingers. "I've waited my entire life for this. You. Head to toe. Inside out. And I'll be damned if I can't see your face and feel every inch of your body the moment I slip in here." He pressed the heel of his palm harder against her and Sienna moaned.

"Don't take that from me, Sienna. I'd never forgive you."

The next tug Beau gave Sienna's hair allowed him to see a little more of her face. But it still wasn't enough. Beau tightened his jaw, patiently panting until she spoke.

"I wish you'd make love to me."

Sienna had been looking at Beau and not the sky when she said it, but all it did was light a fire of determination in him like never before, and Beau wasted no time making that wish come true exactly how Sienna deserved.

Nothing had ever been more important, not football, not goals and dreams of ghosts and demons. The only thing that mattered was the way Sienna's hair fell against his pillow like a halo, the way her eyes squinted but didn't shut the moment he slid inside her, or how it felt like she was hugging every part of him—including his heart—from within as she caged him in her warmth.

His strokes were slow and forceful, Sienna's kisses deep, but her hands frantically moved and clutched at him—his back, shoulders, and his face, which she grasped firmly between her soft hands. Her eyes snapped shut.

"Look at me," Beau panted, trying to find words beneath a cloud of lust. But Sienna didn't, her eyes still shut, her head turned to the side. He lifted a hand, grabbing her cheek with force, his focus on soft and gentle long abandoned. "This. You're going to give me this. *Look* at me," he commanded.

Beau was frantic to see every part of her the moment she let go and surrendered. With a forceful rock of his hips, he drew a moan from Sienna and gathered her full attention, her eyes opening. Beau's hand left her face and returned to the bed, lifting his body to hover higher over hers, so he could see every part of her writhing and clenching as she teetered tightly around him.

"This," he said between thrusts, "is on my wish list."

"Watch," Sienna whispered hoarsely, nails sinking into the flesh of his arms. "And feel."

Beau had never seen anything more beautiful than the intensity behind her green eyes that flashed as she let go, surrendering in delicious spasms Beau continued to chase. He dropped his head, burying his face into her neck and painted the valley with the roar of his release.

Wish list.

chapter thirteen

"DON'T." Beau grabbed the duvet Sienna was pulling up her body. "If you're cold, I'll warm you up. If you want to hide, don't. I waited a lifetime to see this body." He trailed his lips from her shoulder, lingering in the dip of her back before playfully sinking his teeth into the top of her ass cheek. "I've got a lot of ogling to make up for."

Turning on her side, Sienna propped herself up on her elbow when Beau returned to the head of the bed.

"It's a little different from the one you probably ogled as a teenager." She glanced down at the faded, silver stretch marks, the scar that brought a stubborn Grace into the world.

"You're right," Beau said, pressing his lips to hers. "It's even better."

His mouth lingered against hers, and Sienna's lids fluttered shut, waiting for another kiss that didn't come. When she opened them, she found Beau staring pensively.

"What?"

He shook his head. "All that stuff out there," Beau began, running his hand up her side. "I wasn't lying. But I also imagined this moment too."

Even among the familiarity of him, there was a softness to Beau's eyes that was new—something Sienna never wanted to go without. She cupped his cheek, rubbing the stubble of his jaw with her palm before tracing his lips, swollen from their kissing, with her thumb. "Me too."

Beau turned his head, nipping her palm. "But I'm serious, though, about what I said out there," he repeated, a coy smirk creeping across his face. "I *really* meant it."

Sienna was still so warm from their lovemaking she couldn't tell if her cheeks flushed. But her entire body warmed even more from the inside—remembering how his body felt under hers, against hers, the cool glass and smooth wall against her skin.

"You better," she told him, scooting closer so they were chest to chest. "I'm going to hold you to it. I'm adding them to the wish list."

Beau nuzzled her neck, his hand pressing her lower back to pull her flush against him. "I can't get enough of you," he confessed. His words painted a chill across her sensitive skin as he trailed his mouth to her ear and he whispered, "I wish I never will."

Sienna wrapped her arms around Beau. *Please don't. Please don't make me give this up again,* she thought with anguish.

She would have stayed there forever—drunk on the smell of their skin pressed together, hypnotized by the pounding of his heart, as if it were trying to beat out of his chest to join hers. It was the missing piece she had been searching for since he left all those years ago—the connection that Sienna knew didn't come with just anyone. With Beau, it was so deep it had to be molecular.

Sienna now realized she didn't need to sleep with him to know that. His comforting presence over the past month—even the early, hard days—had been enough to quell her aching heart. But her body, now knowing what it had been missing out on, screamed for him, and if her stomach hadn't grumbled hard against his own, Sienna would have begged him to show her something he had mentioned in the living room.

Beau lifted his head. "I have dinner for you." He pulled

away, stepped into his closet, and tossed a T-shirt at her. "Did you really drive out here with no pants?"

Sienna slipped the T-shirt over her head. A waft of Beau enveloped her—clean, masculine, and woodsy—and she wanted to drop back into the warm, disheveled sheets that held more of his scent.

"You're lucky I even bothered with the jersey," she said with a sigh before heading to clean up in the bathroom.

At the sink, Sienna took in her reflection in the mirror—disheveled hair that refused to be tamed and tucked behind her ears, flushed cheeks, smudged mascara. She dried her hands on the neatly folded towel and raised her arms above her head, a smile painting her face at how relaxed her body felt—bordering on deliciously sore in the right places.

In the kitchen, Sienna found Beau at the stove. "I thought you couldn't cook?" She leaned against the island.

"Why do you think I bought that restaurant?" Beau licked sauce off the tip of his thumb.

Sienna laughed. "You can't be that lazy."

"No, not *that* lazy. Sometimes I make ramen noodles." He turned from the stove. "Here, sit. Hopefully, it didn't dry out too much. I wasn't thinking we'd eat this late. You put a wrench in my plans like always."

Sliding onto a bar stool, Sienna crossed her legs. Her stomach grumbled again, and she twirled noodles onto her fork. A moan of delight escaped her lips as soon as she took a bite.

"Told you," Beau said, wiping his mouth. "Truffled gouda fettuccini. Can't beat it."

They ate over small talk and light touches—like the brush of Beau's foot up and down Sienna's bare calf. Sienna pushed the plate toward Beau to finish it.

"Don't tell me you're full. There's still dessert."

"Chipwiches?"

"Actually, tonight, instead of back in time, we're looking at the future." Beau paused, tilting his head. He ignored the confused look on Sienna's face and finished his pasta. "Well, kind of. Past, present, *and* future."

Sienna squinted in confusion. "I'm not following."

Beau wiped his face and stood, reaching for a kitchen towel hanging on the handle of the stove before twisting it.

Sienna quirked an eyebrow. "What's that for?"

Beau twisted the towel, coming behind her. Sienna jumped when he placed it over her eyes, tying it behind her hair. She relaxed when Beau's hands dropped to her shoulders, giving them a gentle squeeze.

"Did you add kinks to the wish list and not tell me?"

"No." Beau laughed, and she could hear and feel him moving away.

"Too bad for me."

He pinched her side, and Sienna giggled.

"A surprise," Beau called out, his voice semi-muffled, letting Sienna know he had moved out of the room. "Your gift."

Sienna frowned. "I didn't get you anything."

Suddenly Beau's lips were against hers. "You just gave me *everything*," he said, giving her side a squeeze.

Still unable to see, the feel of Beau's soft lips and scruffy face, the taste of him, was stronger, bordering on addictive.

Beau placed a finger to her mouth. "Wait. This first."

Sienna could hear the gentle scrape of plastic.

"Open," Beau said quietly.

"Don't tell me it's another kind of cheese."

He was so close that a breathy chuckle tickled Sienna's cheek. He nudged her leg with his. "Just open."

Cautiously, Sienna parted her lips. But before Beau even brought the spoon to her mouth, she could smell it. She gasped as soon as the creamy soft serve hit her lips.

"Dole Whip?" she asked, feeling a drop of chilly ice cream slide out of the corner of her lips.

Beau's finger touched the mess but didn't wipe it. Instead, he smudged it across her lips. Sienna's tongue darted out, licking his finger.

"Dole Whip." The spoon was at her mouth again, and Sienna squealed in delight.

"How?" she asked when Beau brought another bite. "What, did you have it flown in on a private plane, and it's been in the freezer this whole time?"

She lifted the towel from over her eyes, dropping it on the counter, finding Beau rolling his eyes.

"That would be pretty bad for the environment if I flew up *one* cup. Besides, this way, you can have it whenever you want."

Sienna's mouth hung open before Beau scooped more ice cream into it. "You *bought* a machine?"

Beau nodded. "For you. I'll have it brought to your place."

She looked down at the creamy dessert. "For me?"

He nodded again, handing her the cup.

"You bought me a frozen yogurt machine?"

"Unlimited Dole Whip was on the wish list, wasn't it?"

Sienna scooped more, taking another bite. "I haven't had this since I was six."

Beau leaned against the island beside her, folding his arms across his chest with a smile.

Sienna's eyes flew from the cup in her hand. "Another wish come true? How many is that? Two? Three?"

Beau shook his head. "Not yet. But you'll see. Finish that, and I'll show you the second part."

Her eyes widened. "Second part?"

"Just finish it."

Sienna looked down, swirling the ice cream. She offered him a bite. "Help me."

Beau grimaced. "Pineapple."

"Come on," Sienna said, taking another lick, letting her tongue linger a bit before she ran it over her lips. "How about a baby step?" She slid off the stool and stepped in front of him, tilting her head up.

"I already know what you taste like. And for the record, it's way better than that."

"You might be into fancy food, but there's still Cheez Whiz in your cabinet."

Beau laughed, and Sienna stood on her tiptoes, pressing her chest to his. Her ice-cream-covered lips were as close to Beau's as she could get. She smiled coyly.

"Maybe it only needs an à la mode of Sienna."

Beau's tongue darted out of his mouth, swiping at his lips, and Sienna felt a drop of the Dole Whip drip down her chin. She tilted her head higher so it rolled down her neck.

"You could at least help a girl clean up," she said, shivering as Beau's fingers crept under her T-shirt, holding her waist.

Beau hummed in contemplation before lowering his head. "I wouldn't want you to be all sticky," he whispered, and Sienna nearly dropped the cup when he pressed his open mouth to the delicate skin of her neck, his tongue circling to wipe away the cold cream. The heat of his breath, in contrast with the ice cream, made Sienna's legs shake.

"Maybe," he said, letting his mouth follow the trail of the mess, "coming off you, pineapple isn't so bad." He sighed against her. "Actually, an à la mode of Sienna every day would solve a lot of my problems."

"See?" she croaked, leaning farther back as Beau continued to trail his tongue up and down, and she wished the mess was bigger and all over her body. A small moan floated out of her mouth when his hands slid to her back, one dancing up her spine, one gripping her ass. "Told you so."

"What do you think? Is it as good as you remember?" Beau asked when he peppered light kisses along her jaw, pressing her tightly to his middle.

"Better," Sienna breathed out. "You make it better." *You make everything better,* she thought, fighting back the emotion of the realization.

The small, sleepy town of Brookwood? Better, more exciting

with Beau. Dinner? *Always* better and seemingly more delicious with Beau—whether it was peanut butter sandwiches or truffled fettuccini, in a five-star restaurant, his parents' kitchen, or in his apartment. Dole Whip with Beau? *Definitely better. Better than Disney World.*

The hand holding the plastic cup dropped to her side when he kissed her chin. When his lips met hers, Sienna opened her mouth wider, eager for more of Beau's taste that simply was unmatched.

"No, you're not ruining this plan," Beau said, leaning his forehead to hers. "This"—he ran his hands up and down her body—"comes later." He left a small, light kiss at the corner of Sienna's mouth. "There's still part two of your present."

When Beau stepped back, Sienna fell forward into the now empty space in front of her. He pushed off the counter and went back toward the bedroom. She looked at the cup in her hand with defeat.

"Here," Beau said. "Put these on."

"I thought you already knocked me-in-your-clothes off your wish list," Sienna said, taking the pile.

He pulled a sweatshirt over his head and gave her ass a playful slap. "That's ongoing. But I thought you might get cold. Come on, I'll give you slippers. And grab that blanket on the chair."

Five minutes later, donned in too big shoes and sweats, Sienna rode quietly up the elevator with Beau to the roof.

"This isn't only for you, by the way," he said as they stepped off, and he led her down the hall.

Sienna shuffled her feet. *I told him I don't do this anymore.* Sienna didn't want to harp on the past, but some things were too difficult to revisit. She thought about the leather book at home on her nightstand. Beau might have bought all the stars in the sky for her, but that didn't mean she might keep them forever. *But he's trying. He's here and he's trying,* Sienna thought and decided that if Beau brought her to the roof to make a wish, she could at least try to, or fake it at best.

"What do you mean not just for me?" Sienna asked.

Beau pushed open a door, and a chill struck her.

"The Dole Whip was for you."

He pulled her by her hand onto the roof and she clutched the blanket she had taken from the apartment.

Sienna shivered, following Beau to a seating area with lounge chairs. On one of them sat a box.

She pointed. "And that?"

"That's for Grace. And her friend in the hospital."

Confused, Sienna fingered the large silver bow.

"And for other kids and families." He handed her the box. "But you should be the one who opens it."

Sienna sat on the lounge chair, adjusting the blanket around her shoulders, and lifted the lid of the box. There was enough light coming from the side of the building for Sienna to see sequins. She squinted, picking up a pair of Mickey Mouse ears.

"In June, when school is over. Disney World. You, me. Grace. Her friend. Any other kid on the Golden Penny Foundation's list I can get there. We'll shut down Magic Kingdom for a few hours—"

The blanket slipped off Sienna's shoulders, and the box fell from her lap, landing on the floor when she jumped into Beau's arms and wrapped her hands around his neck.

"Thank you. Thank you," she whispered against his cheek, streaking it with her kisses.

Beau snaked his arms around Sienna's waist as he lifted her. "I'd do anything to make you happy," he said with a sigh, cradling the back of her head. "I just wish I could've done this a long time ago."

Sienna squeezed her eyes shut when the pain struck her, that gnawing unease that gripped and twisted up her gut, latching onto her heart. She tightened her hold. *Please don't leave again,* she silently begged. But Sienna knew, if she let those thoughts escape her mouth and flood the space between them with her anxiety, she would send Beau further away on a float of guilt when what they both needed to do was swim closer together.

"You're doing it now. And you're going to make a lot of people happy." She pulled back and kissed him. "Kids. Kids who need it. I don't know how to thank you."

"Do you think Grace will be happy? She's not too old?"

Sienna shook her head, imagining her daughter's reaction. Her ears already rang with the anticipation of Grace's squealing.

"She'll be thrilled." She looked down at the box and empty chairs. "But what's for you here?"

Beau smiled, moving behind her to sit on the lounge chair. "You here." He patted the space between his legs, and Sienna sat, sliding against him as he draped the blanket over her. "I know you don't make wishes anymore," Beau said quietly. "But can you stay with me while I make one?"

Sienna nodded, sinking into his chest as he rubbed her arms beneath the blanket.

"Maybe for the wish to come true, the moment has to be right." Beau found her hand beneath the blanket, winding their fingers together. "This feels like a really fucking great moment."

Sienna let out a breathy laugh in agreement. They remained quiet for a few minutes, and Sienna nearly grew sleepy from the deep, calming breaths Beau took behind her, from his leg knocking lazily into hers as they looked up at the semi-clouded sky. But even with the fog, a few bright stars sparkled.

Beau sat slightly and leaned over, picking up a headband holding sparkly ears. Sienna shifted, watching him.

"You're never too old for Disney World, yeah?" he asked, plopping them on his head, his hair still unruly in the best way possible—from her hands winding through and tugging the dark brown tresses.

"No." She smiled and returned to her position against his chest, nudging him to hold her. "And maybe you're never too old to believe in Prince Charming, either."

★★★★★

"No way."

"Way," Sienna said for the fifth time with a heavy sigh. "Now, there are going to be parameters in place—"

"No way," Grace repeated for the *sixth* time, this time saying it to Beau, who looked at Sienna before scratching his head.

"Way?" he offered with a nod even though it came out as a question, and before Sienna could tell Grace for the *seventh* time that they were going to Disney World, courtesy of Beau, Grace started screaming—and *squealing*—with excitement and launched herself at him.

For Sienna, there was a pause in Grace's squealing and a halt to her own breathing as she took them in—Beau and Grace. *Have I ever made her that happy? Maybe,* Sienna thought, but Grace had probably been five, and it had involved something as simple as chocolate chip pancakes for dinner. But no pang of jealousy struck Sienna when she came across another thought. *This is what she has been missing—the right kind of man to put a smile on her face.*

Grace didn't know her father. Sienna hardly even knew him, apart from his name. Andrew, a guy who drove a Corvette even though he had told Sienna the night they met—the only night they spent together—that he worked a 9-5 job at Best Buy. He hadn't given Grace anything apart from his DNA. Not a pack of diapers, teething rings. He wasn't there for her first shots, he didn't teach her to ride a bike. He never knew just how strong Grace was—how she smiled even when she vomited or played pranks on the first-year resident oncologists.

"What about Molly?" She pulled back to look at her mother, still hanging on to Beau.

And you know what, Andrew? You missed out on a heart of gold.

Sienna sighed. "She needs clearance for travel. Just like

everyone else. Beau is going to make it as safe as possible." She smiled kindly at him, overwhelmed by his generosity in chartering planes for families.

Beau stumbled back when Grace jumped again, wrapping her arms around his neck and kicking her legs with delight. She gasped. "I have to call her!" She sprinted out of the kitchen and down the hall to her bedroom.

"Does she always do that?" Beau asked, rubbing his head. "My ear is still ringing."

"Only when she's really excited." Peeking down the hallway, Sienna made sure Grace was out of sight before walking over to him. "I'll never be able to thank you for this," she said quietly, kissing him. "It's her dream come true."

Beau gave her chin a small squeeze. "I guess some wishes are generational."

Sienna laughed. "Maybe. But don't tell her I'm only in it for the Dole Whip and not the fairy tale part. That's our secret."

Beau wrapped his arms around her waist. "You don't believe in fairy tales?"

"Of course I do." She leaned up to kiss him again before whispering in his ear. "Turns out my favorite one is only beginning."

no wasted moments

DEAR MOM,

The other night, I dreamed of you for the first time since you died.

Now, I didn't see you in this dream. I didn't hear your voice or hug you or anything. I was just waiting, sitting on the small stone wall outside of school in Nashville. It must've been a Monday or Wednesday —when Henry had debate or chess club. Those were the days you picked me up alone.

I knew I was dreaming because my heart was racing beyond belief, and I began to pace, walking back and forth on the empty sidewalk, my eyes scanning the street and the entrance to the school. My whole body had been expecting you, and even though I couldn't see you or your car, I could imagine what your face would look like when you picked me up. You'd roll down the window even though my hand was already on the handle, as if you couldn't wait another second to talk to me. "Tell me about your day," you'd say.

Continuing to pace, I tugged anxiously on the straps of my backpack and began to count my steps. One. . . three. A car drove into the parking lot, but it wasn't yours. Five…seven. . . another car came, but again, it wasn't yours.

It was Beau's truck. His window was already down, and I halted when he pulled up to the curb. "Come on," he said and reached over with his long arm to open the door. "Let's go."

My eyes flew open before I got into the car in dreamland. But Beau was beside me—half on top of me with that long arm draped heavily over my stomach. His face pressed against my shoulder. I turned to look at him, steadying my breathing for a minute before I noticed all the neon stars were still lighting up the ceiling. We must've fallen asleep.

"Beau, wake up," I whispered, pressing my hand to his face. The tip of my finger traced his scar.

He mumbled something, rubbing his head back and forth against the pillow before opening his eyes. He grinned sleepily, and he reached up to cup my face. "This is the best dream."

I laughed. "It's not a dream. And it's one in the morning."

"Shit," Beau said but made no effort to move. He pressed his lips to mine, holding them there, but there was a change to their shape. He was frowning. "I need to go."

"It's okay."

"No, you don't get it. I don't want to leave you. I have to, but I don't want to," he huffed. "But I'm out of time."

What I didn't get was the sudden change in his demeanor, in the way he held my face. It turned into a clutch, sort of a panicked hold. I shimmied, forcing him more on top of me, and kissed him. I didn't want him to leave, and words didn't seem to do enough, so I tried to show him with my body, but as usual, Beau stopped me.

"You're making this hard."

I could feel that I was. "I know," I tried to kiss him again, but Beau lifted himself a little higher, chomping on his lip. I sighed. "Is there something wrong with me?"

Beau's eyes widened.

"You only go so far with me. I'm starting to think I'm not your type."

He dropped down quickly and I gasped from the surprise. "Does that feel like you're not my type?" I turned my head, and Beau lowered, pressing his lips to my ear. "I want it to be perfect with you the first time. Exactly how you deserve." He kissed my neck, nuzzling his nose to it when I shivered. "And after that, I'll never say no, no matter where you ask."

I pressed my mouth into a smile. "You'd do it anywhere with me?"

Beau nodded.

"Okay. An airplane."

He broke out in laughter and then quieted himself. "We're kind of tall for the mile-high club. But yeah, we'll make it work." Beau lifted his head to the star-covered ceiling. "Wish list."

"Wish list," I sighed and let him roll off me so he could put on his sneakers.

"I'll pick you up later."

When we got to the town fair the next afternoon, Beau's mom asked us to help manage her booth—she had packaged up jars of cake, brownies, and cookies prepared to donate the proceeds, something Beau says she does every year. This year it was going to some organization that works to make sick kids happy. But after Beau had opened his third jar of brownies, she fired us. So, we walked aimlessly through the fair holding sticky hands (cotton candy is only second to Dole Whip if you ask me), trying to decide what ride to go on.

"Ferris Wheel," Beau said.

I rolled my eyes. "That is so *lame. No. Let's go on that one." I pointed to some tall catapult-looking thing where people were being launched into the air while upside down.*

"In your dreams."

"You're boring," I told Beau, and when I tried to take my hand from his, he began leading me across the grass lot. "What are you—"

"Boring enough to square dance?" Beau asked over his shoulder as he led me toward the stage.

"No, Beau, come on." It wasn't that I was embarrassed about making a fool out of myself. I mean, that was part of it. I was more worried about the huge crowd of people I was about to make myself a fool in front of. "I hate crowds," I whined, trying to remind him.

Beau stopped. "I really want to dance with you."

I shrugged. "We could wait until prom. I mean, you are taking me, right?"

There was the slightest change in Beau's eyes, a straining, like he was holding back from blinking. But when I dropped his hand, he quickly picked it back up, shaking the look from his face. "Yeah. I'll take you."

"I love white peonies." I giggled when Beau looked confused. "For my corsage."

Beau nodded. "White peony corsage, got it."

I smiled. "Wish list," I told him, sealing the deal. "And there's something else."

"What's that?"

"Something after."

The truth is, Mom, I don't want Beau and I to leave each other without fully being with each other in every way. And I think I've waited long enough.

Beau nodded. "Wish list," he said softly, and I couldn't ignore how his voice cracked a bit. "Since we're here, though, and there's music, and dancing with you is on my *list, can you just give me this one?"*

I let him lead me to the crowded floor because he had some sort of fierce determination within him, even though I don't think Beau really wanted to square dance with me. We folded into line. I had no idea what I was doing, and even with his overconfidence, Beau didn't either. But that was okay. We danced like idiots—going left when we should've gone right, stepping forward when we should've moved back—smiling while laughter escaped between rushed breaths. And when the music slowed, Beau pulled me in, and I rested my cheek on his shoulder.

"I don't want to waste a moment with you," Beau said, and I knew what he meant.

We know how fragile life is because it all ends, and that's sad, no matter if it's peaceful or traumatic or just wrong. Every minute is precious enough that it can be wasted. Beau taught me that. So now I don't wait for my birthday to make a wish. I don't even wait for the perfect star anymore, Mom. Just the perfect moment, and there's no moment like the present.

Beau has taught me to eat the cake (or cookies or brownies), dance while there is music even if your moves are bad, and say what you want to say when you need to say it.

"I love you."

Beau looked down at me like he had something he needed to say too. "Sienna," he began, but then bit his lip and looked away before pulling me close. "I love you too."

Love,

Sienna

the slow break

DEAR MOM,

I wish I could tell you that I'm basking in love right now, that life is a fairy tale, and I've found my Prince Charming. I wish I could tell you that I'm constantly dreaming of that happily ever after, of what life for Beau and me looks like down the line. We'll have kids, definitely (but when I said down the line, I meant WAY down the line). I hope all boys because it makes me smile imagining him running around with a gaggle of shaggy brown-haired rug rats just like him trying to explain an air raid offense.

But all I have to tell you right now is that over the past few days, I've learned that life can go from impossibly high to impossibly low all over a few tenths of a second.

Beau wakes up early now that the season is over—like 5:00 AM early. Some days he goes on a long run—I don't even offer to join him because I hate running, and I know I won't be able to keep up. But other days, like this morning, Beau goes to school, sprinting and training on the empty field.

"4.83," I called out when he crossed in front of me. I had taken one of Dad's stopwatches because he asked me to come and time his 40-yard dash.

Beau's sprint slowed to a jog and then a walk as he continued down the field. "Fuck," he yelled, his hands pressed to the top of his head. "Too slow."

If I wasn't a football coach's daughter, I would've disagreed. But I know Beau wants his 40 to average around at least 4.5 seconds, if not faster. But even though I know that, I tried to make him feel better about it.

"We should do this first thing. Not last. You're tired."

Beau scoffed.

"What?" I asked. "We've been here an hour. It's not a fair test—"

"You know who won't care if I'm tired? Coach Naber at FSU." He took a few deep breaths. "Let's do it again."

"Beau, come on." He continued to stalk away from me to the goal line. "You only need to worry about staying in shape."

He spun back toward me on his heel. "No, I need to worry about staying in playing *shape. That's what you don't understand. You think all the shit I did here"—Beau paused, motioning to the field—"is going to hold up in Tallahassee? It's not. I've got to compete with bigger and stronger guys if I'm going to start."*

"You might do those things and still *not start," I called out to him, and immediately regret laced my mouth, but I continued—because I* am *a football coach's daughter, and I know how this goes, Mom. Guys from all over the country—the best of their high schools—suddenly go to a Division-I school and realize they're no longer the big fish in the small pond. They're a guppy in the freaking ocean.*

"You have to be realistic, Beau."

Beau laughed. "You telling me to be realistic? That's funny coming from the girl who still makes wishes on stars and hopes they come true."

My mouth turned into a downward pout immediately, but if Beau noticed, he didn't seem to care.

"So, you don't think I can start?" Beau asked, his voice twinged with a harsh laugh, and I knew, judging by the way his hands sat on his hips and the wicked look on his face, he was taunting me. "What do you know about college ball?"

I pursed my lips together. "Nothing," I admitted.

"That's what I thought." Beau pointed. "Stand there and time me."

I made no effort to move to where Beau wanted me to go because even though I love him, he was being a total asshole.

"I know that you're too slow to drop into the break. That's because you're tall, I get it. But you turn your shoulder and hip before you drop right into the defensive back on your ass." Beau narrowed his eyes at me. "Almost every interception you gave up was because of that, not because of you being too slow." I lifted the stopwatch from my neck and stomped over to him, slamming it into his chest. "So, stop worrying about shaving three-tenths of a second off your 40 when you're tired, *and keep your body straight and your eyes up."*

I turned and walked off, each step quicker than the last. I could hear Beau call my name, but I kept walking. And when I hit the parking lot, it was a jog. When I got to the sidewalk, I ran all the way home.

Dad was making coffee when I walked in, my cheeks red and chapped from the chilly morning. He took a deep breath. "You better have slept in your own bed last night," he said.

"I did." I wanted to add out of spite that I always *will, but it would've been wasted on Dad.*

"Where were you?"

"With your *wideout," I told Dad, pushing past him to pour myself coffee.*

Dad wrinkled his nose. "What were you doing with him this early in the morning?"

"Whatever it was, it was the last time." I poured steaming hot coffee into a mug. "He's a know it all. You know, you should look at film with him. Most of those passes you thought might be short from your QB? He gives himself up to easily before the drop." I took too big of a sip of my coffee and burned my tongue, cursing under my breath.

Dad laughed.

"What's so funny?"

He shook his head, opening the cabinet. "Maybe you should use that mug more often." He dropped a kiss into my sweaty hair.

*I looked down at the mug in my hand—**WORLD'S BEST COACH.***

"Best girlfriend too, I imagine. Sometimes teenage boys need to be put in their place." He poured his coffee.

I sighed. "Can you meet with him a few mornings a week? He's freaking out about FSU. I'm trying to be patient and ride it out but . . . " I trailed off, shaking my head. "I hate *football."*

"I'll talk with him. But do me a favor and don't give him too hard of a time, alright? Kid has a lot on his shoulders."

"Yeah, well, I hope it's worth it."

Dad grew silent for a minute, leaning against the kitchen counter and focusing on his coffee. "You know, Sienna . . . whatever is happening with you and Beau, I don't want you to get too hung up on it."

"What do you mean?"

"He'll be off to Florida soon."

"In August," I reminded Dad.

"And you'll be down in Austin."

I, of course, know this too, Mom. Because the plan is that even though Beau heads off to FSU in early August, I will follow at some point once I transfer. It might be a year later, but that year will be fine. Or at least that's what I keep telling myself. We had a plan for that—I'll work at the diner this summer and save every dime and penny so I can afford the gas to drive to Tallahassee for his home games.

And even though, standing in the kitchen, I was mad at Beau for kind of being a selfish asshole, I was still planning to stick to that plan—the one that ends with that happily ever after and a bunch of kids running around playing backyard football. The one that ends with him and me together. I haven't made that wish yet, isn't that kind of ironic? It's the one thing I want the most—a real family with the guy I love who already is *family. But there's something that makes putting it out into the universe scary, as if I'm tempting fate.*

But then I remember that it's not just me. Beau and I will tempt fate together. And haven't we already? We found each other again. We'll keep each other this time.

Love,

Sienna

chapter fourteen

"DOWN. FARTHER. LOWER." Beau bit his lip, standing behind Sienna as she squatted. He placed his hand on the small of her back, pushing gently. When she reached her limit and began to rise, he slid his hand to her ass.

Sienna let out a small grunt when she put the bar back. "That's not spotting."

"It's not?" he asked when she turned around, putting her hands to her hips. He rubbed his chin. "Shit. I've been doing it wrong this whole time."

Sienna rolled her eyes. "Yeah. You might want to apologize to your teammates for the groping."

Beau watched as Sienna stepped around him, reaching for her water bottle. "Football is an ass sport," he told her.

"Why do you think I ever bothered watching you play?" She put the bottle down and gave him a playful kick to the leg. "A high, firm butt in tights. Can't beat that."

"They're *pants.* Not tights."

"Keep telling yourself that."

"Are we done here? I've got you for another hour."

Over the past month, Beau and Sienna had fallen into a routine—seeing each other a few days a week between his training while Grace was still at school. Sometimes, they walked around Dallas, sometimes stayed in at his apartment, and occasionally, Sienna had asked Beau to help her in the gym. Nights were more difficult to work around, given Sienna's time spent at Maloney's and Grace. Sienna had asked for more time before having Beau stay at her place, and Beau respected that, stealing her away when he could—when Grace was spending the night at a friend's and not pushing for more time with Sienna after dusk apart from dropping by the bar.

And while he always mixed up her workouts, Beau made sure that there was one exercise they never missed.

Sienna pulled a mat out from the corner and unrolled it. "We're not done. Abs."

"We can work out upstairs in my apartment." He glanced at the clock. He had to meet Chase for lunch in fifty-seven minutes. "High intensity too. Like last time."

"Who told you that was high intensity?"

"Ouch." Beau rubbed his chest, feigning hurt. "But funny enough, the noises that come out of your mouth didn't sound like complaining." He leaned against the wall. "What if I wear my tights?"

She laughed. "Would you shut up and hand me that?" Pointing to a medicine ball, Sienna lay down, waiting for Beau to drop it to her.

"Keep your neck straight," he told her, catching her toss as she did sit-ups on the mat.

Sienna groaned after tossing him the ball, collapsing on the mat.

"Need a break?"

She shook her head, lifting the heavy ball. "No."

"You're not training for the season," Beau reminded her. "Not sure why you feel the need to push yourself so hard."

She huffed. "I'm tired of being soft."

Beau caught the ball and stared down at her, the swell of her hips covered in leggings amplified against the red mat. Sienna squirmed awkwardly, tugging the tank top she wore to hide her stomach. Beau dropped the ball at his side and bent, crawling over her.

"If soft is wrong," he said, pushing up her shirt to kiss the span of her stomach, smiling against her skin. "I'll never be right again. Ever." Sienna giggled when Beau swirled his tongue around her belly button. He lifted his head. "You don't know how beautiful you are, do you? It doesn't surprise me. You didn't back then."

"I know I was *different* back then."

"So was I."

Scoffing, Sienna tilted her head. "It's not the same. There's more of you in the right places." Her hands came down to his shoulders and ran down his arms.

"If you think that *this*"—Beau paused, his hand sneaking from her waist to her thigh, which clenched beneath his touch—"is the wrong place, you're absolutely crazy." He kissed her stomach again, grinning when she quivered. "Same goes for here." His mouth trailed up over her tank top to the opening, letting his teeth sink into the soft swell of the top of her breast. "And god, definitely here."

Sienna sighed beneath Beau as he swept his lips up her neck. "This is a gym." She squeaked when Beau rocked into her. "Where people work out. I'm supposed to be working out."

"It's late morning, no one's coming in. And I told you," Beau said, nuzzling the crevice behind her ear, "upstairs." His hips instinctively flexed when Sienna opened her legs further. "High intensity, low intensity, yoga, whatever you want. We can even workout in the shower. Water aerobics."

"You've got a big season to prepare for, so go easy on the extracurriculars."

Beau shot up as Sienna tugged her shirt back down. "We're supposed to meet at one," he told Chase, who turned his eyes away as Beau adjusted himself through his shorts. He stepped protectively in front of Sienna when she rose from the ground. "You could start calling."

Chase tilted his head. "You could start returning my messages."

Ignoring Chase, Beau looked over his shoulder and whispered to Sienna, "I'm sorry," before clearing his throat. "Sienna, meet my often inappropriate, pushy agent, Chase Matthews. Chase, my girlfriend, Sienna Clarke."

Beau watched Chase's eyes bounce between Sienna and him when he stepped aside. "I believe we met already. Briefly, at the season closer. I guess you were the good luck charm that reminded the world Beau Walker's still got it. I've got you to thank for the headache the LA Bulls have made for me over him."

No, no, Beau fumed internally. *Don't do it, Chase.* But before Beau could interrupt, Chase continued.

"Have you ever been to LA, Sienna?"

Look at me, Beau willed Sienna. *It's not what it sounds like.*

Sienna didn't look at Beau. She merely reached for her bag and hoodie. "You know, I'll head out now. I have some errands to run before Grace gets home from school. It was nice to see you again, Chase."

Frustration strangled Beau as he watched her walk swiftly to the gym door. He bore into Chase.

"Sorry I cock blocked you."

"LA isn't a thing."

"I didn't say it was," Chase said, oblivious. "I just said they gave me a headache. Two actually. I've also got a tension one thinking of all the money you're walking away from. If you're done"—Chase paused, looking at the mat Sienna had lain on—"working out. My car's out front. Run up and change."

Beau let out a huge breath when Chase left the gym, sticking his hands on his head and pacing. He reached for his phone to call Sienna, bouncing his leg anxiously as it rang and rang until going to her voicemail.

Not what it sounds like. I'll explain tonight

He quickly texted her while trying to mentally assure himself as well.

Her reply minutes later didn't provide much more reassurance.

Can't see you tonight need to be at work. Call you later.

★★★★★

"I gotta jet after this. I need to be across town in an hour." Beau looked down at his watch. If he hadn't already scheduled time to train Damien, Beau would have already been in his car on his way to Brookwood to clear up the misunderstanding.

"Oh yeah?" Chase took a sip of his drink. "Where's that."

"North Dallas."

Chase arched an eyebrow. "What's there? Doesn't your girl live out in the middle of nowhere?"

"Her name is Sienna," Beau said, lifting his sandwich. "There's a kid out in that area. Hardworking, quick feet. I'm helping him—"

"You?"

Beau looked around. "Yes, idiot, me."

"You're what, coaching him?"

Beau shrugged. "Sort of."

"Don't tell me you'll abandon next season for coaching—"

"No." Beau rolled his neck. "I won't. Even if I'm exhausted. I'm physically and mentally exhausted. I'll be honest. I *barely* have it in me to do another season. But I need some time to figure out what the hell I'm supposed to do with the rest of my life."

Chase took a sip of his drink. "Why are you so worried about that? Play golf. Go sit on a beach."

"I hate golf."

Chase rolled his eyes. "Learn to crochet then, whatever. I can get you a commentating position in a heartbeat. You're camera handsome. ESPN would eat you up. I mean, come on, Beau. What are we doing here?"

Beau bit into his club sandwich. "We're eating," he said with a full mouth.

"I think maybe you're scared." Chase continued when Beau raised an eyebrow. "Maybe you think you're washed up, and that will show if you go to LA. Maybe you're worried about losing a starter to some D-I hot shot just out of college."

"I'm not." Beau laughed. "You can save the reverse psychology. I'm *driven* by competition. Do you want to know what makes me want to run faster? Fast guys." *I don't know if I want to anymore,* he added in thought. "But let's table the LA discussion, alright? I don't have plans to go out there ever again."

Chase dropped his fork. "You could take a vacation though. Maybe it would be good for you. You're running around trying to wrangle sixty kids and take them to Disney World. When was the last time you lay on a beach?"

Beau laughed. "When I played for LA." He furrowed his brow in thought when an idea struck him. "Maybe you're right. I could use a little time away. Can you get your travel agent on that for me?"

"Beau Walker taking time off? Alright. I'll have them check flights."

Beau tsked, reaching for his water. "I want to go private."

Chase narrowed his eyes. "I mean, that's not usually your style."

"And I want a few days down in Malibu. Find something nice on the beach. Right on Pacific Coast Highway. Ocean view." *Another thing come true for Sienna,* Beau thought with a smile. *Wish list.*

Later that night, after Sienna still hadn't returned his text or call, Beau showed up at her house, eyeing her car and nervously fiddling with his hat.

Henry appeared and shook his head.

"She's at work already?" Beau looked down at his watch.

"Frank picked her up. Her car is giving her trouble." The narrowing of Henry's eyes and the tilt of his head told Beau all he needed to know.

"It's a misunderstanding," Beau defended himself. "I'm trying to—"

"Look, Beau, do me a favor. If you're planning on stringing Sienna along—"

"I'm not," Beau said emphatically, taking a step forward. "I told you, it's a misunderstanding."

Sighing, Henry rubbed his face. "I've done this before with her. Now, she was seventeen back then, of course, everything was *dramatic*, but that doesn't mean you didn't *hurt* her."

Beau clenched his teeth. "I know I did. But this time it's—"

"Different?"

"Yes," Beau professed with absolute certainty.

Henry shook his head, his light brown hair swooping to the side. "Some things don't feel too different, Beau. Like you two doing whatever it is you're doing, and then suddenly it's about football again. And you know something? Back then, it was fine for it to be about football because you were a kid, and look, it got you everything you wanted. But now, she *has* a kid. A pretty great one who went through hell and back. We're all trying to move on, but especially Sienna. What my sister's gone through . . ."

I know. I mean, I don't know. I can't imagine. But I'm trying to do my part now. Behind Henry, Beau caught site of a pair of Grace's shoes beside the door, some sort of sparkly bag on the stairs. *I might have been no good for her then.* It was hard for Beau to admit to the flaw, that years ago, at the peak of his NFL career, he probably wouldn't have been able to be the right kind of support for Sienna as she supported Grace battling cancer.

Pressing his lips together, Beau looked down at the ground. "What you've done for your sister and Grace . . . you're a good man, Henry. Probably a better one than me. And I swear to you, I'm not here messing around. And I'm *not* going back to LA."

"You should be telling her that, not me."

"I will. But I'm telling *you* because I need your help." Henry raised an eyebrow, and Beau continued. "I want to take Sienna to LA."

"I thought you—"

"Just for a few days. Not forever. But . . . there's sort of some unfinished business I want to wrap up with her." *Seeing the ocean. Sail boats. Sunrises and sunsets.* "I was thinking next month. I'd take Grace if she can miss a few days of school—"

"Man, can I give you some advice?" Henry laughed, before adjusting his glasses. "Look, it's cute you come around for Scrabble night, that you hang out with the family. Because Sienna and Grace are a packaged deal. My sister is the greatest mother there is. She's selfless to a fault. Do you know what she needs right now?"

"What?"

Henry sighed. "A little time to be selfish. I'll stay with Grace. She's missed enough school. She wants to be with her friends. Take Sienna. But that's not for free. I want something in return."

Beau raised his eyebrows. "What's that?"

"Mavericks tickets for their home opener next season," Henry said, raising his finger for emphasis. "*Floor* seats."

"You realize I play football, right?"

"I know. And I never held that against you."

Beau laughed. "Fair enough. Consider it done."

"She went to the bar early," Henry told him. "Something about getting that fridge fixed up."

"Thanks, man. I appreciate it." Beau made a mental note to buy a new fridge and not take Sienna's no for an answer. And when he hurried back to his truck, he glanced at her car in the driveway, thinking to buy her a new one too.

Maloney's was quiet when he stepped inside a few minutes later.

"What's up, Frank?" Beau asked, walking up to the bar. There was no sight of Sienna.

"She's in the back if you're looking for her."

When he rounded the corner to the kitchen, a voice brought Beau to a halt.

"This is a Band-Aid. Another seventy-five dollar Band-Aid, Sienna. You can keep slapping them on, but all you're gonna get is another problem next month."

"I'll deal with that next month," Sienna retorted. "So please slap on whatever you need to keep it working until then and your drinks are on the house the rest of the week."

Dylan snorted. "This used to be a lot more fun for me when I was slapping your ass and not this damn fridge."

With quick steps, Beau entered the kitchen. "Dylan, I know you're a handyman, but you play the role of a plumber pretty well," he said, and Sienna's eyes flew to his while Dylan jumped, reaching for his exposed backside and bumping his head.

"Can I talk to you?" Beau asked Sienna through a clenched jaw.

She folded her arms defensively at his question, and Beau quickly reached out, pulling Sienna by her wrist.

"Forward-facing baseball hat," Dylan laughed. "Man means business."

Sienna tried to tug her arm free. "What are—"

"Need to borrow my girl for a second, Dylan," Beau said over his shoulder, leading Sienna to the back door.

"Beau—"

"No," Beau interrupted, pushing the door open and pulling her out to the alley. "You're going to listen."

Sienna shook her head. "Beau—"

"I'm *not* signing with LA." He watched Sienna press her lips tightly together and look at the ground. "They're interested, that's true. I entertained the idea for *one* minute, but that's the extent of it. I need you to understand that."

She crossed her arms. "Chase—"

"Chase is my agent. He's a good guy. He's gotten me through a lot. We've been a team, but we're on opposite sides now, Sienna. Of course, he wants me to go to LA. He wants me to sign a big, multi-year contract. He wants *his* cut," Beau told her. "He wants—"

"What do *you* want, Beau?" Sienna asked, holding her arms out. "Greg wanted football. Chase wants football. Last I checked, neither of them are playing football. *You* are."

"Because," Sienna continued, "you can tell me that you've been playing all along for Greg until you're blue in the face. But you've been playing for a decade, Beau. At what point is it enough?"

"I told you," Beau began, "When I—"

"The Super Bowl. Right. So go to LA where you have a chance at being part of something great then. But I'm staying here." She tapped her foot against the pavement. "Years ago, you asked me not to make you choose between me and your dead brother. I don't even have to say that to you, Beau. Grace isn't *a* choice—she's the *only* choice and I'm sorry, but she comes first. This is where her home is. This is where her friends and doctors—"

"I'd never ask you to choose."

Sienna grew quiet, shuffling her feet. "I could tell you to go. I could say I'll stand by you and see you every minute I can, but Beau, I don't *want* that. I've loved you from a distance before. I won't do it again."

Beau's breath hitched. "Sienna . . . "

"But if you're going to go, let's end things now before it's too late, and I realize that loving you when you're right in front of me is a feeling I might die without."

Beau stepped closer, but she moved back, shaking her head and cracking Beau's heart.

"I won't do it again," Sienna repeated, her promise a form of self-preservation. "I can't, Beau."

"You won't have to." He quickly unzipped his hoodie, wrapping it around her, grateful she didn't move away. "I swear, you won't."

Sienna's lip trembled from the chilly air, and Beau ran his hands up and down her arms. "So, what do you want?" she asked again.

Beau shifted his closed mouth from side to side. "You. You for the small parts, like waking up together. You for the big parts —like seeing *you* wear *my* jersey when I win the Super Bowl." Sienna opened her mouth, but he continued. "But here's the thing, Sienna. I want to win. I've been *trying* to win. But you know what I've realized by losing all these years? The win isn't yanking you from the stands and kissing you under confetti and a big trophy and ring. Because that's a once-in-a-lifetime thing for me at this point." He cupped her face. "The win is you and me for the lifetime, not just one part of it."

Sienna brought her hand up, holding onto his resting on her face and Beau lifted his head to the sky, needing a reprieve from the heavy emotion between them. And that's when he saw a perfect star.

"I wish you're with me for *all* the parts," he said as the shooting star she didn't see passed by. Taking a step forward, Beau closed the space between them. "I don't know what comes after I finally walk away from football. All I know is I want you there for it. And of all the things I wish would come true in this life, the biggest one already has."

Sienna nodded as Beau's lips grazed her temple. "I know. And Greg would be proud of you for getting where you are today."

Beau laughed into her hair. "No," he admitted. "That's not it.

"What is it then?" Sienna asked, tipping her head back to look into his eyes.

"The only wish I ever made for *myself* as an adult was the chance to tell you that I'm sorry. And when Dallas offered me a spot after my accident, that's why I took it. I figured if you were anywhere, you had to be here." He looked around. "I didn't have the balls before to come back to Brookwood and find you and I hate that I waited, but I still hoped one day…maybe I'd get the chance to tell you something else too."

Sienna waited. "What?" she asked, her voice cracking, as if her heart and mind knew what to anticipate.

That I love you. And I never stopped. And I wish to God or the stars, or whatever, *that I always will,* Beau wanted to profess. But somehow, standing in the alley not far from the dumpsters didn't align with the vision of how he wanted everything to play out with Sienna. Even though they were rooted in small, sleepy Brookwood, there wasn't enough space to show Sienna just how much Beau loved her—as high as the clouds in the sky, as deep and vast as the ocean.

"I'm taking you to LA."

The look on her face quickly turned into frustration. "Beau, I *told—*"

Beau grabbed her hand as she stepped away. "How about you and me take the trip to the ocean we always planned?"

Sienna pressed her lips in thought.

"Henry agreed to babysit," Beau offered, hoping it might sway her decision.

"It's not really babysitting when it's his *niece.* But it's a lot to ask."

"Fine, he's *Grace*-sitting." Beau shrugged. "And to be honest, it wasn't a cheap ask. But you're worth it."

Sighing, Sienna motioned over Beau's shoulder. "I have *work.* I can't exactly go. I have a bartender who just had a baby, and I'm working because I can't afford to still pay her *and* hire a replacement. I already have to bring someone to cover when I take Grace to the concert this weekend." She sighed. "Maybe we can see in a few months—"

"Sienna." Beau groaned and took both her hands in his. "If you're going to make me work for it, fine. But don't be stubborn enough to not take the money I'm going to offer. Or to let me buy you a new car."

Sienna scrunched her brow. "There's nothing wrong with my car. I've been procrastinating changing the oil."

"Fine," Beau admitted. "Then I'll change the oil for you. And I'll buy you a new fridge." He paused, remembering how he had found her in the back kitchen moments before. "Were you trying to make me jealous with Dylan?"

She scoffed, yanking her hands free. "Of course not."

"That's a joke, you know that, right? Dylan?" Beau tried to ignore the way his throat burned when he said his name.

"No one is joking."

"You're right. I'm serious about all these things," Beau said firmly. "You'll take the money and hire someone. You'll accept the delivery of the new fridge that will be here tomorrow. And we're going to LA. And when you have a problem, you ask for *my* help, not Dylan's. You're smarter than that. He cornered you in the bathroom."

Sienna looked down at her feet. "It wasn't like that."

"Oh, cool. Glad we cleared that up, then," Beau huffed.

She cocked an eyebrow. "I never got the jealous vibe from you."

"Me?" Beau laughed. "Jealous? Of Dylan the plumber? Get the hell out of here."

"He's an electrician."

"Then he should know better than to play with a fuse," Beau growled, running a hand over his face before conceding. "Fine. I'm jealous."

Sienna pursed her lips, fighting a grin.

"Because he took my place." Beau's hands gripped her hips, and he guided her backward until she collided gently with the brick wall beside the door. Sienna didn't lower her gaze from his. "If you think it doesn't kill me to know that he took a slice of my heaven, then you're a fool. An absolutely gorgeous, stunning, beautiful fool." He pulled his bottom lip between his teeth while his thumb traced the outline of her mouth.

"I gave it to him," Sienna reminded him before lowering her voice, her eyes not leaving his. She moved her hands between them, creeping them beneath his shirt, her nails sliding up the trail of hair to his naval.

That was the end of it for Beau. He abandoned her body only to flip his front-facing baseball cap backward.

"Business is over?" Sienna asked, her lip curling in a curious smile.

"No." Beau cradled her cheeks with both hands and pulled Sienna's face to his, wasting no time parting her lips and sweeping her mouth with his tongue. Sienna's hands had come to rest on his when he backed away, fighting for his closeness. "I wanted to do that, and my hat was in the way."

She took a deep breath, holding his hands against her face tighter. "Do you want to know a secret?" Swallowing, Beau leaned forward, but Sienna tilted her head, moving her mouth to his ear. "I *always* imagined it was you."

Beau sought her lips. "Tell him to get lost."

Sienna pressed a kiss to the corner of Beau's mouth. "He's fixing my fridge."

"I'll order a new one right now."

She sighed, dropping her hands to Beau's chest. "He's a *friend*."

"We started off as friends, too," he reminded Sienna as she went to step aside, but Beau didn't release his grip on her waist.

"You're right. I should've learned my lesson," Sienna quipped before pushing him off her. "I have to get back to work."

Beau held out a hand. "You have your keys on you? I'll change your oil tonight before I head home."

Sienna reached into her pocket, unclipping her car key, and tossing it to him. "Thank you."

Beau pointed a finger. "LA. Next month," he said as Sienna moved past him. "I'll let you know the exact days tomorrow. But look, no matter where I go next season, I don't have a lot of time to waste. I'm trying to make the most of every minute I can with you."

"I'll *think* about it." Sienna opened the door. "But right now, I've got to think about getting an influx of cash into this place quick. From *customers.* Not just friends. Or boyfriends. Even really great ones like you, Beau."

Beau shook off a hard pass from Giles. "*Think* about it," he relented, as if the idea of a weekend away was preposterous. "She said *think*—"

"You can lead a horse to water, Beau," his teammate chimed in. "Fancy, schmancy expensive bottled water or a leaky sewer pipe."

"She's as stubborn as a damn horse," Beau agreed, brushing a scuff from his cleat.

The Sparks' captains' practice—an off-season, unofficial player-run workout—had just ended. It had been grueling but promising, a better vibe than when Beau first signed with the team two years ago. *Maybe there's something here*, Beau wondered, looking around at the players littering the field—quarterbacks, linemen, and running backs dancing, joking, and laughing. *But anything had to be better than last season.*

"My mom's the same way. When women do it on their own for so long, they never stop." Giles shook his head. "You know she still clips coupons? She drives twenty minutes out of the damn way to buy milk because it's ten cents less a gallon. I'll never understand it. But seems your girl is pretty much the same."

Beau nodded, trying to shrug off his frustration.

"She was fine with you footing the bill for that Golden Penny gig, yeah?"

"Maybe. But who could say no to taking sick kids to Disney World? She isn't the Grinch. Just hardheaded." Beau sighed. "She's weird about letting me take care of things, is all."

Maybe that's because I promised I would and left her to do it all on her own, Beau reminded himself.

"Doesn't mean you can't help. Get creative. If things are bad with the bar, how is she going to say no?" Giles pointed out.

"Creative? What do you mean?"

Giles tossed the ball back and forth between his hands. "I mean, if she doesn't want cash, get people all up in her business. How hard could it be? It's a small bar in a small town in the middle of Texas. You're in the heart of Sparks country. Go stand there without your shirt and holler. People will come."

Beau laughed. "I think my ship has sailed, man."

His presence at Maloney's had grown so frequent that it became normal, leaving the regular patrons unfazed. Under normal circumstances, Beau would be elated. But it didn't do much to help him on his quest to get the place booming.

There was hooting and hollering down the field, some sort of dance-off between some of the younger players. Beau laughed and shook his head.

"Were we like that when we were younger?" he asked Giles. As professional as football players were at that level, as dedicated as they were to the sport, at the end of the day, they really were a bunch of clowns who loved to have fun.

Giles turned his head to the crowd and waved them off. "Say what you will about the Sparks. We might not be winners, but we damn sure can put on a show." He laughed, tossing the ball to Beau, and looked at him questioningly when he didn't throw it back. "What?"

Glancing between Giles and the other guys, some of whom had taken to pulling off their jerseys and twirling them above their heads, Beau smirked. “You busy this weekend?”

Giles scratched his head. “Depends on why you're asking.”

“How do you feel about a little creative team bonding?”

chapter fifteen

"YOUR SEATS HAVE BEEN UPGRADED."

Sienna wondered if she heard the stadium attendant wrong through the plexiglass. *Aren't upgrades for plane tickets?* "Sorry?"

"Floor seat ticket holders need a bracelet," the woman said, beckoning for Sienna's arm. "Orange for area closest to stage."

Sienna looked down at the florescent paper bracelet fastened to her wrist as Grace and her friend squealed and danced in delight.

"We'll be so close!" Grace exclaimed, holding up the newest addition to her wrist.

When they left the will-call window and went to stand in line to buy an overpriced T-shirt, Sienna called Beau.

"Don't say anything. That's for Grace, not you. I would've snagged a backstage pass, but I know she doesn't want to meet him with her wig. Next time he's on tour, she's got it."

Sienna raised an eyebrow. "She told you that?"

"She must've mentioned something about it," Beau mumbled. "Don't fight me on this."

Sienna tongued her cheek, unsure why she was annoyed. *Can you give me a reason to* stay *upset?* She wondered what she was supposed to be upset over exactly. *If he says he's not going to LA, then I have to take his word for it, right?* But Sienna's mouth filled with a sour taste, laced with a flavor of the past from when Beau had said then too. She glanced at Grace and her friend, Lilah, and felt wrong frowning when they were beaming.

"Thank you. This is probably the best night of her life. But you know I hate crowds."

"I know you love your daughter more than you're afraid of crowds."

His words tugged on her heart as she recalled him saying something similar during a happy time, just before things went south.

"True," Sienna said, looking down at her wristband.

"Have fun, alright?"

Sienna glanced around. "I'll try. It's not my scene."

"Square dancing wasn't either," Beau pointed out, and Sienna laughed because that was the exact memory she had been thinking of.

"No," she agreed. "But it was fun with you."

"You know what's also fun with me?" Beau asked and answered before Sienna could. "California."

She sighed. "I already had to ask Henry to help at Maloney's tonight. We'll talk about it tomorrow."

"Fine," Beau said with little defeat.

There was enough background noise and thumps that Sienna could hear Beau was busy even with all the rushing people in the stadium. "What are you up to tonight?"

"I'm . . . " Beau paused. "I've got some of the guys here. Movie night. We're, uh, putting a projector up."

Sienna knitted her brow. "Sounds like a heavy projector."

"Yeah," Beau's tone grew rushed. "Listen, enjoy the concert. Let me know when you get home."

Sienna stared confusingly at the phone in her hand when he hung up, unsure of how it felt to have Beau end a call so quickly. But she didn't have time to think too much about it because Grace and Lilah were in front of her, donning matching shirts and shaking with excitement.

"Floor seats!" Grace shrieked over and over as they made their way into the arena as the lighting began to dim.

Sienna sucked in a nervous breath. *Have fun for her,* she reminded herself. She gripped her phone tightly, afraid to lose it in the sea of the screaming crowd. She stepped even closer to the girls. She was more afraid of losing them than her phone but wanted to text Henry and check in.

I'd call but I can't hear anything. Everything ok?

"We are *so* close!"

Everyone is so close, Sienna said to herself. She tried to apologize to someone she bumped into but couldn't even hear her voice over the music.

Henry texted back. **Do we have more rum?**

Rum? Sienna couldn't remember the last rum drink she had poured at Maloney's. It was usually a low-shelf vodka and whiskey type of crowd.

Check stockroom.

"Mom!" Grace's voice was nearly a hum over the music. She looked annoyingly at Sienna's phone.

Sienna quickly opened her camera. "Look here," she shouted to Grace and Lilah.

After she had taken the photo and the girls turned to face the stage again, Sienna held the phone in her hand, staring at the image. *Another moment,* she thought silently. *Another living moment she gets. First concert.* Sienna wanted to stare at the photo forever—at the way Grace's smile stretched ear to ear, how she held one arm up in excitement, the other wrapped tightly around her friend. With the fluorescent lights beaming down from the top of the stadium, Sienna could feel the *life* radiating from the photo. It made her heart burst with joy and twist with anxiety. *More concerts,* Sienna wished. *More happiness and joy and living.*

"Mom!" Grace screamed again, holding her hand out, beckoning.

Live with her, Sienna reminded herself. How many sad, difficult memories had she been focusing on since the fateful day of Grace's diagnosis? How many moments—beautiful, joyful, even if they were bittersweet—did she miss by thinking of the past? She could hear Beau's voice float through her mind.

"I don't spend too much time celebrating in the moment. Seconds later, you might miss something great."

Pocketing the phone, Sienna took Grace's hand and let her daughter spin her in the minuscule space they occupied in the thick crowd.

Sienna didn't know any of the words to the songs—she didn't even like the music that she realized she was *far* too old for. But what she wasn't too old for was having fun and dancing, twirling her daughter, and hearing her loud, living laughter over booming instruments and electronic beats.

Sienna had thought that since it was after eleven, both Lilah and Grace might pass out from exhaustion during the drive home, but instead, a replay of the entire concert bounced around Sienna's car.

"Turn it down," Sienna told Grace. "The ringing in my ears was *almost* gone."

"Can you believe it? We were *right* there! I can't get over it. It was like a dream."

The swooning in Grace's voice made Sienna smile from the driver's seat. She was over the music but not over her daughter's happiness.

Lilah sighed in agreement. "This was seriously the *best* night ever."

Sienna stared at the girls in the rearview mirror. *Thank you, Beau.* She knew that even if they sat in the nosebleed seats as planned, it would've been a great night. But Beau had gone and made an unforgettable one.

Pulling up to Lilah's house, both girls got out, and she was thankful to see a yawn from Grace. "Don't stay up too late watching all those videos over and over," she said, waving at Lilah's mother, who opened the front door. "Call me when you want to be picked up tomorrow."

"I love you!" Grace yelled out over her shoulder.

Sienna waited until both girls were inside the house and sighed. There were a few things Grace asked for that she could say no to these days. Time with friends, even if it meant spending the night apart, was not on that list. So, when Grace asked to spend the night at Lilah's after the concert, Sienna happily said yes, planning to go to Maloney's to relieve Henry and help her staff close out for the night.

Still a few blocks away from the bar, Sienna could hear the noise—music *thumping*. At first, she thought it might be coming from one of the many cars that took up all the spaces—including the one she normally parked in right out front.

"What the hell?"

The line wrapped around the corner caught her attention, and she slowed as she drove by, her mouth gaping as she saw what could have been a hundred—or maybe more—people waiting outside *her* bar. She turned into the alley, where she was certain she could park, but instead found Beau's truck and a loud, bright-yellow sports car she didn't recognize.

Leaving her car behind Beau's, Sienna sprinted to the front entrance.

"Hey, lady, there's a line, and you're cutting it!"

"This is *my* bar."

At the front of the line, Sienna found Henry focused on a clipboard while balancing a large jar of cash between his legs.

"Cover is ten, and that includes one Dole Whip piña colada. If you can't do ten, cover is five, no drink. If you really can't do five, we'll take whatever you've got. But don't be stingy, tonight is for sick kids," Henry said, not looking up from the board. "Entrance fees will be matched—"

"Cover? We don't have entrance fees!" Sienna hissed.

Henry looked up from his clipboard. "Oh. Oh. Shit." He pressed his lips together before his eyes flicked to the line of people behind a fuming Sienna. "It was Beau's idea."

"What is this?" She pointed at the money. "What are you doing? You're supposed to be—"

Henry stood on his toes, ignoring his sister. "Next!" He took the twenty dollars from the couple at the front of the line, handing them bracelets before unclipping the velvet rope. "You need to wait," he told the next woman in line. "We've got a fire code to abide by."

"A fire code?" Sienna asked, completely lost. All of Brookwood could probably fit in Maloney's without worrying about the fire code. "Henry! Who are all these people?"

"Didn't you hear?" The man who had just passed through Henry's barricade asked over his shoulder. "Sparks are in town."

Sienna's eyes widened, boring into her brother, who shuffled awkwardly, focusing on the tally he kept on the clipboard. "Do you . . . want a bracelet?" he offered, avoiding eye contact.

Sienna hopped over the rope, pushing open the door. She huffed at the comments coming about her cutting the line. *I own the place!* She wanted to scream. But when Sienna stepped into Maloney's, she wasn't sure if she was even at her bar anymore.

"Oh, you made it. You've got to try the Dole Whip floats," Frank said, his voice just loud enough for her to hear. "We'll need to order more rum tomorrow though."

Sienna wanted to grab Frank's arm as he passed by and demand answers, but the shock seized her. She didn't know where to look—at the crowd of people or the shirtless grown men dancing on the bar top in football pants.

What the hell?

It took three people bumping into Sienna for her to shut her mouth. Sienna shook her head, eyes scanning. Behind one large shirtless man was Beau singing along and dancing as he stood behind the bar, pouring shots of rum into plastic cups of Dole Whips. He was about to stick a plastic spoon into one cup when he saw her, and his eyes widened larger than a deer caught in headlights.

Sienna took a deep breath and began to fight her way deeper into the crowd so she could get to Beau and wring his neck.

"Sienna!" Beau called out. He tapped one of the men dancing on the bar before pointing at her. The man held out his hand, which Sienna looked at skeptically before accepting, letting out a gasp as he pulled her up onto the bar top so Beau could help her down the other side.

With his cautious eyes and his brown hair sticking out through the opening arch of his backward baseball cap, Beau resembled the five-year-old who once had to tell his mother he and Sienna broke a vase in the living room while conducting an experiment on gravity.

"How mad?" Beau offered her a cup of Dole Whip.

Still flustered, Sienna shook her head. From behind the bar, she could see *more* dancers at the back, and in front of her, all she could see were thick sweaty bodies as they continued to dance and taunt the bellowing, excited crowd.

"Did. . . did you just turn my bar into a strip club?"

Beau fiddled with his hat. "I was going more for the Chippendales vibe." Since Sienna didn't accept the Dole Whip, he gave it a quick swirl and spooned some into his mouth before directing her attention to the bar top. "Running back. Safety. Tight end," he continued, pointing at each of the men on the bar. "Offensive lineman." Beau pointed at the rather large man in the middle, whose confidence wasn't inhibited by the fact that his stomach hung well over the waist of the bottom of his football uniform.

"Defensive backs and wideouts in the back. Quarterback is DJing, but honestly, he's been playing '80s jams most of the night, so I think we might have to sub him out."

Sienna looked around. "And *why* are they here?"

"You needed an influx of cash," Beau said. "And you wouldn't take *mine*. And these guys have been working hard all week. They wanted a little fun. Their Dole Whips are on the house, by the way."

"So, you made them strip."

Beau rolled his eyes. "I'm not a *pimp*. Just a guy helping his girl out is all." Beau took another scoop. "This is the fun crowd, don't worry. They like to let loose. But I've got the other guys contributing even though they couldn't come tonight."

"What?" Sienna asked exasperatedly, bringing a hand to her head. "*What* are you talking about, Beau?"

"One sec." He turned to the machine on the counter and began to fill more Dole Whip cups when Frank approached with a tray, waiting.

She sighed, picking up the bottle of rum. "You pour too slow."

"Don't worry," Beau said, reaching for a rag to wipe away a drop of ice cream that hit the counter. "We'll clean up. How was the concert? Did the girls have a blast?"

"Are you seriously making small talk with me right now?" she asked when Frank took the tray.

"Giles!" Between the dancing players and the music, Sienna hadn't noticed that at the far end of the bar was another of Beau's teammates. "Meet Sienna. Sienna, this is Giles, the team's second-best wide receiver. He also bartended during the off-season when we were at Florida State. No one makes better Jell-O shots."

Sienna's eyes bounced between the two of them.

"This place is great," Giles said. "Hope you don't mind us doing our thing. We wanted to help out."

Help out? "Yeah, thanks," was all she could manage before Beau took her hand.

"You got it up here for a minute?" Beau asked Giles. "I need my fifteen."

"Oh, you work here now?" Sienna asked as he tugged her toward the back, leading her to the hallway where the noise was still loud but muffled.

"I know you're kind of mad—"

"I'm . . . " *I'm what?* Sienna didn't know *what* she was because she had no idea what was going on. "What . . . what exactly are you doing here?"

Beau chewed on his bottom lip and fiddled with his baseball hat. "You wanted a cash influx. Then you can pay your people, fix the dishwasher, take a *break*, whatever."

Sienna peeked over her shoulder at the jam-packed bar. "They all *paid* to get in here?" she asked. "To see you guys?"

"Is that so hard to believe?" Beau asked, sticking his hands on his hips. "We're the Dallas Sparks, for god's sake."

Sienna looked back at Beau. "So you what? Told them your girlfriend wouldn't go on vacation with you because she's too broke to pay for someone to cover for her at work?"

Beau shook his head. "No. I told them that if they matched all the money the bar brings in tonight, they drink for free and get to choose the music." He groaned when Gloria Estefan's "Everlasting Love" began to blast through the speakers. "Remind me not to do that next time."

"Why would they match anything? And match it for what? I don't want—"

"Relax," Beau interrupted her. "You keep the bar money. Don't be greedy. You probably could put a dent in Grace's hospital bills with that."

Sienna squinted. "Then what's their money for?"

"The Golden Penny Foundation. We'll do a team contribution."

Sienna swallowed. "Beau—"

"It'll never be enough," Beau continued. "Disney World. Football games. Concerts. All that shit. Because wishes for sick kids are *priceless*."

Spasms seized Sienna's chest and made her sway. Beau

noticed, reaching out to steady her by the arm. But the contractions simmered into a slower, steady beat, one that matched Beau's pulse, which Sienna could feel through his grip. Shaking her arm free, Sienna jumped, tugging him down for a kiss, one full and deep, filled with the capacity for something she hadn't felt in a long time—hope.

"You make it hard to be mad at you."

Holding her securely by the waist, Beau leaned back. "I thought if I told you about it, you'd say no."

Sienna shook her head, lowering down to flat feet. "No." She looked back at the crowd. "But do I need a permit for the strippers though?"

Beau put his hand on his hips. "They're *not* strippers. And considering the sheriff's wife and her book club are all here, I'd say you're good."

Sienna laughed. "Give me that," she tugged at the bottom of his jersey before taking her shirt off. "Quick. Before someone confuses *me* for an exotic dancer."

Beau lifted his arms, reaching back to pull his jersey off.

"This is my thank you." Sienna smiled. "Me in your jersey again."

Shirtless, Beau leaned against the wall, smirking. "Yeah. But you're ditching the jeans after this."

Sienna bent down, retrieving Beau's hat that had fallen off and placing it back on his head. "If you're lucky. Come on." She took his hand, tugging him. "We've got money to raise. And I actually *love* this song."

For the next few hours, Beau and Sienna laughed and danced behind the bar to awful '80s music, dodging sweaty, dancing players as they slid drinks across to paying customers. When the night dwindled, Sienna told Beau she was going to the bathroom, but instead, she ran to the back, where she found the Sparks' quarterback.

"Can you play 'Everlasting Love' one more time?" she asked, handing him a Dole Whip, which he gratefully took. She gave him an appreciative shoulder squeeze and returned to the bar.

Beau tilted his head up to the ceiling when the song came on. "Again with this song?" he groaned before yelling out to his teammates, "Someone give Gordon a sack and get him away from the sound system!"

Sienna tugged his hand to dance. "Yes. Again," she told him. *And hopefully forever this time.*

Several weeks later, Sienna was standing in the hallway, eyeing the duffle bag she had packed sitting at the front door. *It's too much,* she thought about the long weekend Beau was about to take her on in California. *He's doing too much.*

In addition to buying a new fridge, bringing in several thousands of dollars for Maloney's, and making a substantial contribution to the Golden Penny Foundation, there had been countless dates, including two more after hours visits to the planetarium, a trip to the rodeo, which—much to the happiness of Sienna's heart—included Grace.

But a long weekend—even though Sienna was craving the uninterrupted alone time with him—seemed like too much.

"Are you sure?"

"If you ask me that one more time, I'll go with Beau, and *you* can stay here." Grace was in the kitchen, facing away from Sienna, who nervously tapped her foot. "I can take care of Uncle Henry for three days," she muttered sarcastically.

Sienna folded her arms across her chest. "It's just—"

"Mom." Grace turned. "*Go.*"

Peeking at the front door, Sienna gnawed on the inside of her cheek. Beau was outside, waiting in the car. It *was* only three days, and Sienna had managed to hire a part-time bartender at

Maloney's so Frank wouldn't be left alone. She looked back at the counter—a master list of everything regarding Grace for Henry—which Sienna realized at the moment was quite short. She *was* a teenager. Apart from making sure she took her medication and supplements and did her homework, there wasn't much instruction left to give.

Did I buy the right orange juice? Sienna wondered, heading to the fridge. Grace only liked the kind without pulp.

Grace blocked her. "Go."

"I've never been away from you for this long," Sienna admitted. Sleepovers, now that Grace was healthy, still kept Sienna awake most of the night.

"It's not my fault you're a loser," Grace reminded her with a smile. "I'm just kidding," she sang. "But *go* already, would you? What if you miss the flight?"

"I'll wait until Henry is out of the shower."

"Mom—"

Sienna held up her hands. "Alright." She wrapped Grace up in a hug. "Be good." *Go now,* she told herself, squeezing her daughter's arm. "Henry, I'm leaving!"

"You should've left twenty minutes ago!" her brother shouted from down the hall.

Quickly, Sienna grabbed her duffle and purse and stepped outside, making her way to the black town car Beau was leaning against.

"Everything alright?" he asked, taking the bag from her.

Sienna apologized, sliding in. Beau closed her door and stepped around the car, entering from the other side.

"I hope I didn't make us too late. It's just . . . " She looked back at the house. "I've only ever been away from her for one night at a time. And that was *her* doing, and it's still kind of a new thing."

Beau squeezed her hand. "I feel bad I'm making it hard for you. I'm being selfish. I need you alone for a few days. I'm sure they'll remember to turn off the stove after using it, but do you want to go stick a post it on the back splash to remind them in case?"

Sienna let out a small laugh. "No. No. They'll be fine. I need this too. We won't miss the flight, will we?"

"No," Beau said, rolling her fingers between his.

A soft smile spread across his face, and Sienna leaned against the headrest, turning to him.

"What are you thinking about?"

Beau drew lazy circles on the top of her hand. "I'm just excited to be with you. Take that trip we never took."

Sienna's sigh was laced with a bittersweet taste, thinking back to fifteen years ago, to the innocent naivete Sienna and Beau held when they planned to do everything in one summer as if money and time were no object. They would make it to Disney World, the ocean, and Houston to visit NASA. Yet none of those things had been checked off the wish list before Beau left.

But here they were, in the back of a town car on their way to tick off the literal biggest—nothing was larger than the ocean. Sienna looked back at the house as they pulled away from the curb, seeing the roof where she and Beau used to lie at night.

Better late than never.

"It's hard to make up for a decade in three days."

"You don't have to make up for anything." Sienna shook her head. "We're *past* that."

She held his eyes, hoping her gaze showed she harbored no hate, no resentment. *How could I?* she wondered, thinking of Grace. *If you never left, there might have never been her. Some things just work out the way they're supposed to.*

"I'm serious. I want you to stop thinking that you need to do all these big things to apologize. Actually, I'd *hate* to think you're doing all this just because you feel guilty." Her gut sank at the thought.

"That's not why."

Sienna nodded. *I want to believe you,* she thought. *I want to believe you so badly. And I'm here trying to do just that.* She turned her head toward the window, watching as the small town of Brookwood melted into fields of meadows beginning to bloom.

"It needed to be now," Beau said from beside her. "All of it. I can't . . . I can't quite explain it to you, but it needed to be now, even though I've been thinking about all these things for *years*."

She looked back at Beau.

"You don't believe me?" he asked.

"It's not that . . . " she felt the driver's stare through the rearview mirror. "Not now, alright?"

I don't need another person feeling sorry for me.

Sienna focused on the drive. "This isn't the way to DFW."

"That's because it's not."

"What airport are we going to then?"

"A smaller one."

What Beau meant by a smaller one was an airport reserved for private charter flights. Half an hour later, the town car pulled up, checking in at the gate before proceeding to drive straight to the private jet.

"All set, sir," the driver said, putting the car into park and exiting the vehicle.

Sienna had been staring at the jet so hard she didn't realize he had opened her door. "Beau—"

Beau swung an arm around her shoulder when she stepped out. "Come on."

"You can't be serious." Sienna tugged him to a halt and shook her head. "You have a *plane*?"

"No. I don't *have* a plane. But there's one here that happens to be waiting to take us to LA."

Sienna didn't know what to think. "Why didn't we fly commercial?"

"I told you long ago," he began, his voice lowering. "You and me, we're too tall for the regular mile-high club." He motioned his head toward the plane, holding his hand out for Sienna.

"What. . . "

And then she remembered. In between heated kisses and overstrung teenage hormones, Beau and Sienna had snuck a few naughty items on their wish list—like sex on a plane. She burst into a fit of laughter.

"What's so funny?"

Pressing a hand to her chest, she stifled her giggles. "I must've really made you feel bad for you to work so hard for it."

Beau cracked a grin, nudging her with his hip as they walked to the plane. He pulled her closer, dropping a kiss into her hair. "Don't apologize. Turns out, I kind of like the chase."

chapter sixteen

BEAU DIDN'T JUST like the chase and pursuit of Sienna—he lived for it. Nothing made Beau happier than witnessing the shock and joy that radiated from her with every surprise he pulled out of his hat in an effort, not just to make amends or win her back, to prove she never was the thing he left behind without a doubt.

He had left her behind with too many doubts and too much regret and spent many nights awake wondering about all the missed opportunities—things beyond *her* wish list, ones that included *his* dreams.

All the things Sienna hoped to do in her life were eclectic, mismatched, symbolic of the adventurous little girl who was once his closest friend, the daring side of her teenage personality she thought she had lost when her mother died. There was Dole Whip and sailboats. A fancy five-course meal and a motorcycle ride. Flying high in the sunset and sinking into the dark ocean.

Beau's dreams had a bottom line in common—they all included Sienna.

Football had been *Greg's* dream Beau had silently vowed to fulfill. But what Beau had wished for was *more*—more laughter and memories, breathless kisses and swims in the lake, plans for the future and a family—all with his best friend.

The chase was to get her back, but sitting across from Sienna on the plane, Beau realized everything he did for her brought him a gift as well—learning who Sienna was now. Hardened but compassionate. Cautious but, as he recalled dancing behind the bar the night he hijacked Maloney's, still down for a good time. The quirky things she did made Beau smile—like saved contacts in her phone with the last name first, or how she twirled her right earring when nervous, how her eyes fluttered shut well before he kissed her, as if the anticipation was just as intense as what was coming.

But some things remained the same, even through time, distance, and struggle, like Sienna's listening ear, the ever-present bump in her hair when she tied it back, no matter how hard she smoothed it down. And Beau realized—sitting across from Sienna on the plane with her nose nearly pressed to the window—her love for the endless sky and all the magic and beauty it held.

"You're free to move about the cabin now. Flight time is three hours and ten minutes," the flight attendant said, approaching them. "I'll bring out a cheese plate and the menu for you to look at."

Beau shook his head, not taking his eyes off Sienna. "That can wait, thank you."

"Since when do you say no to cheese?" she teased.

"I'm hungry for something else." Beau tipped back the remaining champagne in the flute and stood, motioning toward the back of the cabin. "*Famished*, actually." He slid open a sleek pocket door, and Sienna followed.

She looked around at the space of the bedroom—the full-sized bed with white sheets and fluffy pillows, the shiny night-stands with matching laps. "Is it still the mile-high club if it's *not* in an airplane bathroom?"

Locking the door, Beau leaned against it, smirking. "I won't tell if you won't," he whispered.

"Wish list," she said, and Beau came up behind her. "I can't remember if it was yours or mine, honestly."

She shivered when Beau pushed her hair to the side, nuzzling the soft skin of her neck.

"Really?" he asked, tasting the space below her ear. "You can't?"

Sienna reached up, winding her hands into Beau's hair, tilting her head back when he nipped at the skin before swiping his tongue to soothe the sting. The soft, sweet moan she let out brought a smile to Beau's face. *Another old thing*, he thought. *She always makes* that *sound when I kiss* right *here.* He hit the spot again, and the noise Sienna released was louder, but Beau didn't smile that time. Instead, he kissed and sucked harder before pulling back, his hands going to her hips to turn her.

"I remember everything," he whispered as if in confession. "Everything we did." Beau wasn't just talking about the nights that tested his dwindling teenage patience and self-control, Sienna writhing beneath him in her bed as they tried—in hindsight, probably not enough—to stay quiet.

Beau was talking about the summer afternoons they spent swimming in the lake, alternating floating along the surface and jumping from the rope swing he had built for her. It was about nights on the roof, where they talked about everything and nothing at the same time. Beau had never let go of those memories. His heart refused to let go of any part of her after his head had made such a drastic mistake.

But at the moment, Beau didn't worry about his heart or his head. This time, he let his body make the decision. His mouth attacked hers furiously, not wasting a moment. And Sienna met him step for step, breath for breath, as she reached for his belt.

"No," he ordered. "You first." Beau stepped back only to lift Sienna's shirt over her head as she whimpered, trying for his belt again.

"Beau—"

Beau swallowed down any objection as his hands crept to her back, unclasping her bra and letting it fall to the ground before sliding back around to her jeans. Sienna panted against him, her hands pulling his hair and sliding down his shoulders and arms. But before she could try again to reach for Beau's pants, he pushed her gently so she fell onto the bed, letting out a small yelp before saying his name again with such wanting his pants grew impossibly tighter.

"Fuck," Beau breathed out, yanking down her underwear and jeans. His eyes spanned Sienna's naked body. She was gnawing on her lip, squeezing her thighs together. Beau grabbed her foot, sliding his hand up her silky calf to pry them open. "Don't ever hide from me." He left a soft kiss on the inside of her ankle, his lips lingering where he could feel Sienna's pulse throbbing, even at the farthest distance from her heart.

"You don't. . . " Her croak turned into a sweet hum as Beau glided his mouth up her bare leg.

Beau sank his teeth into the delicious flesh of her inner thigh, humming happily when Sienna let out a yelp and her hands flew to his hair, clutching his head.

"Who says this is for you?" he asked, lifting his mouth and moving so he was a breath away from her center. "Tasting you. . . " He licked his lips, feeling Sienna's eyes on him. He didn't look away even when she needed to—throwing her head back when his tongue pressed firmly against her. "Watch me. You'll know real quick that *drowning* in you will always be at the top of my wish list."

"Beau..."

His name leaving Sienna's mouth—needy and heavy with want—brought a twitch from Beau's lap against the mattress. But Beau happily continued to drown and drink in Sienna—her taste, her warmth, the quickening of her breathing, how she went from shyly and nervously hiding to anchoring her hands into Beau's locks. Her moans and whimpers as she writhed against him were the song of a siren calling him home and when Sienna met her peak, letting go against his tongue, Beau had to reach down and grip himself through his pants, trying to instill patience. He wanted to linger there, his face nestled between Sienna's legs, lapping, nipping, and kissing until she couldn't take it anymore.

"Beau, please," she whined, squirming.

Quickly, he undressed, leaving a heaving Sienna on the bed with an arm thrown over her eyes.

"No, no," he corrected her again. "Open."

Sienna's dark eyes still seeped with desire—a deepened shade of emerald.

"Look there." Beau pointed at the small window where sunlight broke through the clouds as they flew through the sky. "That's what heaven looks like."

Sienna turned her head, and Beau let her take in the view for a minute before he swept across her body, the contact forcing Sienna to close her eyes with an overwhelmed sigh. Her hips jutted against him, but Beau held off, shifting to the side and pressing his face to hers.

"This," he panted, fighting to keep the rein on his dwindling control. He pressed his lips—still glossy from her—to Sienna's. "This is what heaven tastes like."

He let the taste roll off his tongue, feeding it deeper into Sienna's mouth as she groaned, as if he were pouring the most delicious drink down her throat. Beau's hand danced up her body to break the kiss, his mouth sliding to her shoulder where the sun illuminated the cluster of freckles on her skin, a tiny galaxy with more stars than Beau could ever want because he finally had everything he would ever need.

He traced the cluster with his tongue before Sienna's hands brought his face back to hers.

"And this…" Beau tilted his hips, sliding inside her. Her fingers flexed at his back, nails piercing his skin. Beau hissed, halting, leaning his forehead to hers.

"I know," Sienna breathed against his lips. "I know."

With a heavy gulp, Beau asked, "Do you, though?"

When he began to move within her, Sienna couldn't answer with anything other than the small rise of her hips, the lightest of gasps mingling with his more powerful ones. And as Beau's pace picked up, his own noises intensified, pouring from his mouth with the force of a Hail Mary pass thrown down from the opposite end of the field.

"Fuck, Sienna. I'll be damned if this isn't what heaven feels like."

With Sienna sleeping heavily on her stomach, Beau remained on his side, propped on an elbow. He reached out, letting his finger dance up and down the valley of her spine, smirking when Sienna shivered and scooted closer to him. He pressed light kisses onto her shoulder, his nose grazing her skin, inhaling her delicate scent. Beau smiled when he recognized that some of his own was mixed in with hers too.

Sienna hummed, mumbling something that got lost in the pillow.

"What did you say?" Beau asked, not bothering to remove his mouth from her skin. *A drug. She's like a drug I've been clean of for fifteen fucking years.*

"Everyone needs to do that before they die."

Beau's tongue began to trace light circles that drew goose bumps. "Do what?"

"Sex thirty thousand feet in the air. You were right. It *was* heaven." Sienna giggled when Beau blew a warm breath across the plain of goosebumps.

He sighed, replacing his mouth with his hand when he slid up to her. "No. About that . . . I was wrong."

Sienna knit her brow tightly together. Beau ignored the soft frown lines, focusing on the pout of her pillowy lips, her tangled hair, and the way her eyes sparkled in the aftermath of their lovemaking.

"This is heaven," he said quietly. "Just you and me."

Her eyes softened, and she ran her hand down the side of his face. "It is, right?"

Beau kissed her palm and nodded into it, still not liking the pout that didn't leave her face. "What's wrong?"

"I just . . . I want to stay right here. I don't want it to end."

The uncertainty in her voice tugged violently at Beau's heart, and he covered her hand with his own. *It doesn't have to. I need you to believe that. Believe in me, believe in us, and it won't. Please stop looking at me like you'll think I'll vanish.* But the look on Sienna's face didn't fade, and Beau squirmed uncomfortably. *I broke her. I left her. She had to go through all of it alone.*

"We'll run out of gas at some point," Beau offered, trying to lighten the heavy moment. But the look on Sienna's face didn't falter. "I promise. We're just getting started, alright? I know you love to have your head in the clouds, I'm here to lay the world at your feet. Nothing makes me happier than seeing you happy. Nothing. No draft, no contract, no game or win. Nothing will ever compare to *this*." Quickly, he kissed her. "I'll pull out of the contract if you want me to." Sienna's eyes widened, but Beau continued, "I know it's only a year, but it's a lot."

Beau chewed on the inside of his cheek. Preseason was approaching, and it meant he would be tied to an intense, rigorous schedule from essentially July into January. It meant there would be little time for impromptu drop-ins at Maloney's, that he would be on the road a few days a week.

It means less time for us.

He squeezed Sienna's side tightly as the realization made his chest constrict.

"No," she told him, her eyes dropping from his. "You have one more year left. We have. . . "

"What? We have what?"

Sienna focused on the space between them, winding her fingers with his. "We have forever after."

"I've been waiting for the forever part for a long time, you know? I'm sorry it took me so long to start."

Sienna shook her head against the pillow. "Beau, don't—"

"I can't *not*. I *hate* that I didn't choose you."

"We were kids," she reminded him. "We were young and had no idea how any of this would work. And besides. . . "

"Grace," Beau said. "I know."

He thought back to the final game of last season just a few short months ago, about the lanky, tall girl with the wig who appeared nervous as she walked out from the tunnel flanked by Golden Penny Foundation representatives. But the twisting hands and anxious steps disappeared when Grace and Beau made eye contact, their dark eyes locking and doing something to Beau's heartbeat—giving it a jump.

He hadn't seen Sienna at that point, but Beau realized he had felt her through her daughter. When their dark brown eyes held each other's, it was as if they both said, "It's okay now."

Sienna pulled her hand free and pressed it against his chest. "I don't want to keep thinking about *hurt.* I don't even want to *think* anymore. I've spent years thinking, about cancer, about chemo, about hospital bills." She sighed. "I just want to *live,* you know? I wish I could be that girl with her head in the clouds instead of the one on the cold, hard, realistic ground. . . " She stopped, her lips flattening and tipping into a grin as she peeked out the window behind him. "Well, damn, Beau. You made that come true too."

Beau laughed. "We have three days, just us. Lots of fun. Lots of adventure."

"Like what?" Sienna asked.

"Surprises." He wiggled his eyebrows, pushing back and reaching down for his underwear.

"That looks so painful." She motioned to the scar on his leg. "You never told me what happened."

"Swerved to avoid a pothole right on a gear change. Bike spun out and landed right on my leg. Bone popped right through the skin. It was ugly."

Sienna flinched, and he could tell she was trying hard to hide her grimace. "And you *kept* riding?" she asked, the shock in her voice heavy.

"I did."

"That's terrifying. I never would've gotten back on if that happened to me."

Beau laughed, shaking his head. "When I told you I remembered *everything*, I wasn't lying. I kept riding because I promised to make that wish come true for you. I had to be ready just in case. . . "

"Just in case what?"

Beau bent over so his face was to hers. "Just in case the stars aligned one day and you'd gave me another chance. Or I grew balls and showed up and didn't take no for an answer. Whatever came first."

He pressed his lips to hers before straightening, accidentally stepping on the pile of Sienna's clothes where her phone was. Reaching down, Beau grabbed it, smiling at the photo of her and Grace before handing it to Sienna.

I guess the stars aligned after all.

"We hope you enjoyed your flight, Mr. Walker, Ms. Clarke," the flight attendant said as they approached the door.

Sienna giggled under her breath "They have no idea."

"Perfect flight. Thanks for the lift," Beau said before reaching the steps. "Be quiet," he hushed Sienna, taking her hand. "Or you might earn yourself a reputation among the charter flight staff."

Sienna's hand slipped from Beau's before their feet hit the tarmac. "Please tell me that's for us."

Blinded by the California sunshine, Beau squinted to see the bright red convertible. "If you're going to do the Pacific Coast Highway, you might as well do it right. For the record, it's not the one from *Ferris Bueller's Day Off*. But it's a similar model."

Sienna skipped down the stairs, pushing him aside, her long blonde hair trailing behind in the breeze. She stopped a few feet from the car, admiring it and Beau moved past her.

"What do you think you're doing?" she asked when he reached for the driver's side door.

Beau held his hands up and backed away. "Sorry," he apologized, walking around the car as Sienna jumped into the driver's seat, squealing when she turned on the ignition and the car roared to life.

Sienna shook her head, and Beau watched as her hands ghosted over the steering wheel. She sighed, leaning her head against the seat and turning to Beau. "Wish list?"

"Wish list."

Sienna looked back at the dash, the gear, and the interior's well-conditioned brown leather, which even Beau was impressed by. She pressed her lips together, shaking her head, and he could practically hear Sienna ask herself, "How is any of this real?"

"I told you," Beau said, clearing his throat, and he waited for Sienna to turn back to him. "I'll spend the rest of my life laying the world at your feet if you'd just let me. And that's not just because I'm sorry. That's because all these things. . . you're the only one I want to do them with."

Sienna took a deep breath and nodded.

"Come on, enough wasting time." He motioned to the gear. "Let's see what this baby's got in her."

A smile crept across Sienna's mouth, each minuscule moment and movement lighting up her entire face. *Like the sunrise,* Beau thought, but before he could let himself enjoy just *how* beautiful and happy Sienna looked in that moment, she slid into first gear, and they flew out of the parking lot.

★★★★★

"Okay, hold up. Slow down, or we'll miss it." Beau pointed. "That one."

Sienna slowed the car. "*On* the beach?"

"Ocean backyard, baby," Beau said, eyeing the white house as Sienna pulled into the driveway.

Sienna didn't seem to care about the house because after she turned off the engine, she jumped out of the car and ran around it.

Beau hopped out of the convertible. "Wait!" he called to her with a laugh, though unsure why.

If Sienna's dream was to see the ocean, surely he wasn't going to stop her when they were just yards away. He sighed and grabbed their luggage and her purse, walking up the flight of steps to the balcony and pushing the side door open.

The open floor plan allowed him to see just about everything the home had to offer—a modest but sleek kitchen, a small living area with a large white couch. There were three doors that Beau assumed led to the bedrooms. He dropped the bags outside one and placed Sienna's purse on the counter next to a welcome basket. When he looked up, he was reminded he hadn't brought Sienna to Malibu for the house.

The floor-to-ceiling windows let in light and a view that stopped Beau in his tracks—the seemingly endless sea and sky and the point at which they met.

Beau stepped onto the porch that wrapped around the back

of the house. He ignored the four lounge chairs, the small grill, and the hot tub. Instead, Beau went to the railing, leaning against the smooth wood. The ocean and its rolling waves, the squawks of seagulls, and the beauty of the horizon might have taken his breath away, but Sienna standing on the beach, her long blonde hair tangling in the wind, forced Beau to stop swallowing lungfuls of crisp ocean air.

Beau had spent time in Malibu before—a close escape from his home in Los Angeles years ago while he played for the Bulls. He had surfed, walked along the beach, and watched the sunset with a beer on the back deck of a house not too far from where he currently stood. But he had done all those things in solitude—with no one by his side and only his brother Greg on his mind. And though the beauty of Malibu had been rejuvenating, allowing Beau to rest and recover, the solitude made it seem like a dream instead of real life.

Even though Beau was looking out on the same ocean, his hair blowing in the same wind, it hit differently watching Sienna, who wasn't wasting a moment. The enthusiastic energy radiated so intensely off her body that Beau could feel it from thirty yards away. He thought back to Grace's letter and a line that struck him to his core.

I've never actually been afraid of dying. I'm afraid of missing out on all the things I should do while I'm living.

"Like mother like daughter," Beau said aloud as Sienna stood on the sandy shore, taking in the moment where her wish came true, and Beau wanted to wish with a hope as deep as the ocean at her feet that nothing could be truer than the saying "better late than never."

Loosening his grip on the railing, Beau headed toward stairs that led down to the beach, not wanting to waste any more breaths or seconds of what precious time he had with her. But with each step he took toward her, Sienna stepped farther away, closer to the dark, chilly ocean, losing pieces of clothing along the way.

Her sweater.

Her shirt.

Her sneakers and socks.

"Sienna, that water is freezing. Wait!" Beau screamed, taking three steps at a time.

But no amount of footwork Beau had completed could prepare him for how fast Sienna sprinted to the ocean. He expected her to stop when the water swept at her knees, and she did. She looked back at him briefly, only to turn and dive under a rushing wave.

"Sienna!"

Beau stumbled out of his sneakers. "Shit," he gritted out when his feet got stuck in his jeans. He couldn't be bothered to lose the T-shirt he wore beneath his sweatshirt and scrambled to the water where he couldn't see any part of her—no mop of hair, no warm, creamy skin, or long limb.

But when Beau dove into the frigid ocean, the tide's pull brought his body right up against hers, as if the sea knew that no matter how hard he might fight a current or an undertow, he would find her.

"You're fucking crazy!" he shouted, spitting a mouthful of salty water to the side and grabbing her arm.

Sienna merely continued to tread water against him, her mouth parted, lips already tinged blue. Beau was about to drag her back when her free hand came up to his face, her legs now working harder, knocking into his own.

"I feel like I just woke up."

The goosebumps on Beau's body protruded so strongly from his skin, they felt like knives piercing through. "You what?" His chest heaved, and his muscles tightened. "Are you out of your mind? You—"

Sienna did more than swallow Beau's words. Her kiss warmed his entire body beneath the surface. Suddenly there were no more goosebumps. And even though a moment ago Beau would've done just about anything to get them out of the water, suddenly he wanted to stay wrapped up in Sienna's impossible warmth and float in the freezing ocean forever.

"Maybe." Sienna pulled back from the kiss. "Because I'm still in love with you."

Beau didn't know if his heart stopped beating from the water's temperature or her words.

Sienna reached for his free hand beneath the surface, tugging him back toward the shore. "Come on."

They swam with the tide until their feet hit the sand, their chattering teeth even louder than the roaring surf of the Pacific behind them.

"H-h-holy shit, holy shit." Sienna leaned into Beau's body as if it had any warmth left to give. But she didn't seem to care that it didn't or that their clothes had already blown down the beach.

"Sh-shower."

Beau pointed to the side of the house, and they stumbled in the sand before Beau reached for the door's latch, turned on the hot water, and yanked Sienna under the piping hot stream. Hugging her to him, he rested his trembling chin on her head, their bodies panting, heaving, and clinging together.

But suddenly, the teakwood of the shower door Beau faced transformed into a tree in his childhood backyard, the one Sienna had convinced him not just to climb but to jump out of. He wasn't thirty-four, but seven, clinging to Sienna, who had run over to him and hugged him tightly when she realized he was okay. But before the pain even registered, a smile came to Beau's face as he realized that who was beside you through it all—the fun, laughter, fear, pain, and heartache—was the most important thing.

As a kid, Sienna could make Beau smile even though he had a busted ankle.

As a teenager, Sienna could be the ear that took everything in when no one else would listen.

And as a man, Sienna could thaw his frozen heart with something as simple as her words.

Beau shook off the image of how the sky looked that day and tilted Sienna's head up. "Say it again."

She was still trembling, her lips just beginning to let go of their blue shade. "I love you. I never stopped," Sienna whispered, just loud enough for Beau to hear over the shower. "I only wish that I had been brave enough to tell you sooner."

chapter seventeen

SIENNA HAD NEVER FELT WARMER than the moment she broke through the surface of the chilly ocean. It took a little more oxygen to realize *what* she had actually done—stripped down to her bra and underwear on the beach and plunged into sixty-something-degree water. But before reality struck her, all Sienna could do was focus on Beau bobbing beside her and how good it felt to float and be weightless, something small and nearly invisible in the endless ocean, under the brightest star in the sky—the sun.

But as they stood in the shower and effortlessly passed words of affirmation and promises between them—in only the way it could be between two old friends—Sienna didn't think about how the future might look—if Beau was in Dallas or California—only how it *felt* when they were together. Sienna had never given much thought to reincarnation, but with Beau around, suddenly, she felt reborn. His stubbled jaw pressed into her neck when he smiled against it, the way his hands always knew *how* to hold her, and the look in his deep brown eyes that always let Sienna know he was up to something.

All of it had recharged her so much that she hadn't understood exactly how drained her battery had been.

As they remained under the shower's stream and Beau told

her, "I swear, I never stopped loving you," she wondered if he knew that coming back didn't just give *them* a second chance, it gave Sienna one too.

Hours later, dried and changed into comfortable, cozy sweats, Sienna sat on a lounge chair under the fading sun as Beau grilled, taking sips of beer between flipping burgers and turning kebab skewers. The sight of him—barefoot against the wooden deck, hoodie zipped shut, joggers low on his hips—brought a smile to her face. But Sienna didn't need the backdrop of the ocean, the smoothness of the deck, or the shiny gas grill to feel *happy*. She would have the same smile seeing Beau on the pavers in her backyard, using the charcoal grill that had been at the house since her dad had bought it almost twenty years ago.

"What will it be like?" Sienna asked after they had cleared the dishes. She was back in her lounge chair, watching Beau look for the switch to the small fire pit.

"What?" Beau asked, finally finding it. He backed away from the flame, watching it for a moment before moving to the chair, easing behind Sienna.

She hummed with delight as she leaned against him. "When the season starts."

"Do you want to talk about that now?"

"Do you know what the hardest part of Grace's cancer was for me? It was full of surprises, and I'm not even talking about the diagnosis. You get your treatment plan and *hope* for the best possible outcome. But sometimes, she was too sick or too weak for chemo. Her blood count would plummet, and they'd have to hold off until she was strong enough for it. Or she'd get an infection from being so immunosuppressed. A cold nearly killed her."

Beau brought an arm across Sienna's chest, squeezing her shoulder.

"The unknown and I. . . we're not very good friends these days."

"Well," Beau began, "it varies week to week, depending on what day we play or if we travel. If it's Sunday, Monday can either be an off day or just film and meetings. Tuesday, then, would be totally off. Practice Wednesday through Friday, an all-day thing with training or meetings sandwiched between. Saturday, if we're home, some walk-throughs, but yeah, all day. Game day, I'm at the stadium a few hours before kickoff."

Sienna laughed.

"What?" Beau asked.

"It's not *so* bad."

"If I'm in Dallas, no, it's not because I can come to you. You'll be at all the home games." He lazily rubbed her arm. "Travel weeks, well, it's different. I'd bring you to every single one if I could. But Grace has school, that might get messy."

Even though they were talking about being away from each other, Beau's mention and thought of her daughter warmed Sienna's heart.

"We'll work something out," Sienna assured him.

"It's just a year. I mean nine-ish months."

"I can do a few more months sharing you." Sienna looked up at him.

Beau dropped a kiss to her lips. "You're stronger than me, then." He tightened his hold on her. "I don't want a day without this."

"Me? Or the sunset over the ocean?" she joked.

"Us," Beau clarified.

The sincerity in his voice and eyes overwhelmed her. He held her face, preventing Sienna from turning away.

"Do you want to know a secret?" he asked quietly.

"What?"

Beau's hand left her face, sliding down her body where he squeezed her waist. Sienna turned and straddled his lap.

"There's a wish I've been holding on to since we were teenagers," he said, his tone playful but deep.

Sienna breathed against his mouth when Beau's hands slipped under her sweatshirt. "Oh yeah? What's that?"

"Me. Inside you. " His mouth slid from her mouth down her

chin, forcing Sienna's eyes to flutter shut . "Outside. Under the stars."

"R-really?" Sienna forced out.

Her head fell back, tilting to the side as Beau ravaged her neck. When Beau's hand slid to her ass, pulling her closer, Sienna rocked her hips into him and opened her eyes. She couldn't see anything more than the partition on the side of the deck.

Sienna felt her entire body flush. "It's not dark yet."

"Then I guess we'll have to kill time," he panted, guiding her movements, slowing them down.

And for nearly an hour, during twilight, Sienna was seventeen—letting her fully-clothed body search for Beau's with delicious fury through barriers. There was heavy panting, deep, messy kisses, stops and starts as she ground her hips into Beau, chasing more of the warmth from their friction. And finally, as the world darkened around them and the stars painted the night sky, Beau lifted Sienna, only removing his hands from her hips to tug his pants down and let Sienna do the same.

She climbed back over him, hovering, the heat of her throbbing burning between her thighs.

She lowered herself, breathing deeply before she asked, "Wish list?"

Her eyes fell shut as she strained to keep herself off him. Beau's fingers dug painfully into her hips.

"Tell me again," he said.

Sienna didn't need to hear it the same way Beau did. Because his eyes said it all already.

"I love you."

Following Beau's lowering gaze, Sienna watched his grip loosen and gasped when Beau lowered her down to take all of him in.

"Now. . . wish list."

Beau kissed each word into her neck and let Sienna rock into him, filling her to the brim. She didn't care that they were outside, that even though it would be hard for anyone to see, plenty could hear. Sienna moaned his name loudly and unapologetically, so overwhelmed by the wholeness and completion that she couldn't move until Beau nipped at her ear and gave her ass a slap before leaning back against the lounge chair.

"Ride it."

With his hands on her hips, Beau let Sienna move how she liked—bigger, slow circles tapering into smaller, frantic ones—every change in Sienna's pace brought a new noise from Beau he buried into her skin, but his words stayed consistent.

"I love you."

Sienna let those words wash up her body, pulling his head closer so there wasn't a breath of space between them. She lifted her head to the sky, while he peppered kisses beneath her jaw, biting hard on her bottom lip, knowing there wasn't anything she could possibly wish for in the moment. Instead, when she hit her breaking point, her body tightening, and Beau continuing to tell her how much he loved her, Sienna made a wish for something to stay away—the pain which accompanied his absence she knew all too well.

I wish you won't break my heart.

Sienna read Grace's response to the photo she had sent her.

Ok changed my mind. NOT FAIR. I want to be there.

Laughing, Sienna texted back.

Next time. Promise.

Sienna put her phone down, pulling the towel from her hair. Her body was sore—from all the lovemaking, from the hike she and Beau went on earlier that day, from walking up and down the beach all afternoon. She didn't want to *stop* moving, stop taking every moment in—the sun, the sand, the surf was all a dream. But with and because of Beau, it was a dream come true.

She fingered the soft duvet as she fell back on the bed, her body still wrapped in a fluffy white towel. The soft sound of the waves lapping at the shores sang through the open window of the bedroom, a lullaby luring Sienna's eyes closed.

And for the first time in what felt like forever, Sienna dreamed of her mother.

They were in the backyard of their home in Nashville. Sienna could remember it perfectly—the grass was dewy, dampening her bare arms and legs. Even though it was nearing midnight, the humidity in the air was thick and palpable. Their mother had dragged Henry and Sienna—begrudgingly—from bed and out of the air conditioning on the eve of their eighth birthday, a little over two months since leaving Brookwood.

"I don't want to do this," Sienna huffed before she yawned. "This is stupid."

Her mother groaned. "Oh, come on, Sienna."

"I wish for a Nintendo 64," Henry said from the other side of their mother.

"Shh," she corrected Henry. "Don't say it out loud."

"It's not even our birthday yet."

"I know," her mother took Sienna's hand, squeezing it in her sweaty palm. "But do you want to know a secret? The night before you were born, I wished for both of you."

Henry laughed. "We were already in your stomach."

"That's true. But you weren't you *yet." Her mother nudged Henry's side. "My smart and cheeky boy," she said before turning to Sienna. She reached out, twirling a long blonde lock around her finger. "Or my wild and fun girl."*

"I wish Beau—" Sienna said quietly.

"Don't say it out loud."

Sienna closed her eyes tightly and kept the refreshed wish in her mind. It wasn't a toy or a video game, the inflatable chair she had been begging her parents for. She closed her eyes, trying to manifest the short boy with the dark, shaggy hair, the one who was there for every knee scrape, who never said no to a bike ride or catching tadpoles. Silently, Sienna begged the stars for another chance to be friends with the person who taught her what the word friend meant in the first place —I wish I could go home to Beau.

Sienna shot up, pressing a hand to her head. The shower was running, and she looked at the time on her phone. *I must've slept an hour*. Reaching for the glass of water on the nightstand, Sienna chugged it, trying to clear the heavy sleep from her fuzzy mind. She stood, walking to the window across from the bed, breathing in the ocean breeze.

"Thought you might still be asleep. I was going to join you." Beau came up behind Sienna, yawning before pressing a kiss to her bare shoulder.

Sienna's head fell forward.

"Are you alright?" Beau asked, stepping to the side and pressing a finger to Sienna's chin.

"I remembered something."

Beau shook his head. "What?"

"The first wish I ever made. . . I remembered the first birthday wish I made under the stars." Sienna stammered. "The first birthday we had in Nashville after we moved—me and Henry. That was the first time my mom ever took us out in the yard to make our birthday wish." She shook her head. "And do you know what? I kept wishing, even after it didn't come true for days, weeks, months. . . until my Mom, she dragged me out of it. She just. . . tried to make life *so* fun and exciting it was impossible to remember I was sad leaving you in the first place." Her heart clenched, and she wrapped her arms around Beau. "I wished I could go home to you. To ride bikes or play tag. Run through the creek. And that came true when she *died*."

Beau held her tightly, cradling the back of her head.

"I died with her that day. A piece of me did," she whispered with brutal honesty. "And when we came back to Brookwood, it was like *you* brought *me* back."

Her mind flooded with memories—the early days after her mother's suicide, the way her father's face never looked the same after the love of his life's death. There was packing up their house in Nashville—the house Sienna had been reluctant to move into but hesitant to leave after her mother had made so many good memories in it that the colonial build had turned into a home. There were the early days back in Brookwood when Sienna contemplated running away, wondering why it was fair for her mother to, but not her.

But it wasn't only the deep and harrowing dark loneliness Sienna remembered—it was Beau leading her out of it.

"This," Sienna said, wiping at the flood of tears she had left in the valley of Beau's collarbone. "This has to last forever this time. I can't afford another tragedy to be the reason we find each other again. My mom. Grace." Sienna shook her head fervently. "Our love has to be the reason we *stay* this time."

Beau cupped her face. "It is. I'm not going anywhere, alright? I swear," he promised into her ear as he pulled Sienna back in.

There was a solid reassurance in his breathing, in the desperation in Beau's voice that made it easy for Sienna to believe him.

"Did you really wish for me then?"

Sienna sniffled and nodded. "What?" she asked when she felt Beau's smile against her head.

"Thank you."

Shaking her head, Sienna pulled back, letting Beau wipe the tears from her face. "For what?"

"Maybe you wrote us in the stars with that one."

Hours later, after Sienna had calmed down, tamed her half-dried hair into a tight bun, and put on a pair of jeans and a sweater, they left the house in the convertible. She *let* Beau drive this time, her hand resting on his thigh as they made their way up the Pacific Coast Highway at what appeared to be lightning speed.

"Can a Dallas wide receiver talk his way out of a ticket out here in LA?" Sienna asked, gripping the door of the car.

Beau shook his head. "We're racing the sun. I've got to maximize every minute I have with you."

They drove another ten minutes, pulling into a small harbor. "Come on." Beau rushed Sienna from the car even though she was unsure they could even park where he had.

Sienna paused when Beau continued down the dock. "No way."

"Wish list." Beau reached back, waving his fingers to motion her forward. "Come on."

The Wanderlust was far from the kind of sailboat Sienna had in mind when she was younger. *That one could fit* on *this boat,* she thought, slipping out of her sneakers and accepting a crew member's hand so she could step on. But like everything else with Beau, he somehow managed to not just make her wishes and dreams a reality but a magical, nearly unbelievable one at that.

Sienna gripped the railing as the boat left the harbor.

"Where are we going?" she asked when Beau approached, standing next to her.

"Does it matter?" he asked.

Beau's question made Sienna laugh. Because it didn't matter. Sienna could be behind the bar of Maloney's with sweaty, thick legs and asses of gyrating football players in front of her, on a beach in Malibu, or on the creaky roof of her old home. Sienna knew if Beau was there, it would always be fun.

"No," she said, leaning into him. "It doesn't."

Beau wrapped an arm around her shoulders. "Let's just chase the sun for a while, then."

"Alright."

And that's what they did, sailing off into the horizon—the

point where the endless sky crashed into the bottomless sea. She wondered, as the boat tilted, captured by the wind, and as it bounced, the surf creating a playground for a school of dolphins dancing in their tale, if the horizon wasn't the destination after all.

"This is just the beginning," Beau said. "There's still a lot on your list."

Sienna laughed again. "You're right. A trip to NASA. I also wished I could own a lavender farm one day."

"There's one for sale," Beau said, pointing to the coast. "About forty miles inland. I already checked."

She elbowed him in the side. "Stop it."

"The lavender farm, because your Mom told you what Provence was like. NASA for obvious reasons. Graceland. . . " Beau paused, scratching his head in thought. "Okay, honestly, I can't remember the reason for Graceland."

Sienna shrugged—she couldn't remember either. "My mom loved Elvis."

"We're going to do it all. I promise. And we have plenty of time now." Beau nudged her shoulder with his. "A *lifetime*."

The promise of forever didn't scare Sienna or riddle her with anxiety that if she did *wish* for it, she might jinx their outcome. Instead, she was struck by a peace that could only come from the bobbing of the beautiful sailboat, the nearly setting sun, and the man who had stepped a thousand miles away before. Only now, it was just to the front of the boat. But Sienna smiled, understanding even if he left at the wrong time, he returned at the right one.

She pulled out her phone, snapped a photo, and sent it to Grace.

Her daughter responded immediately with twelve smiley face emojis, followed by another text.

Dreamy. Like a fairy tale.

Sienna responded before pocketing the phone and moving to join Beau.

You have no idea.

Beau held his hand out, letting Sienna squeeze between him and the railing before wrapping his arms tightly across her.

"Goes on forever, yeah?" he asked as they looked out at the horizon.

Leaning her head against Beau's shoulder, Sienna nodded. "I hope so."

i'll come back for you

DEAR MOM,

It's been another week of tension between me and Beau. Oddly enough, during that time, Beau replaced me with Dad, who's been getting up at the crack of dawn with him. I guess that's good. I hate waking up early. What I love is staying up late—on the roof or in bed—with Beau. But that hasn't really been happening. Until last night.

I'd been on the roof for an hour when I heard Beau's footsteps, the thump of his weight on the air conditioning unit, the grunt he let out as he yanked himself up.

"Hey," he said, crawling over to me.

I almost didn't want to talk to him, but I mumbled a "hi" without looking.

Beau let out a heavy breath and then lay down beside me. There was the smallest space between us, which I hated, but I didn't make a move to close the gap. I waited for him to instead.

I realized, after a solid minute and a half of silence, that I might be waiting for a while, and I won't lie, my heart hurt a little bit.

"Why weren't you in school today?" I asked. It was Wednesday, and normally our free periods overlapped. It didn't take long for me to realize he wasn't there.

"I. . . " Beau stopped, as if he had to think long and hard about what he was going to say. "I had to take an exam."

"What exam?"

"I'll let you know if I pass. If I don't, it won't matter anyway." He shifted, lying on his side. "How was your day?"

I can't stand small talk, Mom. You know this. And I hate it even more with Beau because it feels like work *when it's never been that way between us.*

"Fine."

It was cloudy, which bothered me on a normal day. Today it bothered me even more. Because the stars reminded me that there was always light in the darkness. And I felt like I was about to fall into another bottomless, pitch-black pit without a drop of light to guide me out.

Beau's eyes were burning into me—something was going on. I could feel it, sense the wheels turning in his head, the words muddled in the back of his throat. I wasn't sure if he couldn't—or wouldn't—say them out loud, and the thought made my body tremble as my stomach knotted.

Beau scooted closer, but his near warmth didn't do anything to stop my shivering. I wasn't shaking because I was cold, Mom. I was shaking under the weight of the pending doom I worried would fall from the night sky that should hold our hopes and dreams instead.

"Sienna—"

I didn't want to hear my name from Beau's mouth, so I shut him up with my lips. He fought against it for half a second, trying to back away, but all it took was one of my hands on the back of his neck and the other gripping the opening of his T-shirt for him to breathe a sigh into me. I clung to it viciously and almost impossibly tight, like it was my lifeline, like he *was my lifeline that I would fight tooth and nail to hang on to.*

Beau rolled on top of me, our bodies molding together, and even though I've only been drunk two times in my life, I knew *I was drunk on him—his smell, his taste, his weight. It was all impossibly delicious, and for a second, I wondered why anyone did drugs or drank at all. Because there was no high like Beau's body on mine, covering me from head to toe, the feel of him against my thigh or the sounds that left his mouth when I opened my legs and he pressed into the perfect place.*

We moved like that for what seemed like hours and seconds all at once. But I knew this time it wasn't going to be enough for either of us.

"I wish you'd make love to me," I blurted out. My eyes had been closed. I wished only on what I could feel—him, my shooting wideout.

Beau usually was the one to slow things down and when what I said hit me, I thought he might. But this time, he was the one to deepen the kiss, his moves and breathing more frantic, and my body was burning from the inside out as it tried to hang on for the ride.

His face was buried in my neck, his hands roaming my body—under my sweatshirt, up my shorts. He groaned into my skin when his hands found my underwear, wrapping a hand around the waistband. I wasn't above begging. I wanted all our clothes off and no space between us. And Beau was close to wanting that too, because he was about to pull down my underwear and shorts, but then I opened my eyes and gasped—and not in the right way clearly—when I saw the shooting star in the small gaps between clouds. Now it was Beau trembling as he strained to not move.

"Shit. I'm sorry. I'm sorry." Beau's fingers slowly let go of my underwear and slid out from the leg of my shorts. "Sienna?" The concern wasn't just in his voice, it was dripping so heavily from his face I could feel it.

I shook my head. "I don't want you to go." My voice was a whisper against my sobs, but I knew Beau heard it because his face shifted from concerned to heartbroken.

You always said young love was messy, Mom. You told me it's hard to hold on to forever when you still have life to live. But when Beau climbed off me and pulled me against him, our legs wound together, his arms—noticeably thicker after our stupid time apart—wrapped around me, I thought about how maybe it wasn't our love that was messy. It was just the timing of it all. Our friendship had stood the test of time and distance already. So maybe, that's the only option for a love like this. Because our love is effortless and timeless. It's both safe and encouraging. It's the type that makes you dream, that makes you believe in wishing on a star.

"I wish we'll be a family," I said, closing my eyes and visualizing the shooting star from moments ago in my mind. "I want the family we didn't get to keep. I want to be a mom like my mom wasn't—here," I tell him. "I want that with you."

He lost his brother. I lost you, Mom. I lost parts of Dad when you died. And I have to think that two people who cling to each other as hard as Beau and I do deserve that kind of completeness.

Beau nodded against me. I didn't want to tell him again how much I don't want him to go. But Beau responded anyway as if I had already repeated myself.

"I promise," he whispered into my hair. "I'll come back for you."

I wished again, Mom, that I could believe him.

Love,

Sienna

chapter eighteen

BEAU HAD NEVER BEEN the kind of person to need an alarm clock. Years of discipline and strict schedules had left his body on semi-autopilot, often waking by 5:00 AM, even after little sleep. But before he and Sienna went to bed on their last night in the beachy Malibu bungalow, Beau set an alarm for 4:15 because he couldn't risk sleeping through the grand finale.

And even though he and Sienna got little sleep that night, Beau woke a minute before his alarm with a strong enthusiasm that made it seem like he had slept for ten hours and not four. He silenced his phone and rolled over, finding Sienna's body in the darkness and wrapping himself around her, his hand pressing into her smooth stomach, his face resting in the mess of her bedhead.

Sienna hummed and mumbled something Beau couldn't make out. But when her body inched back closer to his in her sleep, he understood.

She's happy.

Beau nuzzled into her warmth, wondering if everything he had done over the last few months—planetarium visits, sunset sailboat cruises—brought Sienna even an ounce of joy that just lying with her brought him. Because even though they had missed all those things earlier, they had also missed out on the simplicity of just *being* beside each other as well—through good times and bad, for better or worse.

How could I ever have been so stupid? He thought, bringing a hand up to brush Sienna's hair to the side. Cringing at the thought of her hurting over Grace's cancer, Beau squeezed her tighter. *I wish I had been there for you. I wish I had been there even if you said you didn't need me, even if you said you were okay.*

He thought back to all the times he picked Sienna up as a teenager, making sure to always ring the bell, shake Coach Clarke's hand. With every date that went by, every time Beau and Sienna left her house, her father would always say, *"You take care of my daughter now."*

But Jack Clarke also knew the reality of Beau's future, what it meant to be a devoted student athlete with professional potential. He had encouraged Beau to reach for the stars, to focus on himself, and not throw away an opportunity that would drag him from Brookwood earlier than expected. *"Sienna will be alright. She's a strong one."*

Beau snuggled closer to Sienna. *You don't know how strong she really is*, Beau wanted to tell her father. *And I'm sorry I didn't look out for her the way I should have.* He could imagine himself having a conversation with Coach Clarke as if it were present-day—man-to-man—apologizing for just how much he had hurt Sienna, showing her father how determined he was to make it right.

Shaking the image off, Beau pressed a kiss to Sienna's bare shoulder before rolling out of bed and stepping into the bathroom. Sienna might have forgiven him, even if she never forgot. But Beau wasn't sure if he could ever forgive himself for painting their past with loneliness and hurting. What he could do, he reminded himself as he left the bathroom and tiptoed into the kitchen to make coffee, was paint the future bright and endless.

Yesterday's boat ride wasn't just about the wish list. Beau had taken her at sunset to show her he would be with her through waves—rough or calm—at the close of each day.

And at sunrise, Beau would show Sienna he planned to be there for the start of every day too. If he wasn't physically beside her for each one, Beau was desperate for Sienna to keep him in her heart.

"Hey, sleeping beauty." Beau ran a hand up and down her arm, kissing her cheek. "You need to get up."

Sienna stirred, rubbing her head against the pillow.

"I made coffee."

"Why?" Her voice was a sleepy gurgle. "It's still nighttime," she decided.

"Not for much longer. Come on. I want to show you something. Get dressed. And wear something warm."

They were in the car fifteen minutes later, Sienna wearing one of Beau's sweatshirts, her hair tied up in a bun on top of her head. Beau turned the heat on max when Sienna's teeth began to chatter.

"I guess your dream car isn't so great for the cold." His breath clouded in front of him.

"Your old truck wasn't either," she reminded him. "I'm glad you upgraded that."

Beau smiled, reversing out of the driveway. "We had good times in that truck."

There had been day trips, picnics in the truck bed by the lake, and drives to and from school. And kisses. Beau pressed his lips together. *And a lot of blue balls.*

Sienna was quiet beside him, and Beau peeked over, wondering if she might have fallen asleep.

"What's wrong?" he asked.

The light was limited in the car, and it was still dark out. But Beau could see that her gaze was distant as she looked straight ahead.

Beau bit his lip. *We had one very bad time in that truck too,* he realized, the memory making him feel sick. Sienna cleared her throat, and he gathered her hand, dropping them wound together in her lap. He didn't want to think about the last time Sienna had been in his old truck, how the small space of it felt enormously empty after she slammed the car door and ran to her house.

Beau continued along the Pacific Coast Highway, trying to think of a better memory.

"Sky diving," Sienna said, taking a sip of her milkshake.

Beau objected immediately with a hard shake of his head. "You're nuts."

"Why not?" she asked.

"Don't you remember how jumping out of a tree worked out for me? How do you think I'll do jumping out of a plane*?"*

She giggled, putting her near-empty milkshake on the truck's dash and climbing into Beau's lap in the driver's seat. He leaned back as much as he could. They were both tall—too tall—for Sienna to be straddling his legs without bumping her head. But they made it work.

Sienna pressed her lips to his, pulling back, her face shifting in thought as she glanced out the window at the meadow

"What?"

Her green eyes flickered. "Hot-air balloon ride."

"We don't have to jump out of it, right?" he joked.

"No," Sienna said, leaning closer. Her breath, sweet from the milkshake, fanned across his face, and Beau licked his lips. "I just want to fly with you. Chase the sun until we bump into the moon."

Beau's nose grazed hers. "Wish list?"

"Wish list."

"Beau." Sienna pulled him from his thoughts. "Where are we going?"

Beau squeezed her hand. "Flying."

Sienna had dozed off during the rest of the ride. "Hey, wake up." Beau stroked her cheek with the back of his hand. "I don't want you to miss this."

The sky was still dark, but light began to peek through from the east of the canyon. Beau got out of the car, moving to open Sienna's door. Taking her hand, he guided her through the relatively empty dirt lot, past a small building. But Sienna's hand slipped from his when she stopped following.

Beau turned to face her, but Sienna didn't look at him.

He glanced over his shoulder at the enormous hot-air balloon about fifty yards away—its hues of red, orange, pink, and purple—matching the sunrise they were about to chase.

"What do you think?" he asked. "No jumping out though." Beau ran a hand through his own messy hair while Sienna remained quiet. *Okay, too grand maybe.* He sighed, toeing the dirt. "Sienna—"

"I think . . . " Sienna began before pausing to swallow, "I think none of this is real. It can't be possible that you make *everything* better than the last." She shook her head, her tongue coming out to wet her lips. "None of this is real, right?"

"Sienna—"

"No. I thought it was a fairy tale before. I thought we'd have that ending before. And. . . Beau, don't do this to me if it's all a dream."

"Stop," he quieted her. Beau reached for her hand balled at her side, gently prying open her fingers and sliding it beneath his sweatshirt. "Do you feel that?"

Her cool fingers trembled against his warm skin, and Sienna nodded.

"It's real. What I feel for you is real—how much I *love* you." Beau paused, tilting her chin up with his free hand. "What we have, what we have had our whole lives, might seem like a fairy tale. But fairy tales have hard chapters. There are villains and bad guys. There are guys who aren't bad but who make the *wrong* decisions. But do you know what those kinds of stories have too?"

Sienna waited for Beau to tell her.

"Happily ever afters."

A small cry escaped Sienna's mouth, and Beau hugged her to him. "Let's get ours for real this time, okay?"

She nodded against him, wiping her cheeks with the back of her hand.

"Chase the sun until we run into the moon, right? Wish list?"

"I said something like that, didn't I?" Sienna's eyes floated over to the balloon. "Big time wish list."

Beau led them to the grassy field, where they checked in with the attendant, Jake, signed release forms, and went over all the rules. After, Jake unhooked the latch. "Ready if you are."

Motioning for Sienna to step into the basket first, Beau followed, keeping his hand on the side.

"We'll be up in a moment."

Beau watched Sienna lean over, staring at the ground that was soon to be thousands of feet away. She turned his way and smiled, holding out her hand so he would come closer. Beau moved behind Sienna, pressing his chest to her back.

"Ready?"

Even though he had asked and she nodded her response enthusiastically, they both jumped when Jake opened the propane, Beau's hold tightening on Sienna.

"Oh my god."

Beau kept his gaze out as they sailed upward, closer to the light. But the fading night left a few twinkling stars that hadn't lost their battle to the sun yet. Beau rested his chin on Sienna's shoulder, kissing her cheek.

Forever, he wished.

"Can you believe this?" Sienna asked as they rose higher.

The excitement and wonder in her voice filled Beau to the brim with nostalgia and took him back to a simpler time of their childhood friendship, when it blossomed into something more as they tested the boundaries as teenagers until he and Sienna could no longer deny their feelings.

Beau leaned forward. "I can believe it."

He dropped his head to her shoulder, looking out and watching the sun rise over the shaded valley, bringing brilliant light to the darkest dips. His body molded into Sienna's, his hands resting on hers atop the gondola they floated in. But what made the moment real wasn't the beauty of the changing light or the excitement and awe of being hundreds of feet up in the air. What grounded Beau in reality amid a magical, dreamy moment was Sienna—her warmth, her quick, excited breathing, the race of her pulse he could feel beneath his thumbs over her wrists.

There was nothing more real than that—the feel of the most important person along for the ride. For half his life, Beau had been so focused on achieving his brother's dream in the clouds that he hadn't realized how much he needed someone beside him on the ground while he pursued it.

"I guess we can't chase the sun until the moon comes back out. That propane tank is smaller than I thought," Beau said, and Sienna giggled.

Sienna nestled closer. "A minute up here is more than enough."

"So, should I tell him to bring us down?"

"No!" she gasped, elbowing him.

Beau leaned closer. "Remember I told you about that lavender farm?" he asked before pointing. "It's somewhere over there."

"Don't tell me you bought it and ruin this for me."

Beau chuckled. "No. But it reminded me of something else I did get for you."

Peeking over her shoulder, Sienna raised an eyebrow. "There's more?"

"Before you get annoyed, it's also for Grace," Beau said in defense, and when Sienna slowly twisted around in curiosity, he continued, "I don't know much about lavender. But I do know the best place to see it is in France. You told me that."

Sienna nodded. "Provence."

"And it happens to be in the summer, when I'll be busy."

"Okay. . . "

"And Grace is out of school."

"Right. . . "

Beau sighed. "Some stuff on your wish list was really a mother-daughter thing. You're going with Grace this summer. Like you planned to do with your mom."

Sienna's mouth fell. "Beau—"

"Of all the people I have to share you with, I'm glad it's her. I hope she'll feel the same about me one day. If she'll have me, I hope we can be a family one day."

Sienna closed the small space between them, hiding her face in his neck. "We already are," she whispered as his arms enveloped her.

"Yeah?"

Sienna sighed against his skin, pulling back. "You can always forgive family, Beau. I forgave my Mom. And I forgave you."

Overwhelmed by the thick emotion behind her words, Beau cupped Sienna's cheek and kissed her. "I want to give you the world," he confessed against her lips.

None of that had ever changed for Beau. The grief that dimmed Sienna's eyes when she returned to Brookwood in high school, and the pain and fear her daughter's illness had drowned them with as they stared at each other fifteen years later on the field had only made him more determined.

Sienna stepped back, smiling. "You already have."

She raised her arms up to the sky and leaned back over the basket, knowing Beau would hold her safely as she dipped. And when Sienna straightened before turning around to admire the view, Beau knew the only thing more beautiful in the world than floating through a sunrise over sweeping canyons was seeing it through the eyes of someone who has walked through the dark for so long.

★★★★★

"Are you okay?" Sienna asked Beau when the plane hit the tarmac smoothly. She tilted her head. "Beau?"

Beau had spent much of the plane ride back to Texas a ball of anxiety, the comedown after such a high trip leaving him wondering if he could stand going back to life on the ground—separate homes, cars, kitchens. It pained him thinking about not seeing Sienna's bed head when she pushed off the covers, stretching side to side as if she was preparing to get out of bed before quickly retreating back to her pillow.

She does that every day.

He frowned.

"I want to stay in the dream," Beau admitted sheepishly, looking at his lap. "I'm not ready to wake up, I guess."

Sienna reached out, taking his hand.

He tried to laugh it off. "I did this for you, and here I am wondering how I can steal you away for another few days. I don't want to wake up without you." Beau grimaced at the thought.

"Then don't wake up. Come for a sleepover."

"Back to the window, huh?"

Sienna smiled sadly. "Grace isn't a *kid* exactly, but I need to have a conversation with her. It's her home too." She shrugged before adding, "And Henry's."

Beau bowed his head forward. "God help me."

Laughing, Sienna ran her hand up through Beau's brown locks. "I'll figure it out. Do you want to know a secret?" She dipped her head to whisper, "I don't want to wake up without you either."

Taking a deep breath, Beau nodded into her lap. It would have to be enough for now.

"You know, it's Sunday," Sienna said as they got off the plane.

"*Scrabble* Sunday," Beau corrected her. "Maybe me sleeping over and exiting through the front door in the morning is yet to be decided, but my seat at the table to whoop Henry's ass isn't." He waved at the driver who was waiting for them. "How's it going, Paul?"

Sienna slid in next to Beau, giving Paul a quiet thanks when he shut her door. "I'll order pizza when we're closer to the house. Any requests?"

"Yeah," Beau said. "Pizza from any place else other than where you got it last time."

"Oh, come on! Zappato's is the best."

"Crust is undercooked."

"Not all of us have a Michelin star chef as our neighbor." Sienna rolled her eyes at Beau when her phone rang from her bag between them. "Probably Grace putting in her request. She only likes white pizza." She opened the call. "Hey, Henry."

Beau knew something was wrong when he felt Sienna hold her breath beside him.

"When?"

He turned his head, watching Sienna pull her bottom lip between her teeth.

"No, no. Not the local hospital. You need to tell them Texas Children's." Sienna brought her hand to her head, the tone of her voice eerie. "No, are you listening? *Not* the local hospital. Call them back. I'll meet you there." She pulled the phone from her ear, closing the call. "Excuse me?"

"Sienna—"

"Excuse me, Paul? Please, I need to go to Texas Children's Hospital in Dallas."

Beau bit his lip.

"Sir?"

"Dallas, Paul." He looked back at Sienna. "And, uh, quickly." Beau scooted closer, lowering his voice. "What happened? Sienna?"

Sienna was busy flipping through her phone before returning it to her ear. "Grace fainted at the movies. She hit her head, they called an ambulance." She held her finger up to Beau. "Yes, hi. I need to be put through to Dr. Barron."

Beau listened as Sienna left a message for Dr. Barron, who he then realized, after Sienna started talking about white count and platelets, was Grace's oncologist.

"She fainted? Could that be blood sugar?" Sienna didn't respond, and Beau wasn't even sure she heard him. "Maybe she stood up too fast and. . . Sienna." Beau put a hand to her shaking arm, and she shrugged him off.

"I need to text Luella to see if she's working today. Maybe she could go down to the ER. . . "

"Sienna—"

She shook her head. "I don't want her alone—"

"Sienna," Beau said more firmly.

Turning abruptly, Sienna shook her head. "No, Beau. It's not her blood sugar. It's not because she got up too fast."

A flash of fear overtook Sienna, the color draining from her face and neck, which he had spent the past three days peppering with kisses, painting with his laughter and smiles. The look on Sienna's face mirrored only one thing in Beau's mind—his parents' faces when he woke up in the hospital after the accident. Even though there was *relief* in his mother's eyes, it was competing with a harrowing, nearly indescribable look. But Beau learned, even at a young age, shortly after he came out of his haze of a concussion, that there wasn't an easy way to describe the look on his parents' faces because there simply wasn't a word for who they were anymore.

Kids whose parents died became orphans. Wives who lost their husbands, widows. Husbands who buried their wives, widowers. But no one knew what to call a parent who lost a child. It just wasn't possible because it *shouldn't* happen.

The phone shook in Sienna's hands, and Beau took it from her as she began to take short, raspy breaths, leaning her head forward.

"Sienna—"

"Could you turn the air conditioning higher?"

She fumbled with the buttons of her cardigan, gave up in frustration, and yanked it over her head, leaving her in a tank top. And even though a sheen of sweat dotted Sienna's skin, she grew paler with each frantic, panicked breath. "Higher, please," she begged, opening the window with one hand and reaching up to make sure all the vents were fully open with the other.

Beau shook his head. "Paul, pull over."

"No," Sienna panted. "We need to get to the hospital." A cool-toned green painted her cheeks.

"Sir?"

"Now, Paul."

As soon as the car stopped on the side of the highway, Sienna flew out the door, stumbled into the grass, and wretched heavily.

Beau was a second behind her, gathering her hair. "It's alright." He made gentle circles on her back, biting back the emotion as her body heaved painfully beneath his hand. "You're okay."

There were another two minutes of dry heaves after Sienna had emptied her stomach. When her body finally stopped convulsing, Sienna stumbled forward, out of Beau's reach, standing with her hands on her hips, taking deep, distressful breaths.

"The plane. . . " he heard Sienna say.

Beau stepped closer, stopping when Sienna whipped around, her eyes frantic, pleading. "What about the plane?"

"The plane, the house," she pushed out. "Can you get those again?"

Not understanding, Beau reached out to try and get Sienna to focus on him, but she moved back. "What do you—"

"I'll pay you back every dime, I swear. I'll sell the bar, I'll—"

"Sienna—"

"I won't let her die in the hospital," Sienna shouted, her words clear, every one punctuated with determination and pain. "I promised her last time, I told her. . . " She shook her head. "She's never been to the ocean either. She'd love the sailboat and that restaurant we went to with the—"

"Sienna, stop." Beau tried again to reach her, but she stepped away, stumbling. "I know, I know it's scary, and you're afraid—"

"You don't know!" Her voice rose, but the words cracked out of her as if they were coming deep from Sienna's shattering heart. "You think I'm afraid?" She laughed. "Of watching her be pumped full of poison to kill the cancer and her immune system while we wait for *another* transplant? You think I'm scared to see her intubated when she gets an infection—a *cold*—that nearly kills her?"

Beau's heart sank.

"We're *all* going to die, Beau. We all die and sometimes it's painful and it's not pretty. And I'm not scared of her dying." Sienna paused, wiping her face with the back of her hand. "I'm *devastated* because she hasn't *lived* enough to know the kind of pain she's already gone through. And I can't ask her to go through it again just because I want to keep her."

When Sienna trailed off, her voice and gaze drifting to the noisy highway behind them, Beau cautiously shuffled closer. With both of his hands cupping her face, he turned Sienna back to him, leaving some space between.

"I've lived without my mom." Sienna sniffled, shaking her head. "Without my dad. Without *you,*" she added before her voice cracked. "But I *can't* without her. I *can't.*"

Beau took half of a step, crushing Sienna to his chest. He wanted to swear to Sienna that she wouldn't have to live without another person—the most important one. He wanted to promise into her hair that Grace's life would be long and full, that Sienna would watch her graduate from high school, college. She would watch her build a life of her own, standing on the sidelines proudly as Grace reached for the stars and made every dream she ever had come true.

But Beau couldn't risk making any more promises he couldn't guarantee. So instead, he held Sienna close and told her the only thing he knew. "You're not living without her right now," he said, squeezing her. "She's still here and needs you. You're going to wipe your face and rinse your mouth and get yourself together. And you're going to do the same thing you did since the moment she was born—show up and keep being strong." Beau wiped a smudge of makeup from under her eye. "And if there's a moment when you feel like *this* and can't keep it together, I'll be here for you this time."

chapter nineteen

LUELLA RAISED an eyebrow from her spot on the hospital bed when Sienna yanked open the curtain. "Did you time travel? Weren't you in California?"

Grace's wigless head peeked out from behind her favorite nurse. "Hi, Mom."

"Hey." Sienna cleared her throat, eyeing her daughter. "How are you feeling?" She gave Luella's shoulder an appreciative squeeze before moving to Grace, trying not to wince at the gash on her daughter's head. "They didn't suture it yet?"

"Little miss thing is demanding a plastic surgeon," Luella said, standing. "She'll need ten or twelve stitches."

Grace sighed as Sienna ran a hand over her short hair. "I *don't* want a scar. What about prom?" She turned to her mother with a pout.

"It's okay," Sienna reassured her. "We have a few weeks. Emily is great at makeup. She'll hide it." She frowned when Grace's lips began to quiver.

Oh, Grace . . .

"I got blood on my wig."

"I'll wash it." Sienna ran her hand down the side of Grace's face. "How do you feel?" *Pale. She's pale. Was she this pale when I left? Was she tired?* Sienna tried to remember their last moment together in the kitchen while Henry was in the shower. "Where's Henry?"

Luella motioned at the door. "He's down handling paperwork. They want to admit her for observation. She hit her head pretty hard."

Sienna sighed as Grace began to cry. "It's alright. A day or two, okay?" She squeezed her hand. "Did they run a full blood panel?" she asked Luella. "CBC, platelets—"

"*Everything*. The attending consulted Dr. Barron. She called the order in."

Luella adjusted her stethoscope. "I have to get back upstairs. But I'll find you after my shift, alright?"

"Luella, thank you," Sienna called as the nurse made her way to the door. She turned back to Grace. "What happened?"

She shrugged. "I don't know. We got popcorn, and then. . . I woke up on the floor. I don't know. Lilah said I hit my head on the counter."

"Have you been feeling off?" She tilted Grace's face up so she could see her better. *Pale, but no dark circles, no bruising.*

Grace leaned against the pillow. "Tired, I guess."

Sienna raised an eyebrow. "What kind of tired? How long—"

"Mom," Grace interrupted. "Tired, like tired. And I have a headache now. I already told the doctor everything. You're making my head hurt more."

Looking down at Grace's lap, she covered her daughter's hands. "We talked about this, Grace. You have to tell me if you're not feeling right."

Grace looked away. "I thought if I told you, you wouldn't let me go to the concert."

A pit grew in Sienna's stomach. *It's been a month since the concert,* Sienna said to herself, biting the inside of her cheek. Her heart twisted. *Please, please let this girl go to concerts and sleepovers and parties and—*

"I want to go to prom," Grace whispered. "I really want to go to prom, Mom."

"You will," Sienna said without hesitation, giving Grace's hands a tight squeeze. *You will even if we start chemo tomorrow. I'll buy you a new wig. Emily will do your makeup.*

Grace began to cry.

"Oh, Gracie—"

"Justin *still* hasn't asked me yet. What if I have no one to take me?" Grace asked, turning her head back to her mother. "I *cannot* go without a date."

Sienna let out a breathy, relieved laugh. If Grace's concern was over not having secured a date to prom that was still a month away, Sienna would worry about hiding the chemo port beneath her dress later—if it came to that.

"You'll have a date." Sienna wondered if she might visit Justin at the diner and put in a little mother's elbow grease.

Grace sighed. "Can you go ask where the plastic surgeon is? I don't want a scar on my head."

Sienna looked to the curtain. "Yeah. And let me go give them your insurance card. Hang tight." She grabbed her bag and moved through the thin partition, bumping into Beau, who she had left at the curb of the ER entrance. "I thought you went home."

Beau shrugged, pocketing his hands. He didn't need to justify his presence to Sienna. She could read it in his eyes. *There's no place else I'd rather be*, the warm brown orbs told her.

"How is she?"

Sienna glanced through the opening of the curtain. "She's. . . tired," Sienna said with a helpless shrug. "I want to see if they've got a plastic surgeon on the way. She's got a nasty gash on her head. And I need to go down to admissions and—"

"Go," Beau motioned down the hallway. "I'll stay with her."

"Oh, no, you won't! I don't have my wig on!" Grace shrieked from behind the curtain.

Sienna palmed her face, but before she could tell Grace that Beau could wait outside the curtain in case she needed anything, he pulled off his baseball hat and stretched his arm through the opening of the partition.

"Do you like the Yankees?" he asked Grace, keeping his eyes on Sienna. Gently, he tossed his hat into the curtained room.

Beau. . .

The gesture made Sienna's knees weak, and she placed a hand on the wall to keep herself upright.

"They're overrated." Grace relented with a heavy sigh. "Fine. You can come in."

Sienna took Beau's hand as he stepped around her. "Thank you," she whispered, trying not to let the emotion seep through. *Thank you so much.*

"It's going to be okay," Beau mouthed before squeezing her hand and joining Grace.

Straightening, Sienna nodded to herself. *It might be okay. It might not.* She turned, listening to Beau tease Grace from behind the curtain.

"See, it was a poor movie choice. The Fast and Furious franchise should've ended after the second movie. Your body was trying to warn you."

Whatever way it goes, it's going to be different, Sienna thought. *Because this time, Grace's team is bigger and stronger.* It wasn't that Sienna believed Beau was the cure-all for whatever news they might receive. But Sienna knew the more people in Grace's corner, the better. And even though she walked through the hospital that had been home to more bad news than good, Sienna's steps were purposeful and brave, her head held high. Because she knew this time, in her bones, that *if* she needed to fall, Beau would catch her.

"Anemia," Dr. Barron said, walking into Grace's room after she had been admitted.

Sienna shook her head, her eyes drifting between Grace and Dr. Barron. "You're sure?"

Dr. Barron looked over her glasses at Sienna. "We're still at levels concurrent with no evidence of disease, but we're dealing with some low hemoglobin." She turned back to Grace. "You've been taking your supplements?"

Grace nodded.

"Seems we need to give you a little boost. We'll do an iron infusion now since we've got you here for a night or two." The doctor motioned at Grace's head.

"Is that instant?" Sienna asked. "Will her iron go up right away?"

Dr. Barron shook her head. "No, not right away. We might see it creep up in a few days or so. But ideally, in a week. I'll run a few other tests. It could be an absorbency issue due to your past treatments that's lingered too long, but likely it's nothing worrisome. We'll have to diligently monitor it." She offered Grace a smile. "My apologies for the many finger pricks to come."

"Can I go to school when I'm released?" Grace asked.

"I think a day or two home is probably a better idea."

Grace groaned. "What about prom?" she asked, her voice slightly panicked. "It's in three weeks."

Dr. Barron smiled. "Did you get your dress yet?"

Sienna laughed. "Months ago."

"Prom should be fine. I want you to lay low with that head. No TV, no screen time. Let your brain rest a little, alright?" Dr. Barron moved to the door. "I'll go tell them to get the infusion started."

Sienna let out a small sigh of relief, not wanting to show Grace just *how* worried she had been. "A day or two here, that's it."

"Yeah, with *no* TV," Grace relented. Her color was still pale but better than when Sienna first saw her.

She rubbed her leg. "I'll have Henry bring you a book when he comes by tomorrow." Sienna had sent both Beau and Henry—begrudgingly—home from the hospital.

When a nurse came in with another IV bag, Grace yawned.

"Tired?" Sienna asked, backing up to give the nurse space.

Grace nodded, her head falling to the side. "And cold."

"Let me get this going," the nurse said as she hung the new bag, "and I'll go grab you another blanket."

Sienna sat on the bed, and Grace leaned her head—still capped by Beau's hat—against her shoulder. "You didn't tell me about California."

Tucking the thin hospital blanket around Grace, Sienna asked, "What about it?"

"Was it everything you wished it would be?"

More. Sienna wanted to say. Instead, she reached for her phone sitting on the table and unlocked it. "Next time, we'll take you." She opened her gallery.

"Are those dolphins?"

Sienna nodded. "A whole pod. The house was right on the beach. The entire wall is windows."

Grace took the phone and began to swipe. "Did you swim?"

Sort of.

"The water was freezing. Maybe we can sneak away for a weekend in the summer." She contemplated telling her about the trip Beau had planned for them to Provence but didn't want to overwhelm Grace, given how exhausted she was.

Sienna watched as Grace flipped through the montage of photos—views of canyons, starfish washed up on the shore, of sunsets. She got to a video and pushed play, and Sienna watched herself hold out the phone while they were in the hot-air balloon, trying her best to capture all that sunrise had to offer. The video was shaky, and she had nearly dropped the phone. But Sienna felt Grace smile against her shoulder when Beau steadied her arm and came into frame, leaning her back just enough over the basket and kissing her.

"It's really like a fairy tale," Grace whispered sleepily. She pressed play on the video again.

The nurse cleared her throat when she entered the room with more blankets, and Sienna stood so she could bundle Grace more.

Grace mumbled a thanks as her eyelids fluttered shut. Sienna sighed, knowing that the adrenaline from anticipating what felt like inevitable news had worn off, and Grace could finally feel the enormous weight of the day.

Grabbing her phone from where Grace had placed it on the bed, Sienna held it to the nurse. "I'm going to step into the hall." She texted Henry before calling Beau, who answered on the first ring.

"Hey," he said. "Any news?"

Leaning against the wall, Sienna took a shaky breath. "Anemia, just anemia. I mean, she's anemic enough to pass out, but. . . " The idea that she should be relieved that such a diagnosis was a victory didn't seem right, but she pushed the thought aside, choosing to celebrate the win anyway. "Her blood's good. No cancer, no—"

"Thank god," Beau interrupted. Sienna could hear the relief in his voice through the phone. "Can she go home?"

"Not yet. They want to keep her here because of her head, and they need to run a few tests tomorrow. The doctor said she's not expecting to find anything, but you know, just in case," Sienna told him. "She's having an iron infusion right now. Poor thing fell asleep, she's so exhausted."

"You must be too," Beau said.

Sienna looked around the hallway of the hospital that had begun to quiet for the night. Her shoes squeaked on the linoleum floor. *Wasn't I just barefoot on the beach?* "Did today start on a hot-air balloon? Or was that last week?" She laughed and then shook her head. "Or was it all a dream?"

"No," Beau answered. "We woke up together this morning."

Sienna sighed, running a hand down her neck. She could nearly feel Beau's face nuzzling against it trying to wake her up while it was still pitch-black outside. "It was a good way to wake up."

"It's my favorite way," Beau added, and Sienna's heart swelled.

"I didn't say thank you. It was the most special weekend. I'm sorry it ended the way it did."

Her mind flashed back to the car ride, the panic that struck her and held her mind captive, taking Sienna down a memory lane flanked by horrible nightmares. But there was something else Sienna remembered—the way Beau handled it.

"Don't ever apologize for that. I only wish I could do more. Do you guys need anything at the hospital?"

"More?" Sienna asked with a laugh. "No. You've done more than enough. Henry will bring her a book tomorrow, but that's all she needs. I'd take a hug, but it can wait." *I wish I didn't hurry him out of here so quickly,* Sienna thought. But even though Beau's presence had been welcome earlier, Sienna wanted her focus to remain on her daughter while they waited for her bloodwork to come back. Her phone beeped against her ear, and she looked at the screen, seeing the notification for a dropped call.

"Stupid hospital service," she mumbled.

"No need to wait."

Sienna's head flew to the left, where Beau approached from down the hall. He stopped a few feet away since Sienna was still in front of Grace's open door and motioned with his head for her to follow him into an empty waiting room.

"You didn't have to come back," Sienna said with a heavy sigh before she walked straight into him, dropping her head to his shoulder.

Beau wrapped his thick arms around her. "I didn't go anywhere," he said into her hair. "I didn't want to be in the way, but I wanted to be here just in case."

Winding her arms around Beau's waist, Sienna nuzzled closer. *Just in case it was bad news,* she thought. *He stayed just in case I needed to fall apart, so I wouldn't have to do it in an empty bathroom stall alone.* Sienna tightened her hold on Beau and stayed silent. Her body leaned against him, not because she needed him to hold her up so she wouldn't fall, but because, for once, it was nice to share in the relief instead of bearing the load of the fear on her own.

"I don't want you to be my just-in-case person," she confessed, her voice quiet but confident. "I want you to be my always person."

"Me too." Beau swayed side to side, and Sienna relaxed into him.

His presence, his hold, told her one thing—*heads or tails, I love you no matter what.*

★★★★★

"That is *not* a word."

"Is too."

"Is not," Beau countered.

Another lighter, familiar voice chimed in. "I think Grace is right."

Sienna pushed up from the far too small, too hard couch. She rubbed the sleep from her eyes, finding Beau across from her on the other side of Grace's bed, focusing on the Scrabble board. Grace sat at the head with her arms folded, and across from her, Sienna realized, was Molly.

"She lives," Grace rejoiced.

"Hi, Molly." Sienna sat. "What are you doing here?"

Grace's friend raised her bald head, turning her focus from the board to Sienna. "Round seven of eight today." She beamed and Sienna smiled back. "I get to ring the bell soon."

"For the *last* time," Grace added, smiling at her friend.

Oh, I hope so, Sienna thought, looking at Molly. She only wanted the same experience for her that she did for Grace—one with an end in sight.

"Take that," Beau celebrated, placing tiles on the board.

Grace looked skeptical. "Wideout is *two* words."

"Is not," Beau sang.

"I think he's right," Molly said, and Beau stuck his tongue out at Grace before giving Molly a fist bump.

Sienna smiled. "How long have you been here?" she asked him. Sienna had hardly slept between all the night checks.

"Came by after my workout," he said, motioning to the box on the high-top table beside the bed. "Brought donuts."

"And books," Molly added before smiling at Grace

Looking at the Barnes & Noble bag, Sienna raised an eyebrow. "Are bookstores even open this early?" Beau shrugged at her. *For you, I guess they can always be open.* But Sienna didn't mind favors being called in when Grace was in the hospital. She turned to the box of donuts, lifting the lid, still too tired to eat. "The nurses definitely deserve it."

Beau reached into the small velvet bag for new tiles, only looking at Sienna when she yawned heavily into her hand. "Do you want to go take a nap at my place?" he asked. "I can hang here."

"And get your butt kicked."

Ignoring Grace's comment, Beau motioned at the door. "Go and get in bed. Joe will let you up."

Sienna shook her head, stretching. "No, that's okay." She raised her hands to remove the messy bun from her head, grimacing at the dirty strands between her fingers.

"Go *shower* at least," Grace told her mother before looking at Molly. "People don't appreciate hair until they don't have it anymore."

A shower at his place is better than one that's basically over the toilet, Sienna thought to herself. "You don't mind?" she asked Beau. "Henry should be here soon."

"Go," Beau said. "I have a call later, but I've got time." He smiled.

"Time to get your ass handed to you, Walker."

"Grace," Sienna warned, standing and offering Beau a grateful smile. "I'll only be gone an hour." Beau's apartment was a ten-minute walk from the hospital. "But if Henry comes before I'm back, go. You've spent too much time here."

And you don't have to. But I really, really love that you did.

Sienna bumped into Luella as she made her way to the elevator. "I'm just running out for an hour. Beau is there, and Henry—"

"Beau has been here since seven thirty this morning," Luella told her.

Sienna didn't know if the nurse was about to lecture her since it technically was outside of visiting hours and he wasn't family, but Luella's face softened into a big smile.

"It's nice to see you have someone on your team. You know I adore your brother but. . . well, you know. . . "

Sienna pushed the button. "I do."

"Do you though?" Luella asked.

Sienna shook her head, not understanding.

"I heard about the Disney trip. And when I clocked in this morning, the ladies told me he was playing catch with a few kids with a ball he made from tape. And what he's been doing for my Damien every week. . . well, we're all thankful for Beau. Kind one, that man. I hope you really do know."

I do. The elevator dinged, and Sienna stepped in. "I'll see you in a bit, alright?"

Sienna felt guilty twenty minutes later because, standing beneath the heavy stream of hot water in Beau's shower, she secretly wished her break from the hospital was longer. But after washing her hair twice and lathering herself with Beau's body wash, she finally turned the water off, drying her body and wrapping herself in the big, fluffy bathrobe hanging by the shower.

She picked up her phone from where she had left it on the bed, smiling at Beau's message.

Henry's here. I'm heading to you so I can steal one kiss for payment. Then I'll send you back.

Sienna typed back curiously. **Payment for what?**

Beau responded immediately. **These two are running around the floor blabbing about how they handed my ass to me at Scrabble. Make it a good kiss I've got a bruised ego.**

Sienna lay back on the bed, taking a deep breath and inhaling Beau right off her skin after using his body wash. "I love that smell," she said aloud before sitting and looking at her phone.

Her phone vibrated in her hand, but instead of a text message, it was a low-battery notification. She stood, walked to the other side of the bed where Beau's charger was, and reached for it, placing her phone down. Her eyes noticed a small Post-it with Beau's handwriting.

Call GPF/Janet re Disney transport.

Sienna fingered the post it.

I love him. I love him so much.

Sienna opened the nightstand, wanting to find the pad and a pen to leave Beau a note telling him just that. But the only paper in the drawer was a folded sheet with Beau's name written across it.

Sienna's eyes narrowed when she recognized the swoop of Grace's half-cursive, half-print writing spelling out Beau's name. The towel she had wrapped around her hair unwound with her head tilted in question, and Sienna pulled it off with one hand while she grabbed the paper with the other.

Dear Mr. Walker,

Alright, I'll be honest. I don't really care that much about football. Don't take that personally. I'm sure you're a great wide receiver, even if your record this season tells me otherwise. But the truth is, the day I decided to submit my application to the Golden Penny Foundation was the day I found out two important things: 1) my stem cell transplant worked, and even though I wasn't cancer free right then and there, the doctors were happy and 2) my uncle Henry bought me tickets to the Simon Gorges concert this spring, and that's what I was going to ask for in the first place. I would've asked for backstage passes but I refuse to meet him without my own hair.

Another thing happened that night. I got up to use the bathroom (sorry for the TMI), and when I walked down the hall, heard my mom crying. It wasn't a happy cry, you'll have to trust me on that. I like to think I know her best. The truth is, she cries a lot. Like a lot, even though she'll never admit it. I hate to make her sound so sad, but she just is so *sad.*

And then I realized that if she couldn't be happy on the day that should be the happiest moment of our lives, she's the one who deserves the wish, not me. So, I made it on her behalf and wished to go to the game so I could get to you. I need your help. I'm about to restart my life, and I need her to do the same. Because one day, I might not be cancer free again. I've been around the block before. They already called my first remission a miracle, and it didn't last forever. I don't think you get two miracles in a lifetime.

The worst part about being sick is that life still happens even when you're too tired to get out of bed, too nauseous to stand. It happens during bone marrow aspirations and chemo. That has been the most unfair part. I've never actually been afraid of dying. I'm afraid of missing out on all the things I should do while I'm living.

And there's another thing. I'm afraid for Mom. I'm afraid she has forgotten what living *actually is, what it means to dream big and chase those dreams. I know that since I was born, she's lived for me. And when I got sick, she lived for me even harder. But what happens if I leave her too soon? Who does she live for then?*

I know that long before me, she had you during a really hard time in her life. She doesn't talk about my grandma very much, but I know a lot anyway. I know that she had a larger-than-life personality, that she went out of her way to make people happy and smile and put others before herself. I know that my mom is a lot like her, and that's what I'm scared about. Because if she's happy like her own mother, what if she's sad like her too?

A tear fell from Sienna's face, landing in the middle of the paper. And then another, smudging Grace's words but not erasing them entirely and not blurring the rest of the letter Sienna wished she had never found but couldn't look away from.

A long time ago, you gave her a reason to move out of the darkness. Friendship, young love, whatever it was. It was what she needed at the time. The darkness is deep for her right now, even if she doesn't want to admit it. I'm not asking you to pull her out of it. I'm only asking you to remind her that there is *a way out if she wants it. She's done it before, she can do it again. . . with your help.*

My real wish is for you to do just that.

Sincerely,

Grace Clarke

PS: It's pretty much a mortal sin to not grant the wish of a sick kid. I'm not technically sick right now, but I have been for long enough. Just make my mom happy the way you did all those years ago. I don't tell her enough, but she deserves it. If you're short on ideas on how to do that, there's a list on the back of this paper.

PPS: This stays between us.

With a tremoring hand, Sienna turned the paper around. She didn't want to read the list, didn't want the hope in her heart, which had swelled with such joyful magic, to deflate back into soul-crushing disappointment and newfound embarrassment. Skimming it was enough for Sienna to know that she had been wrong to trust Beau, been wrong to believe in the fairy tale, the happily ever after. Words like "motorcycle" and "ocean" and "planetarium" popped up boldly as her eyes drifted down.

A quick skim said it all. Because it was like Beau had told her before, *"You can't really say no to a sick kid, can you?"*

hopeless wishes

DEAR MOM,

Going to a lantern festival should've been the best night of my life. I mean, who loves a dark sky and bright lights more than me? Only you, maybe.

But I should've known, even before I got into Beau's truck, that things were. . . I was going to write that things were going to take a turn for the worse, but they didn't take a turn at all, Mom. They ended.

I was getting dressed while Beau was talking to Dad. And I didn't hear everything, but heard enough. Dad said, "You need to do what you feel is right for yourself." There was this disappointed tone in his voice, which he never used with Beau, who said something about "Florida" and "this weekend."

My heart didn't want to connect the pieces, so I walked into the living room where they sat and said, "I'm ready."

But Dad looked like he wasn't seeing me, *but me a while ago—his little girl. He folded his lips and shifted them back and forth. And do you know what was in his eyes, Mom? Pity. It's the worst thing ever to be looked at with.*

Beau was quiet in the car. I shifted, bouncing my leg, fiddling with the radio, smoothing down my dress. Really, I was waiting for Beau to take my hand or squeeze my knee—anything that would wake me up from this dream before it turned into a nightmare.

*I tried to stop my hands from shaking when we took our lanterns and markers. And what I wrote on that paper got smudged by the tears that hit it when I saw what Beau had written on his paper—*I hope Sienna forgives me.

*I looked down at what I had written—*I wish for us forever— *and scribbled it out. I didn't want to waste a wish on someone who was about to break my heart. So what I wished for that night was a family—a real one. I wrote and wrote everything I could, nearly filling the paper lantern. I wished for a father who could show up for his kids, a brother who didn't push me away when I needed him. I couldn't wish for another mom because there could never be one like you again.*

So, I wished that when I become a mother one day, I'd be like you but better. I wished I'd be the one who stays around no matter what, the one who teaches her kids to live, laugh, have fun, and never give up, because even though I knew what was coming—a brick wall of heartbreak—I wouldn't give up.

I know Beau saw what I wrote because his face changed. Pity again, two times in one night.

When we got to the line, my hands were shaking so hard that I couldn't hold the lantern up for the attendant to light the flame, so I handed it to Beau. "I'll wait by the car." I had no idea if he sent his or mine up to the sky. I didn't care

The ride home was quiet. "You're leaving." It wasn't a question.

"This weekend," was all he replied. "I passed the last exam I needed to fulfill my graduation requirements."

I knew Beau would leave one day. But one day wasn't meant to be this weekend and my sadness battled my anger over Beau's nonchalant tone and the quickness of his answer. It was like he didn't think his words would rip me open and strangle my heart.

"I'm moving to Florida to train with a program they recommended. I'll know FSU's offense in and out by the time preseason starts."

"What about prom?" My voice cracked because really what I wanted to ask was "what about everything?"

When Beau said nothing, I knew he never intended to take me to prom.

How stupid is that to ask about, Mom? Beyond, right? But that's all I could think about. Because prom was supposed to be our *night. Prom and what followed were on the wish list. And it's not just about sex. It was about giving ourselves to each other. Then we'd finish school and have the best summer. We'd knock everything else off the wish list someway, somehow.*

Beau didn't say anything about prom. He didn't say anything at all the rest of the ride, and neither did I. I focused on the dark road in front of us as he drove me home for what I felt would be the last time, even though when I reached the handle to open the door Beau swore it wouldn't.

"Sienna." Beau held his hand out—I don't know if it was to stop me or to tug me in for one more hug, one more kiss. "I swear I'll come back for you. But I have *to do this. And I can't do it like we planned before."*

That was Beau's way of saying he couldn't do it with me, even at a distance. I struggled to breathe as he continued. I got that he had to do it for Greg. But why couldn't he do it with *me?*

"I need to be focused and. . . I'm going to have to fight like crazy to start at FSU. If I give it my all, then maybe I can do that. And if I'm thinking about you. . . "

My eyes lit up in anger. "If you're thinking about me, what? You can't remember a circus route? How many steps before you cut for a corner?" I stopped and ground my teeth. "You can't balance me *and football because I'm too much?"*

He stayed silent. The dim lights from the truck's dash let me see two important parts of Beau—his eyes and the scar on his head. I say they're important because they are my favorite parts of him. His eyes because they are warm, comforting, familiar. The scar forever etched into his temple reminds me that when you come back from the brink of death with a second chance at life, you seize it. I get that's what he was doing. He just wasn't seizing it with me.

"You don't get it," Beau said. "You don't know what you mean to me."

"Not enough, apparently."

*"Not enough? Are you serious?" Beau spat angrily. "How about this. I was supposed to finish school early—*last *semester. I was supposed to move to Florida months ago. I didn't stay this whole time because of someone who means 'not enough.'" He stopped and cursed under his breath before continuing, "I stayed because you mean too fucking much. You're all I think about. But you're a know-it-all, right? Any catches I didn't make, any interceptions I caused was because I was too slow on the break, yeah?" I folded my arms across my chest, wishing he would stop talking. "No, Sienna. They happened because my head wasn't in the game. I was thinking about you. How to make you happy. How to say the right thing when you're sad."*

I wasn't sad at that moment, Mom. I was devastated. But Beau didn't say the right thing next.

"I've spent almost a year of my life thinking about how the hell I can erase look you had on your face when I first saw you. You can't even see that." Beau smacked the steering wheel, and even though the horn hadn't worked for a few weeks, I jumped. "I'm trying to make something of myself for you. For us one day."

He was right, though, Mom. Because all *I saw was him not choosing me.*

"Don't act like you're doing this for me," I told him, looking down at my lap. "This is about Greg."

"Well, don't ask me to choose between you and my dead brother because I'd choose Greg."

My head shot up, and Beau must have seen that it felt like he had just slapped me in the face because his eyes flooded with regret.

"I just. . . I need you to be strong, okay? And I. . . I know you'll be okay." He reached out and tried to touch my cheek, but I pulled away. "And I promise, when the time is right, I'll come for you and we'll—"

I didn't give Beau a chance to finish. I sprinted from the truck.

It's been eighteen days, Mom. Yes, I'm back to counting. It's been eighteen days since I went back into the house where Dad was waiting. Eighteen days since I looked at him and growled, "You should've told me."

So, I'm back to where I was, thinking about the seconds and minutes that tick by since life was better. Only it's different now. When you died, I counted the days since a part of me died with you—when you broke this family and decided it was better to stop living with us.

And now, I'm counting again to mark the day I realized the most important person in my life could keep living without me.

Both sting. Both hurt. Both burrow a hole deep into my heart and strangle it.

I'm not writing this from the roof. I'm not writing it from my room with the fake stars blasting on my ceiling. I'm writing it on the floor of my closet where I'll leave this diary. To be honest, I want to throw it in the trash. But for eighteen days, I've been swimming in the deepest hole I've ever known. I can't keep thinking of all the high points of this year, of all the happiness I found again. But I'm wondering—only wondering—if many more days from now, maybe a thousand or more when I'm a little less angry, I'll need to be reminded that stories can be beautiful even if they end painfully and not with a happily ever after.

Love,

Sienna

chapter twenty

"I'M HERE TO COLLECT!" Beau hollered, tossing his keys on the counter beside Sienna's bag. He kicked off his shoes, making his way to his room as Sienna rose from the bed, still wrapped in a robe. "Ah, even better. A payment with interest," he said playfully but grew confused when Sienna rushed to the bathroom.

"What's wrong?" he asked, watching her pull the robe off and slipped back into her clothes. *Maybe I shouldn't have left even if Henry was there,* he thought. *I told her I'd stay until she got back.* "I *just* left. Henry was there already. Grace is fine. She and Molly were watching—"

"Don't," Sienna huffed, sliding on her jeans. "Don't you dare say my daughter's name."

What?

Beau shook his head as she fastened her bra and pulled on her tank top and sweater. "Sienna, what—"

His words were lost when Sienna blew past him, her shoulder bumping into his arm. Beau watched her sprint back into the bedroom and around the bed, hardly pausing except to grab her phone from the charger on his nightstand—where Grace's letter sat.

No, no, no. Shit.

"Sienna!" Beau leaped over the bed, snatching the letter as he sprinted after her. She had grabbed her bag from the counter and reached for the door by the time he came up behind her, slamming his palm into the wood and shutting it.

"Beau." The way Sienna seethed his name made him cringe. "Move."

He pressed his hand harder into the door when she tugged at the handle again. "Wait a second. It's—"

"Beau—"

"It's not what you think."

Sienna spun with such force she pushed Beau's body back, but he kept his hand firmly on the door just above her head. "*Not what I think*? You really can't do better than that? I think it's pretty clear what that is." Her eyes bore into the letter at his side.

No. Look at me, Beau thought before speaking, "It's only been about you and me. And I'm here. I'm still fucking here." He lowered his hand from the door and went to lift Sienna's chin, but she flinched in anticipation before he even got close.

"You *lied*."

"I never lied." Beau shook his head, raising his hand gripping the letter. "Not once."

"Are you kidding?" Her exasperated tone struck him hard. "Oh, you're right. You just didn't tell me. That's called *deceit*."

Her chest rose and fell with heavy, painful breaths, each one feeling as if it was pummeling into Beau despite the distance between them. Her eyes moved to his other hand against the door.

"Let me leave."

"No," Beau gritted out.

Sienna turned and yanked on the handle again with enough force to get the door open, but Beau slammed it shut.

"Enough, Beau!"

"No." He turned the lock and brought both hands to Sienna's shoulders, spinning her. "Let me explain. You have to understand—"

"Understand what?" she screamed, her green eyes swirling

between shades of anger and hurt. "That my daughter wrote *that*. . . that the two of you schemed together because you felt *sorry* for me?"

Beau's eyes widened. "No, God, Sienna, that's not it. Please just. . . it wasn't *like* that."

"No?" she asked. "Then what was it like? You were just living your life waiting for an opening back into mine?"

"I . . . " *Yes and no,* he thought, pressing his lips together and shaking his head. "I don't know. I told you, I saw Grace at the burial, I thought. . . I thought your wish had come true. I thought you might have a *family*. I didn't want to ruin that. And at the game, when I saw Grace and I realized. . . fuck, that was before she even gave me this!" He held up the letter in frustration. "The moment I saw you on the field, I wasn't going to slip away. And I made up my mind the second I realized there wasn't anyone else that I wasn't going to let you go."

Sienna narrowed her eyes, floating her gaze between the letter in Beau's hand and his. "I don't believe you. I can't possibly believe you."

What can I do? Beau wanted to ask. *What can I do to get you to believe me?*

"Congratulations, Beau. It was a great show. Give yourself a pat on your back for being the mastermind who put on the *grandest* production to get my forgiveness while still breaking. . . *shattering* me again." Sienna paused when her voice cracked. "I *told* you it was a dream. I knew this was too good to be real."

Beau ground his teeth together. "It wasn't a show," he pushed out. "It was the real fucking thing. It *is* the real thing. You and me. *We* are the real thing. We're *reality.*"

Sienna began to cry and he grimaced at each tear that left her eyes, every single drop hacking away at all the hope he had built up over the last few months, leaving it a cloud of uncollectable dust between them.

Dropping the letter to the floor, he leaned his forehead to Sienna's, cupping her face with both hands. "God, please, please don't cry. Just believe me. It is real, I swear. I promise." He pressed his lips to her trembling ones. "She brought me back. But I'm staying—"

Hands to his chest, Sienna shoved him. "And you stayed around because—"

"Because I *love* you. Because I've *always* loved you—"

"Don't," Sienna snarled, pushing him once more. "Don't you dare feed me that *bullshit* again!"

Beau stumbled. "I fucked up! I did." He put his hands on his hips, looking up at the ceiling. "But that doesn't mean how I felt about you then or how I feel about you right now is bullshit." His head swung to the floor as he took deep breaths, seeing the letter between their feet. He bent, grabbing the paper. "But this. *Grace* might've brought me back. But I stayed—I'm *staying*," he clarified, moving to the side and leaning against the door. "I'm staying for you, Sienna."

"Get out of my way."

"You think I needed this?" Beau held up the letter that had been crumpled by his hand and stained by Sienna's tears. "When I told you on the plane that I remember *everything* it's because I do. Like the first time you told me you wanted to ride a motorcycle. I brought leftover strawberry short cake and—"

"Shut up," Sienna spat.

"Our first date—the picnic in the meadow—you wore this light-blue shirt that matched the sky. We were rolling around kissing and it was covered in dirt and grass stains by the time I brought you home. That's when you wished for a fancy dinner, the planetarium. It's not possible for me to forget *you*, Sienna. You're ingrained in me." He pled with his eyes. "I already know how hard it is to walk away from you. I won't make that mistake again. I won't."

"I'm sorry," she growled sarcastically. "I'm sorry it was *so* hard for you to become the captain freaking America of college football. I'm sorry it was *so* hard for you to leave small, tiny

Brookwood behind and never look back. It must've been hard to accept all that fame and notoriety, money—"

"I'd give it all up!" Beau shouted. "If I could give it all up and do it differently I would, alright? Do you need to hear that? I never wanted those things!"

Pursing her lips in anger, Sienna narrowed her eyes. "You wanted them more than me." She paused, her body trembling. "And that's okay. I made peace with that. It's not about that. I never wanted you *not* to do those things, Beau, even if I believed you were going after them all for the wrong reasons. You think you owe your brother something, but you don't. You never have. You can honor his memory just by *living,* not living the way he wanted for himself. But don't you dare come back and play the martyr card and tell me how hard it is to be the one who walks away." She shook her head before adding, "Not after reading *that* and knowing how hard it is to be the one left behind."

"It *broke* me, alright? What Grace said, what she wrote. . . it broke me. Because when I saw you at the funeral with her and I left *again,* I thought you were happy. And every day I thought of you, I reminded myself you had a little girl and a family and I kept telling myself it all worked out the way it was supposed to." Beau raised his arms in defeat before dropping them with a shrug. "And now *knowing* how hard. . . how hard everything was for you—"

"Beau!" Sienna shouted. "I don't want pity! None. Especially yours."

"I'm not. . . I feel for you because I care. Because you were my friend first and my love second and that never went away. I could never not care about you."

"You feel *guilty*. There's a difference between that and empathy, Beau." She shook her head as if she were trying to clear him from her vision. "I have to go. I want to leave."

"Sienna, please, you need to know that I remember everything. The good and the bad moments. I remember when I told you I was leaving and you looked at me exactly like you are now —like you *hate* me."

More tears pooled in her eyes. "I don't hate you, Beau. But I *wish*." She paused before gritting out the words, "I wish that I could. Because then maybe this wouldn't hurt so damn much."

"Sienna…"

Wiping her face with the back of her hand, Sienna shook her head. "I have to go. My daughter is in the hospital. And I have a ten-minute walk over there to get it together and not look like I'm afraid or *heartbroken* because the guy who promised me the world over and over again managed to—"

"I will give you the world. That's all I ever wanted, even back then. I told you that. . . "

"You don't get it, Beau. *You* are the world. I might've liked to wish for fast cars and motorcycles and trips as a kid. But I would've been happy right wherever *you* were."

Beau swallowed. "And now?"

Sienna shook her head. "I don't think you want me to answer that at the moment."

"Sienna, please—"

"I need to get back to Grace. I need to think about Grace and get myself together for her and pretend more. Be better at faking it. *That's* what I've learned from that letter. I need to be stronger than I've been before no matter what happens, if she ends up with a recurrence or not. Because the last thing on her mind should be *me*. That's what I need to think about now. Not *you*."

Beau's racing pulse throbbed in his ears and he chewed on his bottom lip. "Can I come by tonight after you guys get home?"

There was an early captains' practice scheduled for the morning, but Beau didn't care. *I'll let her blow off some steam. She'll understand. She'll believe me. This isn't the end, it's not,* he told himself, wondering how Sienna could be standing in front of him and feel miles away. He fisted his hands. *Please, I need to hold you.* Looking down at his sock-covered feet, caging hers that she had slipped into unlaced sneakers, Beau would have done or said anything to go back to the plane, where they had floated through the clouds, their limbs tangled, their hearts beating against each other.

"Not tonight."

He reached out, taking her hand, which hung limply in his. "I'm sorry. I'll never be sorry enough. Just let me make it right, okay? I'll prove it to you, I swear. I'll make it up to you. I'll do whatever you want. Don't run from this. I love you."

"I told you before. This isn't just you fumbling the ball on one play and making the catch on the next and getting a whole new set of downs. I told you, you had one shot and you better make it a good one."

Wasn't it good? Beau thought. *We were happy. We were* just *happy.*

"I love you," was all Beau could manage to say. "I swear, I've never stopped, and I promise I never will."

She closed her eyes tightly, trying to prevent more tears from falling. "I wish you knew how much I want to believe you," she whispered, the heartbreak floating from her words, tearing at Beau. Taking a deep breath, Sienna twisted her arm, pulled her hand from his grasp, and walked out of his apartment.

"God dammit, Chase. Did you put a LoJack on my car or something?" Beau threw the mesh bag of equipment into the bed of his truck.

Chase pushed off from the side door he had been leaning against. "I saw on Twitter Beau Walker's been running some sort of camp in a public park."

Beau looked at Damien walking in the opposite direction

across the field. "I told you I was helping out a friend's son. And for real, you might want to keep an eye on him. Kid's got talent."

"Yeah? Give him my card."

"What's up?"

"I called you the other day."

Three times.

"Yeah, I've been, uh. . . busy."

Beau had been busy not sleeping, looking at his phone every time he got a notification, a text, a call. Apart from answering the realtor listing his parents' home to confirm the upcoming open house, Beau didn't answer the phone. Because the one person he wanted—and needed—to talk to was Sienna. And except for sending him a message requesting time, Sienna hadn't called in nearly two weeks. Not once.

Time. Beau would remind himself. *She needs time, she deserves time.* At best, he hoped time would be his punishment, a penance to pay for not coming forward with a letter that broke his soul. He had thought not sharing it with Sienna would spare her from pain. What kind of mother could read a letter her child wrote regarding her out of concern, heartbreak? And selfishly, Beau knew, deep down, Grace's letter, which was written to bring him closer to Sienna, would only drive her away.

His gut was right.

"What's that?" Beau asked when Chase handed him a folder.

"Two contracts. LA and Dallas."

"Chase—"

"I'm *legally* obligated to present you with both. Sign whatever one you want. But let's lock something in before the NFL thinks you're starting your own peewee camp for underprivileged children." Chase looked around the park before pulling out a pen.

Beau opened the envelope. "Wow. You really got LA to up that offer, huh?" The amount of The Bulls' contract was nearly 50 percent more than Dallas's offer.

Chase shrugged. "Persistence conquers all, my friend. You told me that a while ago."

"Did I?" Beau took the pen, signing the offer to play for the Dallas Sparks for one more year.

"Way back," Chase said, taking the folder. "When I first signed you. When I asked you how far you wanted to take your career, you told me, as far as it would go, that no one works harder than you."

Beau remembered saying that. What he had meant was all the way to the Super Bowl. But his career would more than likely end short of that, and over the last few months, Beau had come to peace with letting go of the dream of being a champion. Because life, he knew now, could be fuller off the turf whether he won or lost.

"I'll send this in today. By the way, that GPF trip is set, your accountant took care of everything. Janet said she'll send out the details."

Beau nodded. "Thanks, man."

"Alright, where you off to today? Your last free Sundays are coming to an end soon."

"Yeah," Beau said with a small laugh. "Guess I should take advantage of them."

If things were different, he would head home, shower, and drive out to Brookwood, picking up a good quality pizza for Scrabble night. He hadn't been included in one since before Sienna and he went to California. He would soak in as much of her as he could—how she tugged the corner of her bottom lip between her teeth when strategizing, shifting her tiles. How she would beam with pride when Grace pulled out an impressive move, how she would absentmindedly bump her knee against his and then do it again on purpose.

Beau was eager for more of those moments. Because in less than two months, he would be in lockdown camp. There wouldn't be very many Scrabble nights for the rest of the year.

Fuck time. There isn't much more left until I go. He bid goodbye to Chase and went home to shower.

When the fog cleared from the bathroom mirror, Beau nodded at himself. "Persistence conquers all." *I'm not giving up on her.*

Scrabble night. I have a standing invite, Beau told himself as doubt crept through his mind when he got out of his truck. He sighed when he walked past Sienna's car in the driveway and up the steps to knock on the door.

"Oh," Grace answered, appearing surprised. She fiddled with the sleeves of her dress as a curious look captured her face before it shifted to one of annoyance. "Ugh. She lied, didn't she?"

"What?" Beau asked.

Grace huffed. "She told me you're at some off-season camp that's like prison where you can't use the phone." She sighed when Beau raised an eyebrow. "Okay, maybe she didn't say it was exactly like that but you know what I mean."

Beau only shook his head. "How are you feeling?"

Holding her arms up as if to show him she was still there, Grace dropped them at her sides. "Good as new."

Beau took in the pink of her cheeks, the absence of circles beneath her eyes. "Good. Can I come in? Did you guys order food yet?"

"We're not playing tonight," Grace told him. "Henry has a *date*, and my Mom and I are going somewhere. I asked why you weren't coming with us, she said you were at camp." She folded her arms across her chest. "What did you do?" she asked, her voice a whisper. "Why would she lie?"

Beau didn't want to tell Grace that Sienna had found the letter and was about to talk himself in a circle when Sienna appeared behind her daughter. He hated her guarded positioning—shoulders tense, mouth closed with a dead stare.

"Grace, give us a second."

Beau watched the look between them, the one only a mother could give a child that said, "get lost."

With another sigh, Grace shrugged at Beau and went into the house as Sienna stepped through the door, shutting it behind her. "What are you doing here, Beau? I told you—"

"It's Scrabble night," Beau offered.

"Well, we're not playing tonight."

Beau nodded. "Yeah, I got that. Grace said you had plans."

"We do." Sienna looked down at her feet, rocking back and forth.

"You know, I think Beau's car gets better gas mileage." They both jumped when Grace opened the door, quickly locking it behind her. "Give me your phone, Beau, I'll look up the address."

"Grace—"

"Mom, we can't be *late*," Grace whined and walked down the steps.

Beau looked between Grace, heading to his truck, and Sienna, who nearly had one foot back inside the house.

"If you don't already know," Grace called out, "the cancer card *doesn't* expire, even if the cancer does!"

Sienna's eyes floated to her daughter, and she locked her jaw tightly, breathing deeply through her nose. "I. . . fine. Let me go grab my jacket."

Sienna left Beau standing on the porch.

"Are you coming?" Grace asked.

I'd follow your mom anywhere, Beau said to himself, quickly jogging down the path back to the street where he had parked by the curb. He unlocked his truck and climbed in, shutting the door.

"Are we busted?" Grace whispered. "Please tell me you didn't tell her about the letter. I just realized this was on the list."

Beau then knew exactly where they were going. The lantern festival had been on the list, and when Beau saw it, it made him grimace. Because he had taken Sienna to a lantern festival before, and instead of bringing them together filled with hope and magic, it left them cracked open and far apart. It had been the last thing they had done together before he had left.

"Don't worry about it," he told her, watching Sienna lock the front door and head towards them. "Nothing you do will ever change how she feels about you. But I've got work to do."

He took a deep breath when she got in, trying to ignore how Sienna still had her arms folded over her chest or the way her head leaned against the window facing away from him.

But no one works harder than me.

chapter twenty-one

SIENNA HAD SPENT two weeks tiptoeing around Grace—saying yes to whatever friend she wanted to go to the mall or diner with after school, plastering an overenthusiastic smile on her face that made her cheeks burn when she did spend time with her. *Look? See your mother? I'm good. I'm great. No need to worry about me,* she would imagine telling Grace. *No need to scheme with the former love of my life—let him know how not great I've been, how much better I had been once upon a time with him. There's no need for him to feel bad that he left this place—left* me*—and never came back.*

Sienna pouted over the thought, reminding herself that Beau did come back the day of her father's funeral and what he saw—sweet, young Grace in Sienna's arms—had driven him away again. *I should've taken that as a sign,* she tried to tell herself as she avoided the sporadic gazes Beau shot her way as he drove. She could hear Grace singing to herself in the backseat of his truck. *It never was meant to work. But I didn't need them to go out of their way to remind me of that.*

After Sienna had found the letter, she had asked for time. But she wondered what difference that made. Involuntarily she found herself looking up at the door when it opened at Maloney's, expecting him to drop in. She would hear a small noise in the backyard at night and wonder if it was him coming for her window. Despite the long hiatus Beau had taken from her life, in a few short months, he had planted himself right back not only in her home or work but in her body and soul. So even though she had asked for time, seeing Beau on her doorstep brought some sort of relief.

She shut the door to Beau's truck and waited for Grace to do the same, grateful for the fresh air after the forty-five-minute drive. There was no space in the truck, no escape from Beau's scent, from his presence beside her as he drove, drumming his thumb against the steering wheel, as if he was fighting against reaching out to hold her hand.

Taking Grace—alone—to the lantern festival had been Sienna's idea, even if she hadn't planned on sending any wishes to the sky, only her gratitude that, for now, her daughter was healthy and here. Selfishly, she wanted to erase the bad taste in her mouth that the last festival had left.

Keep looking at Grace, she lectured herself, watching her daughter walk in front of them, her head tipped up to the sky in awe. *Remember this moment.* Sienna didn't know what tomorrow might bring. But over the past week, Sienna learned that the only thing guaranteed was Beau's ability to break her heart.

Stepping in front of Beau when he retrieved his wallet, Sienna put cash down on the counter. *I want nothing from him. Not even the admission fee.* Wrapping an arm around Grace, she steered them toward the entrance, leaning against her daughter's body but trying to spare her from absorbing too much of the emotion flowing from her—deep-seated, silent cries mourning an end to the dreamiest love story Sienna had ever known. But what stung the most wasn't thinking about saying goodbye to sky-high dreams, private planes, beach backyards, or chasing the sun in spectacular ways. What hurt Sienna the most was that she would say goodbye to the moments between—the ones on the ground when Beau was just there.

"Over here." Grace pointed at the line. "We just write on them? What exactly?"

"Anything," Beau said. "A message. A wish." His deep brown eyes met Sienna's. "Whatever you want. Then send it up, up, and away."

Sienna bounced as the line moved. Grace accepted a lantern and moved to a spot at a free table.

"Grace," Sienna laughed and shook her head as she read her daughter's message. "Nothing more meaningful than 'please let Justin ask me to prom?'"

Grace didn't look up from the lantern. "I am *not* going to the dance alone," she manifested before straightening and handing the marker to Beau. "You could wish for a winning season," Grace joked with a shrug. "Can't hurt."

Beau drummed the marker against the table as he bent. "Probably not."

Sienna turned her head away as Beau wrote his message onto the thin paper carefully, trying not to let her mind take her to the last time she had seen him write on a lantern—the end of their middle.

For Grace: health, happiness, and a date to the prom, followed by, *For Sienna: love, laughter, and unlimited Dole Whips.*

Beau's magnetic stare bore into her so strongly with pleading that Sienna had to look at him. "What about for you?"

He looked back at the table before leaning forward and writing.

For Beau: Sienna's forgiveness.

Sienna tried to ignore that one and looked at the marker in her hand. *A week ago, I had everything I'd ever wanted,* she silently relented.

It wasn't just Grace's health, absent of scares. It wasn't only Beau making love to her thirty-thousand feet in the air. It was a feeling of balance, wholeness, and support—something she only had bits and pieces of since her mother had died.

Sienna's hand spelled out her heart's wish in one word

—*family*—and she stood back, letting Grace take the lantern. The three of them walked into the crowd, waiting for the flame to be lit, so they could lift their hopes and dreams into the night sky and let them land among the stars.

★★★★★

Grace clicked her tongue. "So," she said from the backseat. "How about the Mavericks?"

Beau slowed at a stop sign. "Basketball season is over."

"Right." Grace cleared her throat. "The Yankees, I mean."

Sienna closed her eyes and leaned her head back. The tension in the car was so thick Sienna knew Grace couldn't cut it with small talk, let alone a knife—her daughter would need a chainsaw. *A few more minutes,* she told herself, wondering if Beau was driving slow on purpose, the way he used to do when they were teenagers, savoring the final minutes until her curfew.

Grace unclipped her seatbelt. "Actually, speaking of the Yankees," she began when Beau turned onto their street, "I should give you your hat back. Navy is more your color than mine, Beau." She opened the door of Beau's truck as he pulled up to the curb. "Wait here!"

Sienna went for the door handle when Beau reached for her.

"Sienna—"

"No, not now."

Beau squeezed her shoulder. "Please."

"Please what?" Sienna spat, whipping her head to him. "What can you possibly have to say to me that I don't already know?"

Opening his mouth to speak, Beau shook his head. "I'm—"

"You're sorry. I know. You're sorry, I'm heartbroken and *mortified*." She shook her head. "What else is there, hm?"

Beau rubbed his lips together. His eyes left hers only to look at the house where his gaze lingered. "Do you think," he began, "it was supposed to be this way?"

"Do you mean are we supposed to sit here and end it the *same* way you did the first time?"

"No, no. I didn't even know the lantern festival was tonight," Beau tried to assure her. "I was coming for Scrabble night. I gave you two weeks. We've done more than a *decade* apart—"

"Stop." *My heart can't take this just stop.* "I can't even remember everything on Grace's list in that letter. . . the lantern festival—"

"I thought maybe you told her about all those things, about us."

Grace might have heard a few slips from Henry, might have remembered her father watching Beau's games. She thought back to the game they attended with the Golden Penny Foundation, how Grace had said Beau was "the best damn wideout" her father had ever coached. And that had been true, Sienna knew. Because Beau was central to her father's offense, giving him something to focus on beyond his grief.

Steadying her shaking hand on the dash, Sienna shook her head as the memories from the year they reconnected flooded back—the year Beau had pulled her out of the hell of counting lonely days until infinity, the year he spent painting over the dark drawing of grief she had sketched, streaking it with color, laughter, love.

They might have been sitting in the newest model of a Ford F150 that he bought with his copious amount of money. But when Sienna closed her eyes, she could feel the rumbling of the old truck Beau had to fix with scraps from his father's garage. Sienna's mind went back to that night when he pulled that loud truck up to her house for the last time, a harsh, final goodbye under the false promise of return.

But it didn't matter that Beau had come to her father's funeral because when Sienna opened her eyes and looked out the window, she saw Grace peek out behind the living room curtain.

I did it without you, she thought, wiping her cheek with the back of her hand. *I got through it without you because of her.* The time between Beau leaving and Grace's birth had been a path littered with too much partying, dropping out of school, and pushing the limits and her father and brother away. But Grace's arrival into the world gave Sienna a second chance at living that Beau had stolen when he left and never looked back.

"I'll do it again."

"What?" Beau asked.

Sienna hadn't meant to say the words out loud, but since she had, she continued, "I picked up the pieces of my broken heart and your broken promises once before. I can do it again." Balling her fists, she took a deep breath. "I know you're involved in the GPF trip to Disney World and. . . after that, I'm wondering if you should go to LA."

Beau's eyes widened. "Sienna—"

"Don't stay in Dallas because of me, alright?" She ignored the heartbreak on Beau's face and reached for the handle again. "I should—"

"I signed with the Sparks today."

Sienna shut her eyes but didn't fight Beau's hand coming to her face. "I don't know if you should've done that."

"I did it because the timing is *right*, Sienna, don't you understand that?"

Sienna wanted to swat his hand and run from the car, to choose the flight response when Beau was in front of her, prepared to fight. But the space was too small, and she teetered between the past and present, remembering how awful it felt to run from his truck, back into her home, and begin her life without him.

"What? Better late than never?"

Beau clenched his jaw. "Fuck better late than never, Sienna. It's now or never."

It's about Grace, Sienna reminded herself, knowing she was probably still watching from the living room window.

Beau ran his thumb over her bottom lip. "If you think after *everything*—knowing what it's like to fall asleep and wake up with you, make dreams come true with you—if you think I can just walk away now, you're wrong. Because I won't let you go that easily. Not when I know. . . "

"Know what?"

His other hand framed her face. "What it's like to do life *with* someone right in front of me instead of living *for* someone else who's been gone forever. I want to finish my football career with you in the stands. And I want to figure out what happens next for me with you, with Grace. Even with your brother." Beau's fingers stretched, winding into her blonde tresses. "If you're going to make me run routes down the damn field and back, Sienna, I'll do it. I'll prove it to you. It was never about the letter. It was never about Grace. It's only been about you."

"Beau—"

"If I could crack open my fucking chest and show you that your name has been carved into my heart since we were little kids, I would. *This* scar," Beau said, tapping his temple, "I've listened to it my entire life, and it's about time I listen to the one in my fucking heart. I wasn't honest about leaving in high school, and that was a mistake. I didn't tell you about the letter, and that was wrong. But don't even for one second think *you* were the wrong part when you've been the only right thing my entire goddamn life."

Sienna felt the tears stinging her eyes and pulled her hand to wipe at them. Immediately Beau went to grab her hand. "No. Please don't make a scene. Grace is watching."

Beau fisted his empty hands and dropped his head in defeat, nodding. "Go. I don't. . . don't *say* it's over. Not now. Not when we've just started, please."

Did it just start? Sienna wondered. She couldn't remember her entire life from day one. But the point at which her memories began had to do with Beau. And even when he left, he remained the hero of the small, sleepy town of Brookwood even though he hadn't stepped foot in it in over a decade. He remained her father's favorite player—his best damn wideout—long after he had ever coached him.

Leaving Beau's truck, she couldn't give him an answer. That wasn't just because of hurt. Sienna couldn't say with certainty that what they had could truly ever end.

Sienna looked around the empty living room. *She scrammed,* she thought, turning off the lights and walking down the hallway. Grace's door was open, her head in a book.

"School night so don't stay up too late," Sienna told her, trying not to frown at Beau's baseball hat perched on a notebook atop the dresser.

Grace dropped the book, laying it on her chest. "Mom? Why did you want to go to the lantern festival tonight?"

Shrugging, Sienna shook her head. "I thought . . . I don't know. Those things are kind of special. It's been kind of a crazy time. You deserve it."

Grace ran her fingers along the duvet and eyed her mother curiously. "Have you ever been before? Was it special for you?"

"Once, but…not super special." *It ended kind of like this. Me coming back into the house alone, preparing to stick my face into the pillow and scream and cry.*

"Lights out soon, alright?"

"Mom?" Grace called out as Sienna was about to turn. "I love you."

"I love you too. Get some sleep."

Sienna tugged on her pajamas, plugged in her phone, and placing it on the nightstand where Beau's book of gifted stars sat. She frowned. *It really is almost like last time,* she thought, turning away from the book and pulling back the covers of her bed. Beau had a place in a book in her house long ago, one that she had kept on her nightstand, never worried that Henry or her father would read it—neither of them had enough interest in what was going on in her life. Nothing like Grace. Glancing at a photo of her daughter on the dresser, Sienna wondered if she had gotten her inquisitive nature from her father's side and not Sienna's.

Sienna stiffened.

My diary.

Sprinting to the closet, Sienna pulled out the box of what remained of her old room and dumped the contents. Her senior yearbook, a dried flower Beau had picked from the meadow that she had pressed into the back, her old camera. But her diary was nowhere to be seen. She shuffled through the mess again, looking for the notebook with the deep navy cover, a color close to the night sky on a starless night.

Like Beau's hat, she thought, standing. *Like his hat in Grace's room on top of a stack of notebooks.*

With her pulse racing as quickly as her feet, Sienna quietly pushed Grace's room open, finding her already asleep. She tiptoed to the dresser, lifting the Yankees hat Beau had given Grace. Below it was her diary.

"This is how she knew," Sienna said fifteen minutes later. She had only read the first few entries, but her brain and heart were seized and strangled by emotion with each word about her mother's death, the way it cracked the foundation of the family. And, of course, there was Beau—so much Beau.

How could there still be so many blank pages when there had been so much of our story? she wondered—but her heart knew why. Sienna had written irregularly—an entry here, an entry there—because Beau had pulled her attention and words from the page.

She flipped through the notebook again, only this time, Sienna paused at a back page written by a different hand. Her breath bawled up deep within her throat as she traced the familiar, swirly handwriting—the same she had found on the letter in Beau's nightstand.

Dear Mom,

I went back and forth between typing this letter and having it read with my will (which only includes my old Trolls collection, please split between Lilah and Molly, one day, they will be worth money), but then I decided it would be better served here. I know for a fact you haven't looked at this diary for at least two years (because I've had it that long. . . and if I haven't died yet, you might kill me after this paragraph, but I'll continue in case you decide not to).

We got home from the Sparks' game a little while ago, and you didn't say much on the way home. I realized that I might need to explain myself one day. And if you're reading this, I might already be gone. And maybe you came back to this diary because it's where you went when you lost grandma, and maybe you need it. There are so many blank pages left, almost like they're waiting for you to finish your story.

I didn't really understand cancer when I was first diagnosed. Most kids don't. But after it came back and I was older, I knew what it really meant. The only time I ever remember panicking about having cancer was when I overheard you telling Henry that the doctor said it would take a miracle.

I wasn't a little kid anymore, but I was scared. And sometimes, when you're scared, you do odd things—like dig through your closet, yanking everything out, trying to find a miracle like you stuffed it on a shelf last month and forgot about it.

What I found instead was a box of what was left of this room when it was yours. And in that box was this diary. And in this diary, I found a love story. I won't call it the greatest one I've ever read, only because it isn't finished. But you know me, I'm a sucker for a good romance. You know, boy meets girl, girl punches boy in the face (I can't believe you did that), boy falls for girl. . . in your story, boy broke girl's heart.

But we all make mistakes (like me, reading your diary). And life is too short to have more grudges than forgiveness. Life is too short to spend so much time being sad or heartbroken, to count the days that have passed since life was *better. Every day is a chance for things to be better, Mom.*

Cancer has taught me a lot. It taught me that if you hold on to things, they really stick. The good things we keep fill us up. The bad things become toxic the longer they sit—exactly like cancer.

I don't know Beau. I remember Papa talking about him a lot and watching him on TV. "The best damn wideout I've ever coached," is what he would say every time Beau came on screen. I'm sure he's other things too, even though judging by what I've read, he doesn't really seem to think so.

I don't know what will happen to me. You and I both know that remission isn't guaranteed. So, I'm taking it day by day. I want all my days to be full just in case one might be my last. I hope that I'll have lived long enough to at least see the next chapter in your and Beau's story.

And if I don't, I hope he stands by you when you miss me too much. I hope he does what he did for you when Grandma died—teaches you that it's okay to live and love while grieving and missing. If he did it once, he can do it again if you give him a chance. She'd want that, I'm sure. And Papa. And that's what I want if the time comes and I go before you do. I'm so sorry if that happens.

Sienna brought a hand to her mouth to quiet the sob that broke loose from her chest.

My life has been anything but ordinary. No Dad around, single uncle standing in for Father's Day events. Almost teen mom. I learned to read at Maloney's while you and Emily were unloading a beer delivery. Cancer. But I wouldn't change a thing. Because it's been awesome, thanks to you. I never had to wish for anything because before I'd even think to, you already gave it to me.

I'll fight my hardest to stay by your side because I know you tried so hard to keep me there. But in case it does happen, and I have to go sooner rather than later, know all I want is for you to keep doing all the living I won't get to do. And I want you to do it with the person who puts the biggest smile on your heart (after me, of course).

Love you as high as the sky,

Grace

"Mom?"

Sienna barely heard Grace's voice over her crying. She looked up with blurry vision at Grace standing in the doorway, fiddling with her pajama top.

"What. . . why. . . "

Grace looked between her mother and the diary she held in her lap. "I just want you to be happy even if I'm not around."

Sienna closed the diary. She wiped her face with the back of her hand before holding it out to Grace. "*You* don't have to ever think about that, do you hear me?" She cupped Grace's face. "I'm the mom. You're the kid. Kids don't worry about parents, that's not how this works."

"I do worry about you though."

Sienna was struck with the painful reminder of Grace's letter to Beau and she had to take a deep, heavy breath.

"What your grandma did, she was *sick*. And it's sad we didn't know how sick she was. But me? I'm okay. I'm not perfect. I'm not strong all the time even when I want to be. But I'm *here,* Grace. I know how hard it is to be left that way and I'd *never* do that to you. I want you to know it and believe it. I'm your mom and—"

"You're my best friend too," Grace whispered, approaching the bed and taking Sienna's hand.

"Grace—"

"Who takes care of you?" Grace's voice cracked. "I thought. . . he took care of you back then, you know? When Grandma died, Beau took care of you, Beau made it better. I thought two people who loved each other as much as you two did even all those years ago, well maybe if you had another chance. . . and then *if* something happened to me, he'd be there this time. I didn't know how to contact him, and when the GPF accepted my application, I thought it was a sign."

Sienna lowered her hands, clasping Grace's when she sat on

the bed. "That's what you wasted your wish on?" She waited for Grace to nod. "That wasn't supposed to be about me. It was for *you*."

"I mean." Grace sniffled. "It kind of was for me, too."

"What do you mean?"

Grace's gaze fell to her lap, and Sienna watched her mouth open and close repeatedly, as if she were struggling to find the words. "Do you know I've never been kissed? I've never held a boy's hand apart from Jimmy Martin's in third grade, and that was a dare. Maybe it will never happen. I don't know what *will* happen, you know? It's anemia today. Maybe in a few months—"

"What are you—"

"No, Mom. It might not be anemia next time. And maybe it'll be really bad next time. And. . . I want to know what it's like for someone to look at *me* like I have stars in my eyes, like I didn't just hang the moon, like I *am* the moon. *That's* how Beau looked at you on the field. It was instant. What if I never get a love like that?" Grace's eyes welled with tears and her lips trembled as she fought to keep them at bay. "I thought maybe seeing it in real life instead of reading it in books or watching it on TV would be the next best thing."

Oh, Grace. My sweet, Grace.

Sienna tugged Grace against her, cradling her pixie cut. "You're going to have that kind of love and *better*. I swear, I'll fight as hard as I can to give you that chance if I have to, alright? But don't settle for what's in there. Trust me. You deserve more."

"So do you," Grace said, breaking Sienna's hold. "*That's* why he stayed. To give you more."

Beau had given Sienna hope based on deceit, but he had given her an important reminder too. *"Maybe she was your walking miracle. You just didn't know it."*

Sienna ran her hand along the smooth, hard cover before pushing the diary aside, tugging her daughter onto on the bed, and lifting the duvet over them.

Front to back, Sienna smoothed Grace's hair, which stuck out in different directions from wearing her wig cap earlier, exactly how it grew in as a baby. That head of hair started off light brown and only grew lighter and lighter, until it matched Sienna's. And like then, Grace's hair *was* growing, just as she was now.

When Grace's sniffles and shaky breaths fell into even, peaceful slumber, Sienna pressed her nose to her daughter's and whispered, "You never had to look for one, Grace. You were the miracle all along."

saving grace

DEAR MOM,

I used to count the days since Beau left. It's been over two years. But a few weeks ago, I stopped counting. I didn't mean to. It sort of happened. Well, let me fill you in on what went down until that point.

I did graduate from high school, but I flunked out of college. If I'm being honest, I did it on purpose. Because being at school in Austin only reminded me that I wasn't at FSU, where I had planned to transfer to be with Beau eventually. I didn't care about class, exams, or papers. I never said no to a party or even a guy.

I'm not proud, thinking about my behavior. But for so many days, I felt numb, similar to how I did right after you died. I guess that's because Beau took a piece of me when he left. And I was searching for it wherever and with whomever I could. I was desperate to be put back together, filled up. And isn't it ironic that I felt more complete as a virgin with Beau than I did after the second or third guy I had sex with?

On my intense, wild quest to feel, there was a guy. And we spent the night together. And after weeks of not giving him a second thought, I realized pretty quickly I was going to be thinking of him very often. That's because I was pregnant.

Before I told anyone, I spent many nights wondering if I should end the pregnancy. I barely graduated from high school. I had no plans to go *back to college. I was working at Maloney's in town most nights. And the guy gave me an envelope with less than $200 and told me to take care of it. My thoughts were suffocating, constantly making my heart race, my palms sweat. I hadn't gone up to the roof since Beau left. But one night, when I couldn't breathe, I went up there, and boom, as if it had been waiting for me to lower my head to the shingles, a shooting star soared above.*

I kept the baby, and even though I was nervous, there are no doubts that it was the right thing to do. When she was born, I stopped counting the days that had passed. That's because I'm exhausted, sure. But it's because I don't need to remember the last day I was happy, whether when you were still here or Beau was. This little girl with a head full of hair and curled-up fingers and toes beside me in bed is all the happiness I need. I can't even remember what life was like without her—the good, the bad, all of it.

She also taught me something about forgiveness. I finally forgive you, Mom. I forgive you for thinking we could handle the world without you, that our need for a mother didn't matter in your mind. I can finally say that out loud because I understand your love for us. It's all encompassing and consuming. It's as high as the sky and as deep as the ocean that one day I'll take her to. It's as magical as fireworks at Disney World, more delicious than Dole Whips. Thinking about her as she's nestled beside me, how she'll grow and dream and change the world must be the same kind of high you feel flying—endless.

But for now, I'll enjoy the sleepless nights and cuddles. One day she'll be a teenager and won't want anything to do with me.

I won't write here again. I only wanted to let you know I forgive you, Mom. Because I understand now how heavy your pain must've been to walk away from a love like this. I know it wasn't that you didn't think me, Henry, or Dad mattered. You were in such a dark place you couldn't see how much you *mattered to us. I'm sorry it took me this long to see it.*

Her birth didn't go exactly as planned. She's stubborn already, and after twenty hours of labor, the doctor told me they needed to go in and get her. Henry was with me during the c-section because Dad is so afraid of blood. We were both so nervous, and Henry asked if he could play some music. Do you know what was playing when she was born, Mom? "Amazing Grace"—Johnny Cash's version, your favorite. I feel silly writing all this to you now because I know you were with me in that moment. If I closed my eyes, I could hear you humming out of tune above the music from the kitchen in Nashville. It was always our favorite sound, even if we teased you about it.

She's our saving Grace. It feels like we're a family again, thanks to her.

Don't worry about us. We're going to be alright.

I love you forever,

Sienna

chapter twenty-two

"YOU DRAGGED MAJOR ASS TODAY." Giles eyed Beau as they walked shoulder to shoulder down the hall to the locker room. "What's got your panties in a bunch?"

Beau didn't just drag ass. He ran the wrong routes, and his steps were off. On the routes he did run correctly, he flexed his hands too early, which led to the ball bouncing hard off his palms.

Pushing the door open with a grunt, Beau shook his head. "Nothing," he spat at his teammate. "I'm fine."

I'm fine even though I'm sleeping one hour on, two hours off. I'm fine even though I can hardly eat. Everything tastes the same—bland. He grimaced, thinking of the last delicious thing he had eaten—the blueberry donut he had split with Grace as she set up the Scrabble board and Molly climbed into the bed, sitting opposite her.

Sienna had been curled up on the love seat, snoring gently after finally surrendering to her exhaustion. And even though the hospital room had been filled to the brink with anxiety and fear of the unknown the night before, a new day had come and cleared the air.

That had been nearly three weeks ago.

Beau sighed. Sienna had been right about what she said

before they got on the hot-air balloon. *"None of this was real."* It wasn't, Beau knew. Life wasn't always sunrises and sunsets, jumping into the freezing ocean with no consequences. It wasn't always making love in the middle of the afternoon with the windows open, the cool ocean breeze chilling their skin while their bodies burned together. But that didn't mean life had to be bleak all the time, either.

Beau thought back to the hospital room—to Grace and Molly's laughter bouncing between an IV pole and a monitor, happy echoes between scary words like "biopsy" or "leukemia." Their faces and Sienna's sleepy snores, Beau realized, made the room that had been scary and dark the night before lighter and brighter.

Stripping his gloves, Beau tossed them into his locker before slamming the door shut. *Life is what you make of it and who you make it with.* And there had been no one beside Beau while he was trying to live the way he thought he should—achieving dreams on the turf—instead of living the way he had wanted.

With her.

He pulled his phone out of his bag. Beau had given Sienna a full day before he reached out, but his call went unanswered. And several of his texts.

I can only say I'm sorry and that I love you.

I hope Grace is okay and that you're home.

Can we talk?

Sienna had finally responded earlier in the week.

You need to give me more time.

Beau deserved the unease that struck him when he had read her response. *Maybe I should've told her about the letter.* But what Beau had wanted since the night he walked into Maloney's after seeing Sienna at the game was to pick right back up where they had left off, even if he had told her he hadn't because he didn't want to face the truth. The truth was Sienna had been hurting and carrying the weight of the world on her shoulders when he should have been there to take off whatever load he could at the most, and at the least, just let her know she wasn't alone, to whisper that things would be okay no matter what, to tell her that—heads or tails—he loved her no matter what and wasn't going anywhere.

Opening the message thread to Sienna, he quickly typed.

When you told me about the motorcycle wish, we were on the roof eating strawberry shortcake. It was the night before I took you to the lake.

Beau hit send before sighing and typing again.

I built the swing that morning before I picked you up so you could fly asap.

The winning word in Scrabble on our first Valentine's Day was AXEL.

Placing the phone back in his bag, Beau hung his head and headed to the shower.

I didn't want to waste a second making your wishes come true back then, he wanted to tell Sienna, *so I jumped at the chance to make them all true now.*

But Beau didn't want to type that message or even say it on the phone. He wanted to cup her cheek and grow lost in her scent, the smoothness of her skin, whisper the words against her soft, plump lips. With his body, Beau wanted to show Sienna just how deep his love flowed for her—from top to bottom, inside and out. It was an amount incapable of measurement, one that grew despite distance and time, kept promises and broken ones, small, quiet wishes and big dreams.

Beau's fist clenched beneath the hot stream of the shower in frustration. His love for her was still there, filling him to the brink. And he wouldn't stop giving it to her.

"Thatta boy. Higher knees, higher knees!" Beau watched Damien's feet float through the ladder. "Break!" He tossed the ball, and it landed in the teenager's hands.

Damien took a few strides down the field before looping around, returning to Beau, and tossing him the ball. "Better, right?"

"Way better." Beau handed him a bottle of water and looked down at his watch. "Why don't we stretch quickly. Your Mom said I kept you too long last time."

What Beau had anticipated as being a one-time coaching session with Damien had grown into something semi-regular. It had been Beau who suggested it. Damien, a high school junior, had raw talent that needed to be fine-tuned. But he had a good attitude, a fun personality, and was willing to listen. *Easy to coach,* Beau thought.

"You got plans this weekend?" Damien asked. "Bet you don't get the chance to have a lot of fun once preseason starts."

"You're right about that," Beau said, trying not to be too soured by Damien's innocent words, which just reminded Beau he now had plenty of time on his hands and little plans—apart from the Disney World trip.

Beau would soon be back to full-force football, sleeping in a hotel for a few weeks, isolated only with his team. In the past, it had been something he looked forward to, narrowing down his focus, cutting out loud voices—especially Chase's—gearing up for another opportunity to chase his dream down the sidelines.

But this year, after a few whirlwind months with Sienna, he was dreading it.

Damien sat on the ground, putting his feet together in a butterfly position and leaning forward. "You really hanging up your cleats after this season?"

Beau nodded. "I'm old, man. Can't keep up with fast young ones like you as much as I used to." Apart from him and Giles and a few veteran linemen, the Sparks were stacked with young, fresh talent. That could go one of two ways—amazingly right or terribly wrong.

And I don't know what I'm chasing anymore. A Super Bowl ring? The impossible high that moment the game is called when I drop to the turf on my knees, and then what?

A Super Bowl might have been an impossible high. But Beau knew what a high felt like with Sienna, and there was nothing he could imagine or dream of that could compare.

"Alright, I need to run and meet my mom. Her shift ends soon." Damien stood, throwing his water bottle and gloves into his bag.

Pushing off the grass, Beau wiped his hands on his shorts. "She at the hospital? I'll give you a lift. It's not far from me."

The truth was Beau didn't want to be anywhere near Texas Children's Hospital. It wasn't for fear of running into Sienna since Grace had been discharged. But somehow, the building that housed sick kids had grown even more distressing to Beau. He had left that day with a smile on his face and a skip in his step after losing to both Grace and Molly at Scrabble, heading to his apartment to steal some time with Sienna.

It had been the last time he had really smiled.

He and Damien gathered their things, leaving the park as it grew more crowded. Beau wanted to ignore echoes of his name that seemed to swarm him, and Damien awkwardly looked around, pretending not to notice, until a young boy stopped in front of them.

"Are *you* Beau Walker?" There was a timidness in the little boy's voice but stars in his eyes.

Beau ruffled his baseball hat and looked at Damien. "I think so. Who are you?"

"Bryce Roberts," the boy said, holding out a hand. Beau smiled at his parents standing a few feet away before giving Bryce a shake. "Hey, do you want to play?"

"I can walk," Damien said, holding a hand up.

"No, no, it's alright. Listen, Bryce." Beau paused, squatting down, trying to get as close to eye level with him as possible. "I can't play now, I've got to give Damien a ride home, and then I have some meetings. But this guy right here, me and him, will be at this park next Saturday at 9:00 AM." He spoke loud enough for Bryce's parents to hear. "And I don't know if *you* know, but his name is Damien Holdings. He happens to be the best wideout I've ever coached. And he's going to be the best college receiver recruited in Texas next year, you'll see. So, how about you come play with us next week? Bring some of your friends. Maybe I'll bring some of mine."

Bryce nodded eagerly. "Can we take a picture so everyone at school believes me?" He looked at his mother and then back at Beau, his smile as wide as his face.

Can I really say no to that?

"For sure."

Beau stood, putting a hand on Bryce's shoulder for the picture before reiterating his message to his parents and telling them he'll be there next Saturday.

Damien and Beau continued toward the parking lot where Beau had left his truck. "I'm the *only* wideout you've ever coached," Damien reminded him.

Beau threw his bag into the bed of the truck. "The first," Beau said, glancing over his shoulder at little Bryce who was running across the grass. "But I'm not sure you'll be the last."

"So next Saturday at nine?" Damien said a few minutes later as Beau pulled into the hospital parking lot.

Beau shook his head. "Eight for you. We'll get a workout in first. How old do you think that kid was?"

Damien shrugged, unclipping his seatbelt. "Seven? Eight? Looked like he was my little brother's age."

"Didn't know you had a brother."

"Two of them. Both younger."

Beau pulled up at the front entrance, sliding his truck into park. "They into football?"

"One of them is," Damien said before he reached for the door. "Because *I* am."

"I know how that goes."

No one knows that better than me, he thought, remembering himself at a young age following Greg around, begging his mother to buy him the same clothes and shoes. Only one other person could drag his attention and admiration away from his older brother—Sienna.

"I'll see you next weekend," Damien said, getting out of the car and shutting the door.

Beau quickly rolled down the window. "Hey, Damien, bring your brother, alright?"

"You sure?" Damien asked, dipping his head down. "That kid might tell his whole school you're playing ball in the park."

Beau shrugged. "What's one more?"

Damien nodded, and Beau rolled up his window, watching him walk into the hospital. He was about to put the car into drive and pull away from the curb when there was a knock on the window he had just shut—a frantic, energetic knock.

"Holy shit," Beau exclaimed, rolling the window down. "I could've run over your foot. Then your mother really would kill me," he told Grace.

"So you *are* still in the dog house then."

"You couldn't tell?" He shook his head, the tension between him and Sienna at the lantern festival still thick in his mind. "What are you doing here?"

Grace glanced around. "Henry dropped me off. I'm going to sit with Molly for her treatment while he has brunch with some friends." She sighed. "I'm sorry. I . . . I tried to talk to her about the letter—"

"No, it's not your fault," Beau told Grace as she pouted. "You were looking out for her. I should've handled it better." *A lot better. Like telling her up front and still standing by her.* "She shouldn't be mad at you. I'm the adult."

"Yeah, well," Grace began, "I mean, I did read her diary."

Beau's eyes widened.

"How do you think I knew about all that stuff?" Grace asked him.

Beau had assumed that Sienna had told Grace about their relationship—about the plans they made, the wish list. He never knew Sienna even kept a diary. "I thought maybe she told you."

Grace looked down and shook her head. "No. I think some stuff hurts too much to talk about, even the happy moments, you know?"

It was a punch to the gut that left Beau needing to look away from Grace and take deep breaths. "Well, don't go snooping anymore. No need, alright? I'm sure you'd be pretty pissed if she did that to you."

Grace nodded and rubbed her arm. "Feels like rain," she groaned, tilting her head to the sky. "Great. Just in time for prom tonight. You know, the committee wanted to do it outside this year. Maybe they'll do it in the gym now." She tugged on her wig. "This really doesn't hold up well during flash flooding."

"That kid ask you?"

"No," Grace began. "But Billy Blythe did, and he's *way* cuter."

Beau shook his head with a laugh. "See? Everything works out the way it's supposed to at the end of the day. You should go before it starts to pour. Hopefully it will clear up later."

"Are you going to call my Mom?" Grace asked, ignoring him.

"Grace." Beau sighed. "I . . . "

"She's stubborn as a goat."

"I'm aware."

Grace stepped closer to the truck, placing her hand on the opening of the window. "And sometimes she needs a little push."

"She needs time," Beau said. "I'm trying to give it to her."

"You guys already lost a lot of time," Grace reminded him, and Beau frowned. "Life is short, isn't it?" She tipped her head at the hospital. "I've gotta go see Molly. She's probably on her third popsicle by now. You know, chemo sores."

Beau nodded as Grace backed away from the truck. "See you around, kid. Have fun tonight. Hopefully the rain will hold off, and you can at least get your pictures outside if they move the dance in the gym."

"It's alright. Who doesn't love dancing in the rain, anyway?" Grace waved as she walked away, leaving Beau with his mouth slightly agape.

Wish list.

chapter twenty-three

IT'S SUPPOSED **to rain tonight.**

Peeking at her phone, Sienna rolled her eyes at Beau's message. *Now he wants to talk about the weather?* Earlier it had been about their first Valentine's Day together—which hadn't gone as planned. Sienna closed her eyes, shaking her head at the memory while her heart sank.

It went even better.

Sienna reached to open her nightstand, retrieving the copper coin Beau had gifted her all those years ago. It had oxidized, gentle hues of turquoise now painting the edges. But the message on both sides remained clear even after all the time that had passed—*I love you.*

It hadn't been easy to look at the coin after Beau left high school. Instead, Sienna kept it under her pillow and slid her hand beneath, palming the metal each night. *It was real, right?* Sienna would ask herself. *He, me, us, we were real.* Sienna couldn't deny it as the memories of their year together struck her—rooftop nights, meadow picnics, drives to nowhere in his clunky truck, and the sound and feel of happiness after so much grief.

It took Sienna sixty-three days after Beau had left—and zero calls or emails—for her to remove it from under her pillow. She had erased all traces of him from her room—his shirt, the night light, and the coin especially. His departure smacked her so deep it left a scar she couldn't see but could always feel. And that scar soured the precious memories so much that they began to feel like a dream instead of the past.

It hasn't rained since December. Before we saw each other again.

You mean since before my daughter approached you and let you know what a headcase I've been—a sad, very lonely headcase, Sienna silently scoffed as she caught sight of the diary and sighed. She could forgive Grace—what could a child do that a parent couldn't forgive? But Beau—who had swooped into her life and filled it to the brim with promise and magic under false pretenses for a second time—Sienna wasn't so sure. *Fool me twice,* she said to herself, pushing off the bed, *and it will be the last time you do.*

"Come see our girl," Emily called from down the hall.

"Finally," Sienna exclaimed, leaving her room and heading toward Grace's room. "Is it prom or the—"

"Or the what?"

Sienna was going to ask Grace if Emily had spent the last few hours getting her ready to walk the red carpet for the Academy Awards. But when she saw her daughter standing in the hall donning the green sequined dress, with just enough makeup to amplify her features—and replace the ones chemo had claimed and not returned yet, like most of her eyebrows—Sienna couldn't say anything other than one thing.

"You're beautiful."

But Sienna's observation had nothing to do with the dress or makeup or perfectly curled wig. It had to do with the scar from Grace's old port that she didn't care to hide—the reminder of all she had overcome and battled while smiling her way through.

If I've done one thing right, Sienna thought, *it's this girl right here.*

The doorbell rang, pulling Sienna from her mind. Grace jumped and squealed. "He's here! He's here!"

Emily squeezed Grace's shoulders as she walked toward the front door, but Sienna moved in the opposite direction toward her room.

"Let me get my phone to take pictures." In her room, she grabbed her phone off her bed and hurried back down the hall where she found Grace's date—*not* Justin, but an equally as cute, if not cuter, Billy—slipping a corsage onto Grace's wrist.

"Mom," Grace groaned, rolling her eyes as Sienna continued to snap photos for five minutes. "We're going to be late."

But Sienna didn't want to stop capturing the moment—one she had feared might never come. "You can never have too many pictures."

Standing behind her, Emily placed a hand on Sienna's arm when her phone issued a warning about low memory. "They're going to take more pictures right now," her friend told her, and Sienna lowered the phone.

"Right," she said with a sigh. "Okay, well. Billy? Speed limit, alright?"

"Yes, ma'am." Billy nodded as he reached for the door.

Sienna tried to hide her eye roll as Emily snickered because she knew he was trying to be polite. "Grace, you text me when you get to Lilah's—"

"I *will*," Grace called over her shoulder before slamming the door shut.

Sienna held her breath, standing at the closed door before it flew open and Grace crashed into her.

"I love you," Grace whispered as she hugged her mother tightly.

Sienna could feel her daughter's grin against her cheek as she squeezed her back. "I love you too. Now go and have fun." She guided her back out the door, watching Grace take Billy's hand as he led her to his car.

Emily let out a heavy breath as she came out to the front steps. "What do we know about that kid?"

"He's nice," Sienna assured her friend. "Henry taught him last year." Sienna watched them drive away.

"He's older?"

Sienna nodded. "A junior. But I ran a background check with Henry's colleagues, don't worry. Polite kid. On the debate team. The kind of guy you'd want to take your daughter to prom."

"Go, Grace." Bringing her arm around Sienna's shoulder, Emily sighed. "Did we just send her off to *prom?*"

"Her first." Sienna smiled. "But not her last."

"Wasn't she just eating ketchup right from the bottle at Maloney's?"

The bittersweet memory painted a smile and a frown on Sienna's face. "Sure feels like it." She turned back to her friend. "You should go home and hug your baby. Before you know it, she'll be moving out."

"This mom," Emily began, pointing a finger at herself, "hugged her baby for sixteen hours straight." Her finger pressed against her chest. "I can stay another hour before my boobs explode. And I've got plenty of milk stashed if you have a reason I need to pump and dump."

"Beer or liquor?"

"Go easy on me," Emily said.

Sienna went into the kitchen and grabbed a beer from the fridge, popping the top off and handing it to Emily. "Let me grab a sweater," she told her. "I should've sent Grace with a shawl or something. The temperature dropped."

With the bottle to her lips, Emily motioned at the window. "Must be the rain coming," she said to Sienna before she went to her room. She pulled a sweatshirt out of the bottom dresser drawer and slipped it over her head. Her phone dinged again.

Dancing in the rain was on the wish list.

Sienna threw her phone on the bed and groaned so loudly that Emily came running.

"What happened?"

Hands on her hips, Sienna shook her head at the phone—at

the diary, the book of stars Beau had given her, at the coin she had left on the nightstand and forgot to put away, at the photos of Grace on her dresser.

"Sienna?"

She turned to face her friend. "He did it again."

Emily quirked an eyebrow in confusion. "Who did what again? Beau?" When Sienna didn't respond, Emily sat on the bed. "What did Beau do? Didn't he just take you—"

"Yes, he took me to California. On a private plane. He got a house on the beach. And a sailboat and a hot-air balloon—"

"Hold on, what exactly did he do *wrong* here?" Emily asked with a laugh as she crossed her legs. "I mean, look, it's not that you don't deserve those things—"

Sienna held her hand out. "He did all of those things because Grace *asked* him to." The admission made Sienna's stomach swirl and throat tighten, and Emily waited for her to continue with the beer bottle pressed to her lips.

"She *what*?"

Her phone beeped again, and Sienna silenced it before plopping beside Emily on the bed. She stared up at the dull, blank ceiling. "Grace used her wish for the Golden Penny Foundation to go to the game."

"I thought it was weird. I didn't want to say anything," Emily told her. "But you know Grace, she's quirky. And she wanted to be on TV."

"It was so she could give Beau a letter."

"Okay, and the letter said what? Come back and woo my mom a little because she's had a *rough* ass go over the last few years? And while you're at it, go all out and take her to the beach for a weekend?"

Sienna stared at her friend.

"Oh. . . no, no, it didn't." Emily waited before her eyes widened. "You're lying."

"She. . . " Sienna could feel the emotion creeping up her throat. "She was worried about me."

"Grace is a kid," Emily reminded her. "Mature for a fourteen-year-old, but she's still a kid."

Sienna nodded. "That's right. She's a kid. And she wants to believe in the fairy tale, in Prince Charming coming back to save the day, but . . . "

"Beau is kind of like Prince Charming."

"That's just it. It wasn't real. Any of it."

Sienna sat, looking at the diary to her right, took a deep breath, and began to tell Emily the tale of the year Beau and Sienna had spent together, the adventures they planned and wished for, the promises he broke or waited too long to fulfill.

Emily waited until Sienna had stopped speaking. "So he was at your dad's funeral?"

Nodding, Sienna sighed. "He saw Grace and . . . "

"Thought there was someone else." Emily sighed. "He did come back again—"

"Because of Grace's letter. Not because he had ever planned to. She wrote him the most heart-wrenching and"—Sienna paused, rubbing her chest—"you wouldn't be able to say no to that, you know? None of it was because he *chose* to. Grace gave him a list, and do you know what was on it? Beach vacation. Dole Whips. A motorcycle ride." The paper with Grace's handwriting flashed before her mind. "Do you know where she got it? From here." She held the diary, and Emily took it. "All those things, they were on our list. Beau's and mine. We never did them before. We were always supposed to."

Emily flipped through the diary. "So, it was like a bucket list you two had?"

"We called it a wish list," Sienna said softly, but she offered nothing else before rising from the bed. "You can read it if you want. Enough people have."

A half hour later, when Sienna had finished her beer and lay on the couch, Emily appeared with the diary. Sienna could tell she had been crying as she sat on the couch and wrapped her in a hug. "I want you to know that you raised the most special human on the planet, and if I'm half the mom to Abigail you are to Grace, I'll know I've done something right."

Sienna returned the embrace. "You're a great mom. I mean it, go be with your baby. I've kept you here long enough."

"Before I go, I need to tell you something."

"What's that?"

Emily looked down at the diary and sighed. "I read fast, but. . . you talked about a wish list, but there isn't one written here. Just lines here and there where you mention it."

"We never wrote it down," Sienna said.

"Was the hot-air balloon ride on it?"

Sienna nodded, her mind flashing to Beau's truck when she had straddled him after getting milkshakes at the diner.

"Prom was, I saw that entry." Emily shifted on the couch, pulling out Sienna's phone from her back pocket. "But what about dancing in the rain?"

Sienna furrowed her brow. "What do you mean?"

Handing her the phone, Emily shrugged. "I didn't mean to snoop. I saw the message."

Dancing in the rain was on the wish list.

Sienna's heart raced as she remembered the day—or night—when Beau had crept into her room with the night light and kissed her under a neon ceiling for hours, staying until after midnight so he could be the first to wish her a happy birthday.

They put dancing in the rain on the wish list that night.

"Maybe he didn't need Grace's help after all," Emily said with a sigh. "Maybe he remembered. That's not for nothing."

Opening the diary, Sienna began to scan the pages. She was looking for mentions of dancing in the rain, of hot-air balloon rides, of chasing the sun until they ran into the moon. But there were no mentions of that in Sienna's handwriting as she searched line by line. Those things, Sienna realized—and *everything*, just as Beau had said—he remembered.

Emily gave Sienna's leg a gentle squeeze.

"And maybe, that wish you made about wanting a family? About wanting to have the life you used to have before your mom died? Well, that came true, it only looked different is all. And when I said Grace was special, I meant it, but I mean it more now. Because she's the wish that gave you everything you ever dreamed about—everything, even if it came later than you hoped."

After Emily left, Sienna couldn't go anywhere and sat frozen on the couch, eyes focusing on the diary sitting on the coffee table in front of her. The notebook held her wishes and dreams, her ups and downs, her happiness and heartbreak, each penned deeply into the yellowing pages, standing the test of time.

Sienna stood from the couch and went to her bedroom, where she wanted to collapse into bed. But he was there as well—in his book of stars, in the coin she had left beside it on the nightstand. She picked it up again, flipping it back and forth.

"Heads or tails, I love you no matter what."

Sienna's breath tripped up the back of her throat, and her body grew impossibly warm despite her earlier chill. She took a deep breath. She had been asking Beau for time, but Sienna realized she needed space. And with quick steps, she was in Grace's room, sliding the window open and reaching for the trellis she hoped would still hold her weight.

The moment her palms flattened against the familiar, rough shingles, the tightness in Sienna's chest eased, her lungs reinflated to capacity, and the air above her cooled her body. It didn't matter that the sun hadn't set and the stars hadn't woken yet.

Lying back, she had nearly forgotten how much space there was on the roof for her thoughts to breathe—from the perfect heavens to the imperfect ground and back again.

And before she even had a minute to think about what she would say to Beau, a smooth engine, a heavy door shutting, and quick, hurried footsteps that matched the uptick in Sienna's heartbeat cut through the air. She immediately sat.

"What are you doing?"

Beau's fast pace came to a halt, and Sienna scooted to the edge, cautiously eyeing him from the patent leather dress shoes, up the slim fit black pants, to the crisp white shirt beneath his jacket and stopping at his bow tie.

"Shouldn't I be asking *you* that?"

Sienna pressed her lips together. "What's that?" she asked, pointing to the small plastic box he was holding. A smile she couldn't hide spread across her face. "Cake?"

Beau looked at the box and back at Sienna. "Are you going to let me come up?"

"I guess I couldn't really stop you."

Beau wasted no time and, before Sienna knew it, hopped on top of the air conditioner. "I *know*, the trellis is quieter," he said, pulling himself up on the roof. "But you always climbed better than me."

Sienna wanted to stop him so he didn't ruin his tux, but she couldn't find the words. Her body ached for him, and instead of telling him to stop, she pushed up on her knees and went to him. Her movement made Beau freeze.

"I *know* Grace didn't know about some of those things." She pursed her lips together. "I never said anything to her—or *anyone*—and I never wrote them down or—"

"I told you," Beau said, shaking his head. "I remember *everything*." He was still on all fours facing her as she sat back on her knees. "I know you thought—"

"You know what I *never* thought about before?" Sienna asked. "Fate."

Beau's Adam's apple pushed forward from the strength of his swallow.

"Because a lot of *bad* things have happened in my life. And I never wanted to stop and think that I was just destined to be covered with sadness or death or whatever. But if *this* isn't fate, you coming back because of Grace, because of everything she went through, I don't know what is."

Hesitantly, Beau crawled closer, finally sitting down. "I came because of her. But I came back for *you.*"

"I believe you," Sienna said with a fervent nod.

It was impossible not to, and not just because Sienna realized that Beau had never forgotten her—or what they had together—but because as they were sitting so close together, all Sienna could see was Beau's eyes—dark and warm. Even though they had grown older, grown apart, his eyes remained the same. They were the eyes of her best friend, who he was at the start of it all. The only thing that had changed about them was *how* they looked at her—with admiration and laughter in the beginning, with concern and care later. And now, they only looked at her with love—the kind that fought through distance and space, the touches of other people, heartbreak and anger, forgiveness.

The love Beau's eyes held, Sienna had realized, could only have been written in the stars.

"The only reason I wish you had told me about the letter—"

Beau's frown interrupted her. "I'm sorry—"

"I just wish we had gotten the hard part out of the way sooner, that's all." She shook her head. "I still would've been mad. But somehow, someway, I know we would've ended up in the same place as right now." She looked at the space between them and lifted her hand to cover Beau's, feeling the relief leave his body as his head bowed when he flipped his palm up and wound his fingers with Sienna's.

Sienna looked at their hands clasped together, how easily they fit.

Then. Now. Always.

"I'm sorry. You know I'm stubborn."

"You are," Beau agreed before looking up from their grip on each other. "And strong. And beautiful. And kind and smart. And I hope something else." He slowly inched closer but with no hesitancy this time, as if Beau could see her chest cracked open, leaving her heart for his taking again.

"What?"

"Mine."

"Always," Sienna promised without hesitation, her mouth capturing Beau's in a kiss so whole and deep she had hoped he would swallow down her vow.

With that kiss, Sienna was lost in the familiarity of Beau's taste—both from weeks and decades ago at the same time—the continuity of their relationship full and bodied and something Sienna couldn't get enough of.

Beau moved his hands to hers, now at the back of his neck. "Wait," he mumbled before kissing her once more before leaning back. "Wait. I have something for you."

Sienna tried to steady her breathing as Beau reached for the box. His thick fingers fumbled to open it, but when they did, a small corsage made with a white peony sat inside—her favorite.

"Will you go to prom with me?"

Before Sienna could say yes, thunder boomed. But she didn't jump, only lifted her face to the sky when heavy rain began to paint her cheeks.

"Shit. Or not," Beau said, clicking his tongue. "I mean, we could go. . . or we could just dance in the rain," he added with the smallest twitch of a smile. "What do you think?"

Sienna shifted against the roof, feeling the thick piece of copper in her back pocket. "For old time's sake. How about we flip a coin?" She lifted her hips and slipped it out of her jeans, watching Beau's eyes fill with emotion as they found the old copper coin. She ran her finger around the rough edges. "Heads or tails?"

Beau didn't miss a beat.

"I love you no matter what."

Sienna gave it a flick, and the coin flew from the roof before plummeting to the ground.

"What is it?" she asked Beau.

Neither of them had followed the coin's trail, and their smiles mirrored each other's.

"Doesn't matter."

Beau backed away and hopped down loudly onto the air conditioning unit before jumping to the ground. Sienna followed to the edge. But she didn't slide further to the trellis. She swung her legs to the edge and jumped into the arms Beau held out, waiting for her, their bodies sliding and melding together. Her chest warmed beneath her soaked clothes when Beau leaned his head against hers.

"Wish list?" he asked against her lips.

And before Sienna gave her answer, Beau began to lead them, their feet slipping and sliding along the soaked grass of her front yard as his hands both delicately and firmly spun and dipped her to nothing more than the music of their breathy laughter and racing heartbeats.

"You've ruined this," Sienna said, bringing her hands between them, loosening his soaked bow tie and the button beneath it. "I don't mind though. I actually do love an open collar."

Beau spun her again. "Next year, it's the whole nine yards. Corsage. Fancy dress. Tux. Limo."

Sienna laughed, running her fingers through the damp hair at the back of his neck. "I'll have to chaperone. They don't let parents crash prom."

"What about football coaches?"

Sienna steadied herself against his chest, blinking heavily through the rainfall. "What about next season?"

"I'm playing with the Sparks next season. But that's for *me*. Fuck the Super Bowl. You know what I want? One happy moment after a game lifting you over the rail of the stands. Just once. *That's* why I'm playing."

Sienna swallowed. "And after?"

"And after, I've got some time on my hands. And you know, what else I realized recently? I don't mind kids. And I love an underdog. Maybe there's something for me in Brookwood. I looked back at their record. They've been god-awful for the last three years."

"Really?" Sienna asked.

"Really. But first"—Beau paused, pulling her back to him—"I'm going to keep dancing in the rain with you. And then, I'm taking you inside and not sneaking out the window tomorrow. Or the day after. And soon, we're going to the happiest place on earth and putting some well-deserved smiles on kids' faces."

The rain continued to pour down on them as they danced to silent music no one else could hear. But no storm—a sprinkle or hurricane—could prevent Sienna from seeing the love Beau held for her that poured out of his warm brown eyes.

"*This* is the happiest place." Sienna yanked on his lapel. "Us. Together."

"Better late than never, yeah?"

"No," Sienna said emphatically, kissing him. "Better *now* than never."

epilogue

one month later

"I'M GOING to need another one of these," Beau said, tossing the now bare turkey leg into the trash before wiping his mouth and hands with a napkin. "How's that Dole Whip? As good as you remember?"

Sienna looked down at her ice cream, stirring it with a spoon. "It is. But the one at Maloney's is better," she told him with a wink.

"Because it's got rum in it," Henry reminded her, and Sienna waved him off with her hand.

Beau wrapped an arm around Sienna's waist, pulling her to his side. "What do you think? Are they too old?"

Sienna looked at Grace and Molly, walking linked at their elbows. Every moment, one would turn and point at something, the other going in that direction. "Definitely not," she said, catching the look of wonder painted across her now fifteen-year-old daughter's face. She smiled at a little boy who walked along with them, holding his father's hand. Charlie had the same cancer Grace did. He had finished his second round of chemo in time to join the trip to Disney World. And even though there were dozens more children who had their wish come true that night, Sienna's heart pained. *But so many others didn't,* she thought, trying not to let the frown that came to her face be too evident. *There's no frowning at Disney.*

"We'll do it again next year."

Sienna laughed. "Next year, you'll be on a football coach's salary," she reminded him.

Beau fiddled with the Mickey ears headband he wore. "I'm. . . I'm not taking a salary."

"No?" Sienna asked.

Beau shook his head. "They're using that money for something else."

"What's that?"

"I don't want to tell you now and jinx it. We're still waiting for approval from the superintendent."

"Approval for what?" Sienna playfully nudged his chest. "Tell me."

Beau took out his phone, pulling up a picture—a rendering. He zoomed in and handed it to her. "For the Clarke-Walker memorial stadium."

Sienna's eyes left the phone to meet his.

"Your dad never coached my brother," Beau told her. "But I think they would've been a good team."

Sienna nodded, taking Beau's hand when he put the phone back into his pocket. "Probably. But *you* were his wideout."

"And now you inherited me," Beau joked, and Sienna giggled as they kept walking.

"My wideout also happens to be incredibly handsome, sweet. . . " She paused, looking at the gaggle of children who had begun to gather in front of Cinderella's castle. "And he's also got a big heart. Maybe the biggest and best one of anyone I've ever met."

Beau ignored her comment, but she could see the flush in his ears as they walked past a street lamp. "I could be something else, too."

"What's that?"

"Your husband. How do you feel about being Mrs. Wideout?"

Sienna nearly stumbled, and Beau's hand fell to her waist to keep her upright.

"Okay." He laughed. "Maybe *not* your husband."

"No, no it's not that," Sienna began. "You're already my family," she told him. "Always have been. Always will be. I don't need to wear a ring for that."

"I do, though," Beau told her. "Need you to wear a ring."

Sienna rolled her eyes. "Is this about Dylan?"

The tension between Beau and Dylan had simmered, but Beau hated that he was still one of her most regular customers at Maloney's.

"No. But we spent a lot of our relationship keeping this *quiet*," he said, lowering his voice. And Sienna knew Beau was right.

"Can I tell you something?" Beau didn't wait for Sienna to answer. "I promised your Dad I'd always treat you right." He reached out, twisting a long blonde lock around his finger. "So, this," he said, as his hand trailed down her side, grabbing her left hand, "is important to me."

Sienna pressed her lips together, fighting the smile. "Okay. But not today." Her eyes flickered behind Beau, where Grace, Molly, and Henry had gathered. "It's Grace's day."

"What Grace wants, Grace gets," Beau said with all sincerity, and Sienna nodded in agreement, knowing if it hadn't been for her daughter, there would be no them at that moment.

They moved closer to the castle as the sky darkened, anticipation buzzing among the members of the small crowd, who all released a collective gasp of awe when fireworks lit up the sky, painting it with specks of neon reds, purples, and blues.

But Sienna wasn't looking at the fireworks. She was looking straight up, as if her eyes were drawn to the shiniest, sparkling star right above their heads.

Happily ever after, Sienna silently wished. Then she tugged on

Beau's shirt to get his attention away from the show and held up her left hand, wiggling her bare ring finger.

"Wish list."

full circle

Dear Mom,

I've been meaning to write sooner. I had repacked this diary after we moved out of the house, which Henry still lives in. We bought Beau's parents' old home, which he never ended up selling. But a lot has happened since then. There's too much for me to write, so I'll just have to hope in my heart that wherever you are—I hope it's with Dad—you witnessed it for yourself. Things have come full circle in the strangest of ways, in a way I can only believe fate had something to do with it.

Grace's cancer changed us all. It changed her physically and emotionally, but in a manner that made her determined to seize every moment of life and not waste it.

It changed me too—it hardened me. Her suffering made me no longer believe in anything—love, happiness, wishes, and dreams. I was shrouded in a sense of doom but too afraid to step out of it, even when things were turning around.

Grace's cancer changed Beau. I once wrote that she had given us (me, Henry, and Dad) a new sense of purpose when she was born. Her disease brought Beau back to me, it opened his heart to realize that he made a difference in people's lives—that he matters. He's retired from the NFL now. He got a standing ovation—tens of thousands of people on their feet honoring him—at his last game. What a moment. I know Dad would be proud. I know his brother would too.

The day after that game, I found out I was pregnant, and I knew in my gut it would be a boy. And it was. You have a grandson—Jack Gregory Walker. He's almost four and a handful. But we're so lucky and blessed he came when he did. Beau has more time on his hands now that he's retired. And get this, he stepped into Dad's old shoes. He's been the head football coach at Brookwood High School for several years now. The team is alright, but each season gets better.

We began to run weekend training camps for kids all over Texas after Beau retired, and we haven't stopped. The turnout is huge every time. Beau has some of his old buddies helping out, Henry built the website. It's all free. We only ask if anyone has a little cash to spare to donate it to the Golden Penny Foundation. We owe a lot to those people. And every little bit helps. Wishes for sick kids are priceless.

I'm writing from Malibu, where we came to celebrate our wedding anniversary. I love thinking about the day—how handsome Beau looked in his sleek suit (with an open collar of course). We married at the planetarium beneath the stars in the auditorium. Henry officiated and Grace was both the best man and maid of honor. She gave a speech for the ages, had everyone laughing and crying—including dozens of former NFL players. She amazes me, my Grace. I know she would amaze you too.

I never knew I could love something as much as I love star gazing, but wow, do I love looking out at the ocean from the back deck. Beau bought this house he once took me to for a long weekend. We've been coming out here as much as possible because Grace—who continues to be healthy—is now at the University of Southern California. She's studying theater, which I think is a good fit. But she's not the only student in the family.

I've gone back to school. It hasn't been easy—especially with Jack—but Beau and I make it work. He supports me more than I ever probably could have supported him while he still played. I make it to class, I study, sometimes at Maloney's, which has been renovated and is no longer a money pit. I'm hoping, in a few years, I'll be a nurse. Better late than never, right?

So, see? We're doing alright—more than alright. It's just taken a little more of a detour than I would've preferred. But life is full of them. And the major one we took—Grace's cancer—brought all of us to a better place, even though it was the longest, bumpiest one of them all. Her fight meant something bigger than we could've possibly imagined.

I wish I could tell you Beau and I sit outside every night to look at the stars. But we're exhausted. Having a kid in your midthirties is a lot different from when you're twenty. Beau usually does bedtime, and I'd say five out of seven days a week, he falls asleep with Jack after reading a dozen stories. I never waste one of those moments to make a wish. I look at my boys sleeping—they're nearly identical—and focus on Beau and wish away. After all, he's still my shooting wideout.

What do I wish for, Mom? Just one more day. I try to pack each one with more laughter and happiness than tears and sadness. You never know what could happen.

I don't let Beau sleep the whole night in Jack's bed. I feel terrible his neck is all cramped, but after a few minutes of staring I wake him and we lean on each other as we trudge down the hall into our bedroom. Even though this was Beau's family home, we did minor renovations and upgrades, but my favorite thing we did was frame the coin Beau gave me all those years ago and hang it on the wall. I look at it every night I go to bed and smile.

It might seem silly to frame a double-sided coin. But I don't need to see both sides. I know—heads or tails—Beau and I will love each other no matter what.

Wherever you are, tell Dad I say hi. Tell him he's still Grace's hero even though she's grown up. Let him know his grandson, even as a toddler, has the arm of a quarterback (the broken TV is a testament to that) and the speed of a wideout. But if he wants to play soccer, teach, or be a pilot, that's fine too. We only want for him what we do for Grace, to follow his dreams and no one else's.

Jack sings out of tune to songs like you. He lights up rooms and hearts and makes everyone's day better without trying. He's the best of everyone who had a role in bringing him into this world, even when they weren't around. Both of our children are.

You can tell Dad Beau kept his promise.

Love,

Sienna

dear readers

I always tell people you don't have to publish a book to call yourself an author. You just have to write one. But sometimes, motivation is lost (honestly, it's part of the process). What makes it easier is knowing you have an audience waiting. Thank you to those who have been with me from the beginning and waited for *When You Wish Upon a Wideout*. And thank you to others who have come around recently. I hope you all came for the game, but stuck around for the party and emotional rollercoasters that tend to paint the pages of my books.

If it's not too much trouble to ask, I would love if you share your feelings on Goodreads and Amazon. Readers' ratings and reviews make a huge difference in the success of an author's work.

I hope you stick around for what I have coming this summer —Crosby and Maxine's story. It's a high stakes, forbidden love tennis romance with an age gap. As always, I promise it will be a sports romance with both heat and heart.

Thank you dearly,

Cathryn

acknowledgments

The following people were instrumental in making sure this book was finished and put out into the world.

My husband Hamza: It's ironic that as a writer, I'm at a loss for words here, but I am. I can't express just how much I love you and the family we created together, or the right ones to explain my gratitude for your encouragement to write, even when the world was upside down for a moment.

Thank you to my family who doesn't just support my work, but does so proudly.

And a special thanks to my mom—Catherine—who is undoubtedly the greatest grandma in the world and looked after my kids over the last summer so I could get a head start on this book. I like to think that at the heart of *When You Wish Upon a Wideout* is a love story, but it's also about the mother daughter relationship. I'm so lucky that everything I learned about being a mother came from you, Mom. Thank you also for sharing with me the ins and outs of cancer journeys—the ones as the patient, which you've lived through more than once, and the ones of the nurse and caregiver, which is a huge part of who you are.

An alternative time line story is not easy to write or edit. So thank you to my editors—Jeanine and Nancy—for your careful reading and making sure final book is far better than the manuscripts I sent you. And to the other MVP of my editorial process —my beta readers MK, Lo, and Davis—I actually could not have moved forward without your help. I love football, but I'm no player. Your voices are heard in these pages.

To my ARC team: thank you for taking a chance on Beau and Sienna's story, for believing in it when it was just an idea (I'm looking at you, Ellen). Your hype means the world and makes a huge difference to little indie authors like myself.

To my Breakfast Club—I sometimes wonder if we will still be meeting every Thursday for breakfast when we are in our sixties. I'm sure we will, and that we will still be complaining about our kids while gushing over their photos between sips of coffee. I'm certain that *if* I'm still writing books at that point, your support will be there too. I love you all, my found family, and I can't imagine my life without you.

And lastly to those who were with me day to day—the staff at Books@Cafe and Coffeebean here in Amman, and my "office-mates" Najwa and Jihan—who know when I need a break from writing.

also by cathryn carter

The Fourth Down Series

Fourth Down Blitz

Fourth Down Fumble

about the author

Cathryn is a native New Yorker but currently lives in the Middle East with her husband and two children. She often can be found in the corner of one of Amman's many coffee shops with her laptop. When her head isn't in a book or she isn't writing, Cathryn enjoys building enormous structures out of Magna-tiles with her kids. She loves swimming in the Atlantic Ocean, floating in the Dead Sea, and traveling during non-pandemic times.

You can find her on Instagram and TikTok @cathryncarter-writes or by visiting her website www.cathryncarter.com

Made in the USA
Monee, IL
24 March 2023

30486877R00231